# Emerging Practices in Cyberculture and Social Networking

# Emerging Practices in Cyberculture and Social Networking

Edited by

Daniel Riha and Anna Maj

Amsterdam - New York, NY 2010

The paper on which this book is printed meets the requirements of "ISO 9706:1994, Information and documentation - Paper for documents - Requirements for permanence".

ISBN: 978-90-420-3082-4
E-Book ISBN: 978-90-420-3083-1
©Editions Rodopi B.V., Amsterdam - New York, NY 2010
Printed in the Netherlands

# Table of Contents

.

# Introduction

## *Daniel Riha & Anna Maj*

The chapters in this volume are a selection of the most significant research presented during the 4th Global Conference on *Cybercultures: Exploring Critical Issues*, held as a part of Cyber Hub activity in Salzburg, Austria in March 2009. This multi-disciplinary conference project is a successful rebirth of the 2003-2005 conferences held previously in Prague in the frames of the ID.net *Critical Issues* research project. The enriched materials presented here are the results of in-conference discussions as well as later research and further reflections on the topics covered.

Being a contemporary dominating cultural paradigm, cyberculture is an important subject for a wide range of researchers representing various disciplines. Thus, the idea of the interdisciplinary exchange of knowledge through presenting results of diversified research projects seems to be crucial for their further development at both local and global levels. The research problems connected with cyberculture (or rather cybercultures) nowadays are those arising in the field of philosophy, psychology, sociology, culture, media and game studies, IT studies, engineering, design and law.

One of the fundamental topics raised during the conference was the issue of access analysed at various levels, especially users' access to information and technology with regard to the notion of diversified competencies, knowledge and disabilities as well as accessibility of the content and interface.

The question of access has become a serious political issue. Moreover, it concerns not only the never-to-be-solved problems of geo-economic nature such as 'digital divide' or those of socio-psychological provenance such as 'competence gap'. In the networked paradigm of global economy, the access to certain vulnerable data may provoke serious political or economic crises as well. It is no longer possible to feel safe and keep the ideal of isolation when everything is connected to everything else, every citizen of the global village has potential access to powerful tools which can make him/her an important source of information or its transmitter and amplifier.

Politics today is more about moderating than about controlling - or at least it is evolving into this direction. Yet, on the other hand, viral politics - as viral marketing - is commencing to prevail. Gradually one can observe political actors becoming fully conscious of the situation and using this knowledge. Sometimes it is positive for citizens, and sometimes it is not. It gives new hope for social communication, disrupting the old top-to-bottom model and changing it into a bottom-to-top one. But on the other hand, it is sometimes a new threat for an individual. New communication tools can have democratising potential but this power is understood by the authoritarian leaders, who are afraid of people and of the freedom encapsulated in new technologies. The result of a systemic reaction can be very painful for society and this sad side of emergence of cyberculture can be noticed in some parts of the world.

Access also means accessibility and usability of content, various technologies, communication systems and devices. It is an important tool of inclusion of all marginalised groups of society: the elderly, children, poor, stigmatised or disabled. It is an important problem for contemporary responsible design, especially web and interaction design. The issue concerns designing assistive technologies but also social networking environments and various possibilities of social interaction, wiping out the stigmas or 'communication gaps'. This is, of course, an important issue for contemporary pedagogy, e-learning and for the entertainment business. Therefore, open access and user-friendly architecture can be also a good marketing formula to attract attention of new target groups.

The other important issue is the user's involvement in the process of development of technologies and devices - client's incorporation into the creative process and the idea of user-friendly interfaces as well as their implementation. The issue refers to the growing competencies and will of interaction, especially connected with the so-called 'Net generation' that is beginning to enter the job market and business. This generation is the one that was raised in the environment of digital technologies, especially computer games.

This is the result of earlier emergence of personal computers at home, which built a creative environment of work, education and entertainment and programmed users for other interactive needs. Individuals, who are eager to cooperate with a service provider if the goal is beneficial for the whole community, now express this demand clearly and globally. But on the other hand, it results in the emergence of grassroots projects and actions, which develop information and communication possibilities of all Internet and mobile devices users.

These issues are connected with the problems of gaining control, maintaining control, and the lack of control as associated with privacy and its loss. This subject implies ideas of control over the dispersed and decentralised system of the Net itself and of the content distribution in the context of Web 2.0 architecture and the cultural trend of sharing.

Grassroots journalism, sharism, social tagging, bookmarking or networking are evoking many positive processes but also provoking an unprecedented loss of privacy. This implies the possibilities of personal data stealing or abuse of intimate information. The problem lies in the unawareness of possible malicious usage of social media and the need to emphasise advantages and disadvantages of social networking. This consciousness will emerge, but it first needs to be tested. But digital maturing of virtual communities is in process. It will result also in collecting the knowledge on system vulnerabilities, and will teach to what extent digital traces should be treated as digital footprints, and to what degree one's privacy could be revealed and to what degree it should be protected.

These issues provoke questions on changes in education and the increasing need to provide cyber-education for various groups within society in view of their specified profiles. The necessity to broaden the abilities of an average user and the demand to constantly increase teachers' competencies are the challenges for educational systems. These problems are widely analysed in the presented book with reference to interesting local examples of different forms of implementation of new ideas and methods of creative teaching of media and through media, i.e. with the use of 3D environments, games, machinima and social networking websites. The questions of evolution of competences in media and information literacy are today fundamental for the future of educational system and therefore - for the shape of future society. The changes are necessary, as the old paradigm of literacy has been loosing its ground to new generations of 'digital natives'.

The relation between the real and the virtual is the next important issue raised in the book. Crucial terms analysed in various contexts became 'interaction' and 'interactivity'. The problem concerns virtual environments, game design and human-computer interaction, user-generated content connected with the ideas of openness, folksonomies and wikinomics. The ontological questions are transforming today into judicial or psychological problems concerning our existence in both real and virtual environments.

Digital data loss or an attack on an avatar - may be seen as nothing serious, but in fact it can be felt as a real harm, despite the digital nature of its object. The virtual is therefore no longer the opposition of the real, it is its aspect, even if it still sounds strange. We perceive them both through our senses and through our bodies. These questions should be taken into consideration also by designers of virtual environments, video games and communication systems.

Both the constantly emerging and growing virtual communities and the convergence of new media create new possibilities of communication. The current situation enables media users to develop, often subconsciously, their skills and various types of communication behaviour, which results in new models of perception and thinking - thus, new patterns of culture and new forms of society. On the other hand members of this new society design new technologies, software, devices and communication solutions that change world even more quickly, rebuilding interrelations between the elements of the social system. This opens possibilities for new visions of cyberculture and humanity.

However, cyberculture, being shaped by global and information marketing provided by major IT companies, largely depends on the Web users' willingness and their access to the global information product. Web 2.0 can be, without any hesitation, regarded as such a product - moreover, a successful one. But the label '2.0' quickly changes into '3.0', as the novelty is one of the priorities of marketing. What does it mean for the users and for future communication? The authors specialising in various disciplines try to find answers to these and other important questions of our contemporariness and future.

Concluding, we should remember that even if potentially well-known and mature, cyberculture is still vivid, paradoxical and hybrid. Therefore, it is not easy to indicate the most important problems from anthropological, sociological, psychological, pedagogical, political or judicial perspective. Although today very important, tomorrow our problems may seem to be naive. But cyberculture will never become old; it will rather disappear or evolve to a different form of culture. There are multiple emerging issues and each day introduces new solutions, every new software or device gives new hopes and raises new questions about the future. And in this perspective the content of this book is not going to fade away with new inventions - now it presents challenges of emerging cyberculture issues, one day it will become the record of our times, interesting from anthropological or archaeological reasons.

This book consists of ten chapters and has been organised into four parts which are dedicated to four important aspects of emerging practices in cyberculture and social networking:

PART I:        Access, Power and Social Marginalisation in Cyberculture
PART II:       Cyber-Governance, Cyber-Communities, Cyber-Bodies
PART III:      New Concepts in Education and Entertainment
PART IV:       Web 2.0 and Social Networking

The first part is comprised of three articles on topics of access and power as well as on different aspects of domination and marginalisation, which are of great importance for contemporary societies and future development of digital media.

*Nils Gustafsson* explores the borders of social tendencies and viral politics in his essay 'This Time It's Personal: Social Networks, Viral Politics and Identity Management'. Social media are analysed here from the point of view of identity design and management, whereas social networks are regarded as a form of collective gatekeeping of information and a post-institutional way of civic self-organisation. The author proposes a new model of political viral campaigning using social media and operational terms as 'viral politics' and 'temporal elites', which are fundamental for the understanding of this communication process.

*Anna Maj and Michal Derda-Nowakowski* in their essay 'Anthropology of Accessibility: Further Reflections on the Perceptual Problems of Human-Computer Interactions', show the context of accessible design, especially for people with visual impairments but also for other groups of users that can be marginalised by the process of acceleration of the development of technology. The authors emphasise the fact that nowadays competencies to operate technologies have become fundamental cultural competencies. Problems connected with the 'proper' design, which means openness, standardisation, usability and accessibility are analysed here with the background of some influential technological solutions and inventions, and is regarded as an anthropological problem of communication process and information flow.

*Christina Neumayer, Celina Raffl* and *Robert M. Bichler* in their essay 'Politics and Social Software: Recommendations for Inclusive ICTs', reflect on social media's potential to strengthen citizen movements through disseminating patterns of collaborative creation. The authors suggest that social networking can be more effectively used as a powerful tool for political and ideological purposes and for struggling with the digital divide or other forms of social marginalisation. The authors focus on the inclusive use of new media increasing social power due to various tools such as social software that may have impact on political activism enabling a participatory attitude to social issues.

The second part of this book presents two articles focused on three important levels of the digital order - cyber-governance, cyber-communities and cyber-body, which enormously influences our digital existence.

*Melissa de Zwart* and David *Lindsay* in the essay 'Governance and the Global Metaverse' analyse an issue of increasing importance-multidimensional coexistence of juridical systems and digital culture. The authors examine various problems, such as ideas and methods of governance, legitimacy and power distribution in the context of 3-D virtual worlds, games and social networking websites, raising questions on the conditions and implications of the ways in which cyberlaw functions in different digital environments and also in offline reality of state law. These issues are crucial for global culture and cybersociety as they concern questions of the code being the law itself, freedom of users (or its lack) and the power of service providers.

*Donata Marletta* in her essay 'Hybrid Communities to Digital Arts Festivals: From Online Discussions to Offline Gatherings' shows the possibilities for anthropology of cyberculture or ethnography of media, science and design. The author examines new forms of connectivity and modes of community forming, especially those connected with the Internet communication and a wide spectrum of new media festivals, digital art competitions and conferences on ICT and its social impact. The research perspective presented here sheds new light on parallel online and offline existences of digital communities. The essay indicates important factors of the evolution of the meaning of virtual communities and cyberspace itself.

Part three examines emerging ideas in the field of education and entertainment, which are connected with new modes of learning, perception and cognition as well as new communication practices and competencies connected with creativity and the knowledge of specific tools:

*Jef Folkerts* concentrates on the issues of perception, interaction and semiosis in the essay 'Playing Games as an Art Experience: How Videogames Produce Meaning through Narrative and Play'. Game design and playing are regarded here as an important semiotic activity where meaning is constructed by designers and constantly reconstructed by players. The issue of imagination produced by games is the core problem analysed by the author in the context of other kinds of cultural mass production. Games are regarded here as the following step of evolution of artificial environments used for creation and recreation of social and personal imagination.

*Daniel Riha* 'The 3-D Virtual Library as a Value-Added Library Service', discusses the functionalities the Library 2.0 shall deliver with the focus on 3-D library service and analyses the assumptions for the establishing of the long-term user community from the wider historical perspective. The concept of the 3-D Virtual Library, realised in 2004 for the University of Constance Library is compared against the actual 3-D library concepts.

*Theodoros Thomas* in his essay 'Cyberculture: Learning New Literacies through Machinima' concentrates on cyberculture teaching, a new context of education process and alternative, participatory forms of knowledge distribution. Basing on realisation of an educational project concerning cyberculture and digital literacy, the author analyses problems and challenges of teaching new media skills. The knowledge of cyberspace, virtual communities and environment, basics of image, video and sound processing and digital storytelling skills which was acquired during the academic course, were later applied by students to prepare their own machinima projects.

The fourth part of this book, presenting papers concerned with the various aspects of the development of Web 2.0 trends and the global rise of social networking practices, gives three interesting local examples of the social use of digital media:

*Natalia Waechter, Kaveri Subrahmanyam, Stephanie M. Reich* and *Guadalupe Espinoza* in their essay 'Youth Connecting Online: From Chat Rooms to Social Networking Sites', presents results of empirical research on social networking of American teenage users and the modes of their activity. Teenagers are eager to use social networking websites as well as other communication tools which expand their offline social networks but also let them create online social networks. The researchers study behaviour, attitudes and needs of young Internet users in order to understand the dependencies between their online activity and psycho-sociological development of emerging adults.

*Chand Somaiah's* 'Cybergrace among Eating Disorder Survivors in Singapore' considers the implications for ethical storytelling. Illness has been understood as learning to cope with lost control. Cyberspace then to the author might serve as a medium for semblance of lost control. The potential impact of online eating disorder support groups and blogs for shaping individual and collective identities has been examined.

# PART I

# Access, Power and Social Marginalisation in Cyberculture

# This Time It's Personal: Social Networks, Viral Politics and Identity Management

## *Nils Gustafsson*

**Abstract**

This chapter deals with political mobilisation and participation in social media. The main focus is on the importance of Internet-mediated social networks in providing a 'media filter', functioning as a kind of collective gatekeeper to spread news and information perceived as important, in contrast to the image of the single individual media consumer faced with an insurmountable mass of information. I argue that by investing one's personal *ethos* in spreading information and encourage peers in the personal social network to political participation, vital news and calls for action spread quickly. A form of *viral politics* ensues that, in concordance with traditional types of mediation and formation of political opinion, might provide a basis for a new type of political elite in competitive democracy. Drawing on earlier research concerning the effect of social capital created by weak ties on political participation, I argue that social networks organised online provide a new type of post-organisational weak ties, functioning as *maintained social capital* building institutions, encouraging to and organising actions of civic engagement. I also argue that, contrary to the common belief that various forms of Internet-mediated political mobilisation constitute a more inclusive, emancipatory and egalitarian politics, it could also be the case that the growing importance of viral politics reinforces the traditional inequality in political participation and influence in society. More specifically, a case is made for the need for more thorough conceptualisation of new modes of participation: spontaneous, individualised, 'unorganised' forms of action. Two concepts, *'temporal elites'* and *'viral politics'* are developed for describing how social network membership and density determine how people are recruited to political campaigns. The theoretical assumptions are further illustrated by the preliminary empirical findings of an ongoing study of Swedish Facebook users and their attitudes and behaviour concerning political participation in social media.

**Key Words:** Social Networks, Political Participation, Virtual Mobilisation, Facebook, Social Capital, Elite Theory.

*****

## 1.     Introduction

This chapter starts with a short background of the academic discussion in the field and giving a rationale for why new concepts are needed. After a brief introduction to the phenomenon of social media and social network sites, the concepts of viral politics and temporal elites are developed and explained. The chapter ends with an empirical illustration of viral politics at the individual level, reporting the results of a study on Swedish Facebook users.

An ongoing discussion in democracy research is concerned with the question of whether the level of political participation in the industrialised or post-industrial countries is sinking or not. The reason for why a high level of participation in society is perceived as important is that it is thought to be an essential part of well-functioning democracy, at least by proponents of the lines of thought in democratic theory associated with concepts like participatory, deliberative, or 'strong' democracy and theorists like J. S. Mill, Benjamin Barber and David Held. By participating, citizens learn and grow as individuals, thereby bettering and emancipating themselves as human beings and contributing to better governance.[1] Mass participation is not seen as a *sine qua non* by all democratic theorists. Proponents of what David Held calls competitive elitist democracy, like Max Weber, Robert Michels and Joseph Schumpeter, underline the need for a competent political elite and restrict the role of the masses to voting, in effect selecting between competing elitist groups.[2] As I will argue below, participation in internet-mediated social networks, *viral politics* might be interpreted as the emergence of a new type of political elite rather than mass participation.

An academic debate concerning political participation in post-industrial countries has been going on for the last few decades. The main idea is that social capital, as theorised by among others Bourdieu, is correlated to the level of participation.[3] The debate goes in two lines of argumentation. The line championed by, among others, Robert Putnam, maintains that political participation is decreasing as the level of social capital in society wanes with increasing individualisation and political apathy.[4] Another line, represented by, among others, Russell J. Dalton and Pippa Norris[5], argues contrarily that the forms of participation are merely changing and are taking on new forms, as post-materialist values become more salient.[6] Instead of enrolling in political parties and other formal organisations, citizens are now to a greater extent canalising their engagement through various types of protest, such as boycotts and buycotts, civil disobedience, internet activism and through the means of informal networks.[7] These tendencies arguably run parallel to the global nature of several contemporary political issues, as well as the circumscribed autonomy of the nation state and increasing complexity of governance relationships.[8]

Another debate of interest for this chapter concerns the effects of the ever more dispersed and advanced use of digital communications technologies - e-mail, web pages, mobile phones, social media - on political mobilisation and participation. Within political science, this discussion tends to be focused either on the causal effects of such technologies on the level and type of social capital, which is thought to spur participation, or on the effects of social or 'new' media use on political knowledge and attitudes, also thought to spur participation.[9]

However, it is also important to remember that technology itself cannot be taken as a given. The design of social media is deeply related to existing social structures and ideologies in society. Services might contribute to increased elitism, surveillance and competitiveness. The interfaces they use might be produced by and for certain types of people - stereotypically young, web-savvy, able-bodied people. Thus, whether social media platforms will have beneficial or adversarial effects on grassroots mobilisation depends in part on active choices of designers.[10]

The discussion about social media and social capital is also linked to assumptions of the increased importance of social networks in late modern society.[11] In this case it is also possible to distinguish between different strains of thought present in the debate. On the one hand it is argued that the dominant effect is a decrease in social capital; on the other hand it is argued that new communications technologies in combination with a waxing network society are in fact contributing to an increase in social capital. A third position maintains that the internet and other arenas of digital communication function as a useful compliment to traditional types of social capital.[12]

Concerning the effect of social media on political knowledge - together with education an important factor behind political participation - the discussion also divides into an optimistic and a pessimistic strain. Some researchers have found causal effects of social media on political knowledge and participation in empirical investigations, explaining the effect with the 'surprise effect' of unexpected political social media content, offsetting the effect of already politically interested people actively searching for political information on the internet.[13] Others have pointed to how social and other digital media correct mistakes in traditional mass media, reinvigorate the public sphere and provide a base for a more diverse political discourse, peer production, citizen journalism, and so on.[14]

Empirical evidence has, however, also been provided for the hypothesis that social media in combination with other types of media, producing an overall wider media choice for consumers, have resulted in a larger knowledge gap between politically interested and disinterested citizens, most strikingly so in the work of Markus Prior.[15] The American political scientist Matthew Hindman presents convincing empirical evidence for that in the blurry field of 'Internet politics', there is a strong tendency to winner-takes-all behaviour, power law distributions and a reinforced influence for traditionally strong groups in society in his book 'The Myth of Digital Democracy', deploying terms like 'Googlearchy' to describe how a few heavily linked web sites completely dominate discourse in the American political universe.[16]

It is fair to say that there will be no consensus on whether social network sites and other forms of social media, or the internet in general, are 'bad' or 'good' for 'democracy', whether that means a more oligopolistic or more fragmented public sphere, a more or less emancipated electorate, centralised or decentralised decision making, etc. Soon enough, the technologies will become so ubiquitous that they turn invisible to us, and the amount of new research dedicated to establish causal relations between 'the Internet' and 'democracy', or between 'social media' and 'democracy' will decrease.[17] However, a few unclarities must be sorted out. In the debate between techno-utopians and techno-dystopians, false dichotomies are abundant. Social media does not make everything new. Old hierarchies remain. But still, everything is not quite the same. The inequalities in representative democracy prevail, but are transformed as political strife and discourse take on new shapes and new actors are involved. It is also important to distinguish between what is, what could be, and what ought to be.[18] Proponents of deliberative democracy would like to see an informed public evolve through a more inclusive digital public sphere, but if what we actually have is an elitist competitive democracy, that should be taken into account. And empirical research departing from a competitive democratic model should not be confused with saying that there ought not be a more egalitarian political system or that it is not possible for the digital public sphere to facilitate informed deliberation on public issues. It is my strong belief that students of Internet-mediated politics, as in all other fields, must be aware of that. That this chapter departs from a view of representative democracy in post-industrial countries as unequal and that political mobilisation aided by social network sites might even increase power inequality does not mean that I as an author support elitism. I am actually a huge fan of egalitarianism.

As much as the field of political participation and mobilisation aided by social media is emerging as an interesting and important field of research in the social sciences, it is still an under researched field. It lacks standard definitions and it though the interdisciplinarity of web research makes it fascinating and vital, it is also a crossroads for heaps of theories and classic literature in so many established disciplines. As a web researcher, it is difficult to know all. The reason for why I have chosen to develop new concepts for network-driven political mobilisation (viral politics) and for the emerging sub-group of people in the stratas of political power using this phenomenon as a successful way to political influence (the temporal elites) is that I do not find that there are really good concepts available for talking about these things. I believe that taking parts from classic democratic theory and classic elite theory and using them in combination with newer work on the information flows in social networks for interpreting this confusing world of Twittering rebels and Facebooking anarchists is a productive way of moving forwards.

The next section will give a short introduction to social network sites and develop the concept of viral politics.

## 2.        Social Networks, Social Network Sites and Viral Politics

Social network sites are a prominent type of the various forms of user-generated social media that sometimes are grouped under the term 'Web 2.0'.[19] Quoting the by now minor classic 2007 article on social network sites by Danah Boyd and Nicole Ellison, they are:

> web-based services that (1) construct a public or semi-public profile within a bounded system, (2) articulate a list of other users with whom they share a connection, and (3) view and traverse their list of connections and those made by others within the system.[20]

By using social network sites, it is possible to maintain off-line connections in an on-line environment, making it possible to communicate with close friends as well as casual acquaintances regardless of where they happen to be situated in time or space. It is also possible to form more or less contemporary groups, connecting people from different networks on the basis of common interests, membership in formal organisations, sharing jokes or promoting political and social causes. Another typical feature of social network sites is the interconnectedness with other types of social and mainstream media. It is easy to upload or link to media content, post it to your personal profile or to a group, or forwarding it to the contacts in your network, as well as integrating your personal profiles in different types of social media. To take an example: someone draws your attention to a funny video clip of a politician making a fool of her- or himself on television. You favourite it on your personal YouTube page, post it on your blog with a comment, tag it (assign a label to it in order to find it easily later) and store it on your del.ici.ous folksonomy page, forward the blog post to your Facebook profile, post a tweet (write a short blog post on the microblogging site Twitter) with a link to your blog post about the video clip, pass it along to your friends via e-mail, through Facebook, an SMS, etc. Your friends will in their turn assess whether they think that the clip is worthy of passing on, forwarding it or not. Someone might edit the original footage, adding music, snippets of other clips, texts, thereby creating a mash-up, a new piece of media, which in its turn might be passed around.[21] Different tools allow the interactive audience to discuss and see how other people have interpreted and rated the media content. There are special services available that collect the forms of media content that are most circulated at the time. In the end, the sharing of the media content might in itself be a story worthy of mentioning in mainstream media, thereby creating a feedback loop between the different forms of media. In effect, your social network provides a media filter for you, passing on media content that are found to be especially interesting.

This is the art of viral sharing, one of the defining characteristics of the contemporary media structure. Perhaps most applied to the logic of new marketing techniques, it is also a concept most useful to describe how post-organisational political mobilisation might occur through activist mediation.

The buzz word concept of viral marketing came into use in the mid 90s and was connected with marketing strategies on the Internet.[22] The basic idea is that in a world where the Internet makes it possible for anyone to be a publisher, it is difficult, if even possible, to shout down the immense mass of information produced. Thus, the best way to reach out is to make consumers themselves do the advertising by sharing information about products with their friends.[23] An early well-known example was the way that Hotmail automatically attached the line 'Get your free email at Hotmail' to every outgoing message sent by a Hotmail user. The recipient then knew that 'the sender was a Hotmail user, and that this new free email seemed to work for them'.[24] Campaigns for the Google webmail service Gmail and the music streaming service Spotify used the social networks of their customers in that it was only possible to sign up for the service through invitation from a user.

The metaphor of the virus builds on the notion that the spreading of the information is similar to the adoption pattern of a virus, with 'spatial and network locality', only with a much wider scope and velocity than had been possible in the pre-Internet era. Viruses 'thrive on weak ties'.[25]

Viral sharing can be defined as 'getting the right idea into the right heads at the right time'.[26] The features needed for any media content to be truly viral are evocative images and consistency with existing world views in the minds of the audience. In the field of political and social activism, I call this phenomenon viral politics.

The use of the term 'viral' in this context is not uncontroversial. According to Henry Jenkins, the concept of viral media pictures transmitters of viral messages as passive individuals passing on unchanged pieces of information - involuntary hosts infected by an evil virus. In reality, a core feature of so-called viral sharing is that transmitters are empowered to change the message and fill it with new meanings. And while viruses replicate themselves, communication depends on acts of human will. Instead, Jenkins suggests a new concept, spreadable media, which would basically mean the same phenomenon but with a strong focus on the active role of consumers/citizens.[27]

The reason I choose to keep viral as a concept is basically that it has been used for describing the phenomenon of my interest in other spheres of human communication for more than a decade. Although I admit that the metaphor does not hold all the way through - Jenkins is right in his critique - I do not find using 'spreadable politics' a viable way to create a functioning concept. That would take an even greater effort to explain what the concept contains. Taking into account the weaknesses of the wording, I thus suggest viral politics to mean the rapid sharing of evoking media content in social networks online in the realm of political and social activism.

The place of social network sites in relation to other media is complex. On the one hand, the high-modern media structure of the 19th and 20th centuries, characterised by the sharp boundary between consumers and producers of media content and the professionalisation of journalism, seem to give way to an ecological media structure characterised by a blurring of boundaries between producers and consumers and the rise of citizen journalism.[28] On the other hand, the monopolistic tendencies of media concentration and cultural homogenisation become more articulated as generic content flourishes in movie theatres, television, radio, newspapers, magazines and bestsellers. A defining characteristic of this ecological media structure is convergence.[29] Much of the content passed around in social media sites emanate from traditional media outlets. YouTube started out as a channel for purely user-generated content, but ever since the beginning, users have uploaded large amounts of copyrighted content.[30] The reverse is also true: mainstream media try in various ways to reach out to their audience by inviting readers, viewers and listeners to comment, share, upload own media content or rework existing content.[31] Thus, it is not correct to describe or define social network sites or social media in general as the opposite of traditional or mainstream media. That is also true in the realm of politics. Although social media sometimes are viewed as a playground for grassroots mobilisation, traditional political actors like political parties and interest groups are using these new communication tools for enhancing the internal organisation, political advertisements, and tapping into new mobilising structures.

The effects of sharing political media content on political participation using social media is an under researched field. Previous research has established a strong connection between social capital and political participation; in particular, the link between weak ties and participation. According to Mark S. Granovetter, 'people rarely act on mass-media information unless it is also transmitted through personal ties; otherwise one has no particular reason to think that an advertised product or an organisation should be taken seriously.'[32] This relationship has been found in the political field in several empirical studies. Jan Teorell's 2003 study found that as the number of weak ties increases, the likelihood of participation also increases. Although education is a very strong predictor for engagement in societal affairs, people still have to be recruited. If a person's social network is large, the chance that he or she will be asked to participate is higher.[33]

The importance of the personal dissemination of media content and calls for action is not new. The qualitative difference with social network sites and social media is the efficiency with which information can be spread.

Organising weak ties in social network sites allows for an individual to stay connected to brief acquaints also when moving to another geographical area, thereby creating maintained social capital. This offsets the deterioration of social capital in society as a product of increased mobility.[34] Online relationships are provisional, but off-line relationships in an on-line setting are not.[35] This affects the size of the network.

As the size of social networks increases, the chance for any two people being connected to each other also increases. The Small World Pattern explains the expression 'It's a small world' exclaimed by 'newly introduced individuals upon finding that they have common acquaintances'.[36] Small World networks are composed both of small groups of people dense ties and of larger groups with weaker ties. Important for networks to grow extremely large is the existence of individuals with a wildly disproportionate amount of connections, being able to connect a large number of smaller dense groups with one another: 'In fact, social networks are not held together by the bulk of people with hundreds of connections but by the few people with tens of thousands.'[37] New communication technology enhances the stability of these networks, making it easier to connect to other social networks.

The velocity of viral sharing implies that millions of people can be reached through word of mouth in a matter of days. Whereas meeting in person, phone chains, or other older methods of spreading rumours or information, took days and months to pass on media content to a larger group of people, social media reduces this time to a matter of minutes. Spreading a message through your personal network through social media will, by the logics of maintained social capital and the small world pattern, through viral sharing reach a global crowd at short notice (provided that the message is attractive enough to be virally shared, which is an essential part of viral politics.).

The social forces behind viral politics are, as stated above, not new. I would like to point this out one more time because it is often assumed that technology is changing human behaviour in revolutionising ways. However, human culture and basic biologic factors tend to change slowly. The reason that viral politics can be seen as a partly new and potentially transforming factor in political life is the increased velocity and scope of the communication.

In spreading media content to their personal network, individuals manifest their commitment to their existing beliefs and move closer to political action. They also invest their personal status as an acquaintance -

their ethos - in forwarding a message through their social network. This is probably just as much a strategy of identity management - what kind of person do I want to be in the eyes of my peers and what does this piece of information tell them about me? - as a will of influencing society. I will return to this in the final part of this chapter. By finally reaching into mainstream media, the content will reach people who already does not share that commitment.[38] Through the electronic organising of social networks, the 'personal' information flow increases and the threshold for participation is lowered.

### 3.      Temporal Elites

The era of the Internet - first during the 1.0 wave in the 90s and later during the 2.0 wave in the mid- and late 2000s - has sometimes been seen as heralding a new dawn for inclusive, non-hierarchical politics. In some ways, the increased importance of social media has led to the dilution of the power of traditional political actors, at least when it comes to opinion formation. However, I would like to argue that the dynamics of social media does not merely change existing structures in society: old rules of thumb for who participates - and thus has influence over agenda-setting and political outcomes - still apply. It can be the case, quite contrarily to some popular notions of the age of social media, that networked politics of the kind described in this chapter might actually increase elitism in society as well-connected social networks, political knowledge and technical skills become more even important to build effective campaigns. In this section, I try to provide a preliminary sketch of how a partly novel group of highly skilled people in the network society becomes increasingly more influential as viral politics becomes a political strategy in the everyday life. I call this group of people 'temporal elites' to denote their limited influence to certain fields and the highly unpredictable success in exerting influence over policy outcomes and agenda-setting.

Viral politics emanates from political entrepreneurs, that most often will be directly affected people of a certain event or phenomenon (the 'victims') and/or groups and organisations, both NGOs and political parties devoted to this particular cause (Burma Action Committee, Doctors Without Borders, Amnesty International, United Nations, Oxfam, political parties or politicians). In some cases, they will be individuals acting only on behalf of themselves, but usually being a part of a wider network of people sharing views and notions of political strategy. These individuals spread information and media content by word of mouth to wider groups of people through personal interconnectedness. If successful, the content/information will catch on and spread rapidly through the mechanism of viral politics, influencing the formal political system directly through personal contacts with political representatives and indirect through the feedback loop provided by mainstream media.

The political entrepreneurs of a successful campaign of viral politics form, together with temporary supporters of the cause to be found in interconnected social networks, a temporal elite, having the necessary knowledge, skills and (perhaps above all) the motivation to promote the cause.

Sometimes, the concept of elite is put in opposition to the concept of democracy. It can however also be seen as an important part of well-functioning democracy, as in the tradition associated with competitive democracy, where the electorate is seen as fairly passive between elections, choosing between political alternatives depending on track record or promises, thus legitimating political representatives:

> a small group of political leaders [...] with perhaps an intermediate section of more active citizens, who transmit demands and information between the mass and the leadership.[39]

The political entrepreneurs serving as a backbone of the temporal elite associated with viral politics are a group of people that fit well into this description of the intermediate section of David Miller's competitive elitist democracy model evident in the quote above. I would argue, though, that to the group of key political entrepreneurs in viral politics should be added a wider group of people, also belonging to the elite in the respect that they help spreading the campaign and provide a bandwagoning force for a successful cause to break into the traditional mass media outlets, but distinguished from the 'mass' by their political interest, knowledge and activism. In order to bring this group of people into our understanding of the temporal elites, I would like to point to Robert Putnam's classical model of political stratification.

In the model, based on empirical studies of national elites in various countries in the 1970s, the citizenry is divided into six strata, organised to form a pyramid of power:[40]

1.      Proximate decision makers: incumbents in key official posts. This is normally a very small group of people.

2.      Influentials: powerful opinion makers and people to who decision makers look for advice - high-level bureaucrats, interest group leaders. This is also a small group.

3. Activists: This stratum is made up of the group of citizens who take active part in politics - as members of a political party or on a more private level. This is a larger group of people.

4. Still larger is the stratum of the attentive public, which consists of citizens who follow the political debates as some kind of spectator sports. They rarely do something actively.

5. The big bulk of citizens are the voters who have very limited, if any, political influence. They vote and that is it.

6. Finally, the nonparticipants do not even vote and have no politic power what so ever.

The temporal elites would therefore serve to modify the second and third stratas, where the political entrepreneurs, or the core of the temporal elites, fit into Putnam's group of influentials, while the wider group of activists neatly fit into the group of activists. The major difference posed to this model of political stratification by the concept of temporal elites proposed here is that the political entrepreneurs of the temporal elites contain people who would not normally be counted as influentials. The initiative taker of, for instance, the 2007 Support the Monk's Protests in Burma campaign, a Canadian exchange student, was very influential in that the campaign gained hundreds of thousands of followers globally and forced governments and corporations to rethink their policies towards Burma/Myanmar, but a Canadian exchange student would not normally be counted to the group of 'powerful opinion makers'. The activist's stratum is also challenged by the temporal elites as they are made up by individuals participating in politics in a plethora of ways: organised, unorganised, postorganised.

According to Karl Deutsch's concept of the 'Opinion Cascade', the flow of information and persuasion between these political strata flow from the top down: emanating in the political and socioeconomic elite, transmitted by the mass media and opinion leaders to the mass public.[41] Could it be the case that the stability of the downward flow of information might be distorted by the rise of digital media, rising levels of education, post-materialist values, and that 'opinion leaders' should be constructed in a more inclusive way, and also that influence might flow upstream as well as downstream? The concept of temporal elites would point in that direction.

This new concept of elites does not mean that classic elites are not important; on the contrary. Financial and political elites are becoming increasingly powerful in an era of multilevel governance, ruling through networks, hiding behind markets, making power invisible where there used to be a throne, although it is also true that power elites are not as stable as before.[42] The temporal elites might instead be seen as a potential counterforce, or at least complementing traditional elites in democracy. The brave new world of viral politics, networked individualism, and general social media carnivale, might not be a quick-fix for the problem with the unequal power distribution in representative democracies, but it is also not a reason to prophesy doom for all mankind: new developments should be compared to the status quo, not to an unattainable democratic ideal of total inclusivity. It is, however, also important to point out that, for those who have an ideal cherishing democratic equality, the potentially disproportional representation of a young, well-educated generation of native born citizens might widen the political elite in society, but also put more influence firmly in the hands of the well-off. Having said that, studies of political participation conducted in the past five decades have consistently shown that well-educated people with a high socio-economic status are more likely to participate than others. Technology alone will not offset this structure.

I would like to finish this section by elaborating on how the flexibility of Internet-mediated communication might lead to more people being able to join the ranks of 'activists'.

An often-mentioned sociological phenomenon in the field of Internet sociology is the power law distribution. When analysing, for example, the contributions to a Wikipedia page, one of the most characteristic features is the huge difference between contributors in the number of contributions made and the size of each individual contribution. Some individuals contribute substantially more than others, and the 'normal' contribution is typically very small in size (compare with the discussion above on small world networks). There is no point in analysing average contributions, because the number and size of contributions among contributors is not normally distributed. Instead, the nth position has 1/nth of the first person's rank.[43]

The same is true for civic engagement in the setting of the post-organisational viral politics of social networks. A few individuals (political entrepreneurs) invest a very large amount of time in a political or social cause. These individuals constitute the inner core of the temporal elite associated with the cause in question. As they spread information about the cause in their social networks, some people will feel encouraged to invest an equal amount of time and join a temporal elite, some people will invest less, and most people will do little or nothing. The possibility of flexible engagement makes it attractive to more people to engage, as they can easily adapt the work effort put down to their personal priorities.[44]

The total sum of engagement may be equal or even higher than before, despite decreasing levels of membership in formal organisations devoted to social and political causes. The emergence of temporal elites and viral politics might in this way save democracy, although what will be saved is not the egalitarian ideal model of democracy, but the elitist realist model we actually live in.

## 4. Identity Management and Annoyed Participation

In a 2008 study, a small number of Swedish Facebook users were interviewed, using virtual focus groups, about their attitudes towards political content and mobilisation on the social networking site.[45] The participants were divided into two groups, one of which consisted of individuals who are active or have recently been active members of formal political organisations, while the other group consisted of individuals not having a formal political engagement.

I will cite a few of the results here in order to put some light on how complicated motives and actions of participants in viral politics are, and how further research must take that into account.

There were no major differences between the answers from the politically active participants and the non-active participants concerning the attitudes to political mobilisation in Facebook, except for the fact that several politically active participants reported that they have incorporated Facebook among other forms of communication in their formal political engagement. The participants in the focus groups had generally a sceptical view towards political campaigns in Facebook. Many of them maintained the notion that participating in political campaigns online in various forms filled mainly two functions: building your public or semi-public identity by expressing political views and concerns; and being an excuse not for taking a more active part in a campaign. Off-line activity was viewed in general as being more important or real:

> To me, most Facebook causes seem utterly pointless as political/opinion forming tools. My impression is that they function more like markers for a group or an attitude that the user wants to identify with. Quite simply they become statements that you pose with on your Facebook page. It's really the same function as the summary of facts on the user profile, although they give a more active and engaged impression. (Participant)

The respondents also complained about the large number of requests for support from political campaigns, among an enormous number of other types of requests and invitations, leading to Facebook fatigue and a general reluctance toward any type of action.

However, most participants reported that they had actually taken part in off-line activities as a direct result of mobilisation using Facebook. They also reported, without exceptions, that they were indeed members of various groups on Facebook supporting political and social causes. One participant described this seemingly paradoxical behaviour as 'annoyed participation'.[46] It was also clear, interestingly enough considering the importance of recruitment through social networks traditionally found in network studies and political participation studies, that who sent you a request to participate was just as important for whether one of the participants would join a cause or campaign as the subject itself.

This might be an indicator for people engaging in viral politics might not be aware of their own importance for a successful campaign and that empirical evaluation of the proposed model must be aware of this.

## 5.        Conclusions

This chapter has tried to establish two new concepts in the academic debate over the development of political participation in the light of changing uses of computer-mediated communication. Viral politics, with connections to viral marketing and network theory, is used to describe a way of dispersing information through social networks, evident in later years and possibly an important ingredient in political participation in an era of networked individualism. Temporal elites, with connections to classic elite theory and to elitist democratic theory, denotes the people behind viral politics: a group of individuals, well-connected, well-educated and motivated to take an active part in politics, but not necessarily through joining political parties or even interest groups. It is my hope that these concepts might be found useful as the study of viral politics and of political participation in social media takes a much-needed empirical turn, informed by developing political theory.

# Notes

[1] These propositions are made by a score of democratic theorists. Pippa Norris lists Rousseau, James Madison, J. S. Mill, Robert Dahl, Benjamin Barber, David Held and John Dryzak in P Norris, *Democratic Phoenix. Reinventing Political Activism*, Cambridge University Press, Cambridge, 2002, p. 5.
[2] D Held, *Models of Democracy*, Polity Press, Cambridge, 2006, pp. 125-157.

[3] P Bourdieu, 'The Forms of Capital', in *Education: Culture, Economy and Society*, A H Halsey, H Lauder, P Brown & A Stuart Wells (eds), Oxford University Press, Oxford, 1997, pp. 46-58.

[4] R Putnam, *Bowling Alone: The Collapse and Revival of American Community*, Simon & Schuster, New York, 2000.

[5] R J Dalton, 'Citizenship Norms and the Expansion of Political Participation', *Political Studies*, vol. 56, 2008, pp. 76-98; Norris. See also B O'Neill, 'Indifferent or Just Different? The Political and Civic Engagement of Young People in Canada.' Canadian Policy Research Networks Research Report, 2007.

[6] R Inglehart, *The Silent Revolution. Changing Values and Political Styles Among Western Publics,* Princeton University Press, Princeton, 1977, esp. pp. 262-321.

[7] M Micheletti, *Political Virtue and Shopping: Individuals, Consumerism, and Collective Action*, Palgrave Macmillan, Basingstoke, 2003.

[8] G Stoker, 'Governance as Theory: Five Propositions', *International Social Science Journal*, vol. 50(155), 1998, pp. 17-28.

[9] M Cantijoch, L Jorba, and Gallego, A, 'Exposure to Political Information in New and Old Media: which Impact on Political Participation?' Paper presented for delivery at the 2008 Annual Meeting of the American Political Science Association, August 28-21, 2008, viewed on 10 August 2008, <http://www.allacademic.com/meta/p_mla_apa_research_citation/2/8/0/1/0/p 280108_index.html>.

[10] see C Neumayer & C Raffl and A Maj & M Derda-Nowakowski in this volume.

[11] M Castells, *The Rise of the Network Society*, Blackwell Publishers, Cambridge (MA, USA), 1996.

[12] B Wellman, A Q Haase, J Witte and K Hampton, 'Does the Internet Increase, Decrease or Supplement Social Capital? Social Networks, Participation, and Community Comitment', American Behavioral Scientist vol. 45(3), 2001 pp. 437-456. See also J Boase, J B Horrigan, B Wellman, and L Rainie, 'The Strength of Internet Ties', Pew Internet and American Life Project, viewed on 10 August 2009, <http://www.pewinternet.org/pdfs/PIP_Internet_ties.pdf>.

[13] Cantijoch et al., p. 8; K Sweetser and K L Lee, 'Stealth Soapboxes: Political Information Efficacy, Cynicism and Uses of Celebrity Weblogs among Readers', *New Media & Society*, vol. 10(1), 2008, pp. 67-90.

[14] Y Benkler, *The Wealth of Networks*, Yale University Press, New Haven, 2007, esp. pp. 176-272.

[15] M Prior, *Post-Broadcast Democracy: How Media Choice Increases Inequality in Political Involvement and Polarizes Elections*, Cambridge University Press, Cambridge, 2007.

[16] M Hindman, *The Myth of Digital Democracy*, Princeton University Press, Prinecton, 2008.

[17] On the invisibleness of established technologies, see D Beer & R Burrows, 'Sociology and, of and in Web 2.0: Some Initial Considerations', *Sociological Research Online*, vol. 12(5), 2007, viewed on 12 August 2009, <http://www.socresonline.org.uk/12/5/17.html>. For an early influential example of a study linking the mere existence of the Internet to democratisation, see C Kedzie, 'Democracy and Network Connectivity', *Proceedings of the INET'95 International Networking Conference*, Honolulu, Hawaii, 1995, viewed on 12 August 2009, <http://www.isoc.org/inet95/proceedings/PAPER/134/html/paper.html>.

[18] R Putnam, *The Comparative Study of Political Elites*, Prentice Hall, Englewood Cliffs, 1976, p. 3; L Lundqvist, *Det vetenskapliga studiet av politik*, Studentlitteratur, Lund, 1992, pp. 60-63.

[19] The expression Web 2.0 is, of course, controversial and disputed. For one summary discussion, see Beer & Burrows.

[20] D Boyd and N B Ellison, 'Social Network Sites: Definition, History and Scholarship', *Journal of Computer-Mediated Communication*, vol. 13(1), 2007.

[21] The history of the mash-up is described in S Howard-Spink, 'Grey Tuesday, Online Cultural Activism and the Mash-up of Music and Politics', *First Monday, Special Issue # 1: Music and the Internet*, 2005-07-04, viewed on 17 August 2009, <http://firstmonday.org/htbin/cgiwrap/bin/ojs/index.php/fm/article/viewArticle/1460/1375#h5>.

[22] Two early magazine articles made use of the term: J Rayport, 'The Virus of Marketing', *Fast Company*, Issue 6/December 1996, viewed on 17 August 2009, <http://www.fastcompany.com/magazine/06/virus.html>; S Jurvetson and J Draper, 'Viral Marketing', *Draper Fisher Jurvetson*, 1997-01-01, viewed on 17 August 2009, 2, <http://www.dfj.com/news/article_26.shtml>.

[23] J Leskovec, L Adamic, and B Huberman, 'The Dynamics of Viral Marketing'. *ACM Transactions on the Web*, vol. 1(1), Article 5, May 2007, p. 2. viewed on 18 August 2009, <http://doi.acm.org/10.1145/1232722.1232727>.

[24] Jurvetson and Draper, p. 1.

[25] ibid; Rayport, p. 3.

[26] H Jenkins, *Convergence. Where Old and New Media Collide*, New York University Press, New York, 2006. pp. 206-7.

[27] H Jenkins, 'If it Doesn't Spread, It's Dead' *Confessions of an Aca/Fan*, 2009-02-16, viewed on 26 August 2009, <http://henryjenkins.org /2009/02/if_it_doesnt_spread_its_dead_p.html>.

[28] R Silverstone, *Media and Morality. On the Rise of the Mediapolis.* Cambridge University Press, Cambridge, 2007, p. 90.

[29] H Jenkins, 'The Cultural Logic of Media Convergence', *International Journal of Culture Studies*, vol. 7(1), 2004, pp. 33-43.

[30] A Webb, 'Interactive TV: Viewing Rights', *New Media Age,* 2007-03-18, p. 23.

[31] H Jenkins, *Convergence.*

[32] M Granovetter, 'The Strength of Weak Ties', *The American Journal of Sociology*, vol. 78(6), 1973, p. 1374.

[33] J Teorell, 'Linking Social Capital to Political Participation: Voluntary Associations and Networks of Recruitment in Sweden', *Scandinavian Political Studies*, vol. 26(1), 2003.

[34] N B Ellison, C Steinfeld and C Lampe, 'The Benefits of Facebook 'Friends': Social Capital and College Students' Use of Online Network Sites', *Journal of Computer-Mediated Communication*, vol. 12(4), 2007.

[35] R Silverstone, *Media and Morality: On the Rise of the Mediapolis*, Polity Press, Cambridge, 2007, p. 117.

[36] Granovetter, p. 1368.

[37] C Shirky, *Here Comes Everybody: The Power of Organizing Without Organizations*, Penguin Press, New York, 2008, p. 217.

[38] A Chadwick, *Internet Politics: States, Citizens, and New Communications Technology,* Oxford University Press, Oxford, 2006, p. 27.

[39] D Miller, 'The Competitive Model of Democracy' in *Democratic Theory and Practice*, G Duncan (ed), Cambridge University Press, Cambridge, 1983, p. 134.

[40] R Putnam, *The Comparative Study of Political Elites*, pp. 8-15.

[41] ibid., p. 13.

[42] U Bjereld and M Demker, 'The Power of Knowledge and New Political Cleavages in a Globalized World', *International Review of Sociology*, vol. 16(3), 2006, p. 501.

[43] C Shirky, pp. 122-130.

[44] M Joyce, 'Civic Engagement and the Internet: Online Volunteers', *Internet and Democracy Blog*, 2007-11-18, viewed on 1 March 2009, <http://blogs.law.harvard.edu/ idblog/ 2007/11/18/civic-engagement-and-the-internet-online-volunteers/>.

[45] N Gustafsson and M Wahlström, 'Virtual Mobilisation? Linking On-line and Off-line Political Participation among Swedish Facebook Users: Courtesy and Irritation', paper presented to the *XV NOPSA Conference*,

Tromsö, Norway, 5-7 August, 2008. This study will be followed up by a more extensive round of focus group interviews in late 2009.
[46] ibid., p. 12.

# Bibliography

Bjereld, U. and M. Demker, 'The Power of Knowledge and New Political Cleavages in a Globalized World'. *International Review of Sociology* vol. 16 (3), pp. 499-515.

Beer, D. and R. Burrows, 'Sociology and, of and in Web 2.0: Some Initial Considerations', *Sociological Research Online*, vol. 12(5), 2007, viewed on 12 August 2009, <http://www.socresonline.org.uk/12/5/17.html>.

Benkler, Y., *The Wealth of Networks: How Social Production Transforms Markets and Freedom.* Yale Univerity Press, New Haven, 2007.

Boase, J., Horrigan, J. B., Wellman B., and L. Rainie, 'The Strength of Internet Ties', *Pew Internet and American Life Project*, viewed on 10 August 2009, <http://www.pewinternet.org/pdfs/PIP_Internet_ties.pdf>.

Bourdieu, P., 'The Forms of Capital', in *Education: Culture, Economy and Society*, A. H. Halsey, H. Lauder, P. Brown & A .Stuart Wells (eds), Oxford University Press, Oxford, 1997.

Boyd, D. and N. B. Ellison, 'Social Network Sites: Definition, History and Scholarship'. *Journal of Computer-Mediated Communication*, vol. 13(1), 2007, article 1 (unpaginated).

Castells, M., *The Rise of the Network Society.* Blackwell Publishers, Cambridge (MA, USA), 1996.

Chadwick, A., *Internet Politics: States, Citizens, and New Communications Technology.* Oxford University Press, Oxford, 2006.

Dalton, R. J., 'Citizenship Norms and the Expansion of Political Participation'. *Political Studies*, vol. 56, 2008, pp. 76-98.

Ellison, N. B., Steinfield, C. and C. Lampe, 'The Benefits of Facebook 'Friends': Social Capital and College Students' Use of Online Network Sites'. *Journal of Computer-Mediated Communication,* vol. 12(4), 2007, article 1 (unpaginated).

Granovetter, M. S., 'The Strength of Weak Ties'. *The American Journal of Sociology*, vol. 78 (6), 1973, pp. 1360-1380.

Gustafsson, N. and M. Wahlström, 'Virtual Mobilisation?: Linking On-line and Off-line Political Participation among Swedish Facebook Users: Courtesy and Irritation'. Paper presented to the *XV NOPSA Conference*, Tromsö, Norway, 5-9 August 2008. Available via the author's website: <www.svet.lu.se?ngu>.

Held, D., *Models of Democracy*. 3$^{rd}$ edition. Polity Press, Cambridge, 2006.

Hindman, M., *The Myth of Digital Democracy*. Princeton University Press, Princeton, 2008.

Howard-Spink, S., 'Grey Tuesday: Online Cultural Activism and the Mash-up of Music and Politics'. *First Monday, Special Issue # 1: Music and the Internet*, 2005-07-04, viewed on 17 August 2009, <http://firstmonday. org/htbin/cgiwrap/bin/ojs/index.php/fm/article/viewArticle/1460/1375#h5>.

Inglehart, R., *The Silent Revolution: Changing Values and Political Styles Among Western Publics*. Princeton University Press, Princeton, 1977.

Jenkins, H., 'The Cultural Logic of Media Convergence'. *International Journal of Culture Studies*, vol. 7(1), 2004, pp. 33-43.

———, *Convergence: Where Old and New Media Collide*. New York University Press, New York, 2006.

———, 'If it Doesn't Spread, It's Dead', in *Confessions of an Aca/Fan*, 2009-02-16, viewed on 26 August 2009. <http://henryjenkins.org/2009/02 if_it_doesnt_spread_its_dead_p.html>.

Joyce, M., 'Civic Engagement and the Internet: Online Volunteers'. *Internet and Democracy Blog*, 2007-11-18, viewed on 1 March 2009,<http://blogs .law.harvard.edu/idblog/2007/1118/civic-engagement-and-the-internetonline-volunteers>.

Jurvetson, S. and J. Draper, 'Viral Marketing', *Draper Fisher Jurvetson*, 1997-01-01, viewed on 2 December 2009, <http://www.dfj.com/news/article_26.shtml>.

Kedzie, C., 'Democracy and Network Connectivity', in *Proceedings of the INET'95 International Networking Conference*, Honolulu, Hawaii, 1995, viewed on 12 August 2009, <http://www.isoc.org/inet95/proceedings/PAPER/134/html/paper.html>.

Leskovec, J., Adamic, J., and B. Huberman, 'The Dynamics of Viral Marketing'. *ACM Transactions on the Web*, vol. 1(1), Article 5, May 2007, 39 pages, viewed on 18 August 2009, <http://doi.acm.org/10.1145/1232722.1232727>.

Lundquist, L., *Det vetenskapliga studiet av politik.* Studentlitteratur, Lund, 1992.

Maj, A. & M. Derda-Nowakowski, 'Anthopology of Accessibility. The Perceptual Problem of Human Computer Interaction' in this volume.

Micheletti. M., *Political Virtue and Shopping: Individuals, Consumerism, and Collective Action.* Palgrave Macmillan, Basingstoke, 2003.

Miller, D., 'The Competitive Model of Democracy' in *Democratic Theory and Practice*. D. Graeme (ed), Cambridge University Press, Cambridge, 1983.

Neumayer, C., & Raffl, C. 'Politics and Social Software: Recommendations for Inclusive ICTs' in this volume.

Norris, P., *Democratic Phoenix: Reinventing Political Activism.* Cambridge University Press, Cambridge, 2002.

O'Neill, B., 'Indifferent or Just Different?: The Political and Civic Engagement of Young People in Canada.' Canadian Policy Research Networks Research Report, 2007.

Prior, M., *Post-Broadcast Democracy: How Media Choice Increases Inequality in Political Involvement and Polarizes Elections.* Cambridge University Press, Cambridge, 2007.

Putnam, R., *Bowling Alone: The Collapse and Revival of American Community*. Simon & Schuster, New York, 2000.

———, *The Comparative Study of Political Elites*. Prentice Hall, Englewood Cliffs, 1976.

Rayport, R., 'The Virus of Marketing'. *Fast Company*, Issue 6/December 1996, viewed on 17 August 2009, <http://www.fastcompany.com/magazine/06/virus.html>.

Shirky, C., *Here Comes Everybody: The Power of Organizing Without Organizations*. Penguin Press, New York, 2008.

Silverstone, R., *Media and Morality: On the Rise of the Mediapolis*. Polity Press, Cambridge, 2007.

Stoker, G., 'Governance as Theory: Five Propositions'. *International Social Science Journal*, vol. 50(155), 1998, pp. 17-28.

Sweetser, K. and K. L. Lee, 'Stealth Soapboxes: Political Information Efficacy, Cynicism and Uses of Celebrity Weblogs among Readers'. *New Media & Society*, vol. 10(1), 2008, pp. 67-90.

Teorell, J., 'Linking Social Capital to Political Participation: Voluntary Associations and Networks of Recruitment in Sweden'. *Scandinavian Political Studies* vol. 26 (1), 2003, pp. 49-66.

Webb, A., 'Interactive TV: Viewing Rights', *New Media Age*, 2007-03-08, p. 23.

Wellman, B., Haase, A. Q., Witte, J. and K. Hampton, 'Does the Internet Increase, Decrease or Supplement Social Capital?: Social Networks, Participation, and Community Comitment'. *American Behavioral Scientist* vol. 45(3), 2001, pp. 437-456.

**Nils Gustafsson** is a Ph. D. Candidate at the Department of Political Science, Lund University. His dissertation project, *Viral Politics* (working title), is a study in the effects of social media on political participation.

# Anthropology of Accessibility: Further Reflections on the Perceptual Problems of Human-Computer Interactions

*Anna Maj and Michal Derda-Nowakowski*

## Abstract

One of the most important problems which appeared in the computer mediated civilisation is the usability of content for people with limited abilities of perception and interaction. Digital communication has shown all inconveniences of hitherto prevailing 'interfaces to knowledge' and of communication devices in the range of their usability and accessibility. Traditional ergonomics ensured comfort of using the devices mainly to users without disabilities. The Net revealed the existence of the vast global community of disabled people who wants to come out of the ghetto of their own dysfunctions and participate in other communities. The Internet is often the only chance to cross the barriers of this specific exclusion.

The Web design should take into account the aspect of various disabilities of the users. There exist both formal and informal instructions of accessible design. In some milieu of designers of interfaces and internet applications and content managers publishing of content and materials which are accessible is even a sign of 'good manners'. Therefore, there is a grassroots discourse of accessibility, which is conditioned socially. It is often contradictory to the discourse of global corporations, embodying their own non-standardised solutions. The struggle of the 'able-bodied' community for the accessibility of the content for people with dysfunctions of perception is a new form of global thinking about creation and maintenance of communication standards. It is often connected with the generation of open access to the content referring to Creative Commons licenses and technologies of Open Source.

The chapter analyses some procedures of improving the effectiveness of communication and interaction with computer in the process of web designing. It shows some examples of community initiatives connected with accessibility and everyday problems of disabled people. Ideologists and designers of usability and accessibility within the range of human-computer interaction are precursors of this new way of thinking about the needs of online communities which are aiming at the 'noble simplicity' enabling to encode complicated symbolic content - simplexity. Usability understood in this way exceeds the limitations of political correctness with its compulsory necessity of double coding and decoding of meanings.

**Key Words:** Accessibility, Usability, Assistive Technologies, Design, Simplexity, Human-Computer Interactions, Perception Disabilities, User-friendly Interface, Cultural Competencies.

*****

## 1.      Introduction

Ideologists and designers of usability and accessibility within the range of human-computer interaction are precursors of the new way of thinking about the needs of online communities which are aiming at the 'noble simplicity' enabling to encode complicated symbolic content - simplexity. Usability understood in this way exceeds the limitations of political correctness with its compulsory necessity of double coding and decoding of meanings. Such anthropological situation may become a natural bridge between the world of those who can see and those who are blind or other communities with limited access to the content. The reflection on the roles of mechanisms of social content-generation and visualisations of communication obstacles, both on-line and off-line, is necessary. There are various artistic and scientific projects, which resulted in real changes of architectural solutions or development of their accessibility.

The change in accessibility in symbolic and mediated communication is also a chance for revolution in thinking about the physical space. Thus, the Net impacts not only the architecture of information but also the architecture in traditional meaning. This way of thinking about the Network, communities and the new ergonomics of communication is therefore a kind of introduction to the reflection on new society lacking communication obstacles and on further evolution of humans connected to the computer, active in social terms due to technological interfaces and independent of limitations stemming from biology or traditionally understood dysfunctions.

> In both perceiving and visually representing the natural organisation of objects, we are supported by the mind's powerful ability to detect and form patterns. With matters of the visual mind, the school of Gestalt psychology is particularly relevant. Gestalt psychologists believe that there are a variety of mechanisms inside the brain that lend to pattern-forming. [...] Humans are organisation animals. We can't help but to group and categorise what we see. [...] The principles of Gestalt to seek the most appropriate conceptual 'fit' are important not only for survival, but lie at the very heart of the discipline of design.[1]

John Maeda, a new media artist, researcher and designer develops his narration about simplicity and design telling the story of development of iPod menu - its three phases: the first model of the interface (a jog dial with four buttons located circularly around), its complication into four buttons and a jog dial (separated) and simplification (integrated into one scroll dial). The last step - simplification led to its limits - provoked both the commercial success and marked new trends of interface design. It should be noticed here that this kind of simplicity contribute to economise maximally the activities of the user. Most often such a design is favourable for a contemporary user. However, this kind of usability is not so simple to use. Maeda shows the example of good quality design failure on the level of the user inability to use the device. He recalls his brother-in-law's lack of competencies in using the newest iPod just after getting it as a Christmas present. This situation can be regarded as a result of design, which demands from the user the knowledge of the previous interfaces and the ability to manipulate them.

Human-Computer Interaction (HCI) is in fact a kind of cultural competence. Being one of the most important abilities in contemporary information society, paradoxically it is not taught anywhere; a user needs to acquire the knowledge by himself. There are no ideal interfaces - as we still need to 'learn machines' - but the good ones are stemming from the specific patterns of culture. Machines are learning these paradigms but also teach them to us, becoming the interpreters of humanity. This is the part of cyborgisation of culture, described as early as in 1964 by Marshall McLuhan in his classical idea of the extensions of man.[2]

## 2. Social Networks and their Users

The fundamental problem arising in cyberculture in the context of human and machine interactions was symbolically captured by an anthropologist, Michael Wesch, in the title of his popular YouTube film: *The Machine is Us/ing Us.*[3] Therefore, the question of designing interfaces and devices regarding the users' needs and abilities is not marginal. The report of Pew Internet and American Life Project indicates that the presence of older generations in Internet is lower than the young (over half of Internet users is between 18 and 44 years old) - but within 10 years (with ageing boomers generation) the situation may change.

> The biggest increase in Internet use since 2005 can be seen in the 70-75 year-old age group. While just over one-fourth (26%) of 70-75 year olds were online in 2005, 45% of that age group is currently online. [...] Instant messaging, social networking and blogging have gained ground as communications tools, but email remains the most popular

online activity, particularly among older Internet users. Fully 74% of Internet users age 64 and older send and receive email, making email the most popular online activity for this age group.[4]

The problem of cultural competencies in human-computer interactions is central to contemporary design, which needs to be the anthropology as well. Sometimes users' activity crosses the imagination of the designer. That was the case of Nasza-klasa.pl [Our-Class.pl] - Polish social networking website similar to Classmates - where a person who wanted to become a new user had to ask directly the website designers to broaden the age categories for potential users. The given categories were prepared for the users aged up to 90, whereas the asking person was 95 years old[5]. The two young designers did not predict in their economy of thinking about human-computer interaction that also this age group can perform such an activity as social networking. This situation lets us suggest that web design is mainly directed to young people, which seems to be logical regarding the Pew Internet research quoted above but possibly is not a good rule for the next decade. Thus, web design should develop in the direction of diversification of the potential users.

There are of course such interfaces as smart homes, which support the users, especially aged and with disabilities, but these are not only pure interfaces but also habitats. HCI design is de facto the problem of technological imagination concerning target groups. It depends on multiple functionalities built in the interface. The idea of usability of interfaces is at the moment one of the most significant matters within the ideology of 'proper design'.

Functionalities of interfaces and the necessity of usability are the ideas connected with anthropological problems of Web 2.0 design. In fact, the rules of HCI are a kind of web design savoir-vivre and cultural competencies. Designers in a form of ritualised competition watch each other in order to maintain the standards of usability and develop more user-friendly interfaces. From the anthropological perspective, we can see in this process both the patterns of culture drifting into the direction of political correctness and 'the battle for standards'. One of the main assumptions of design 2.0 is separation of content, appearance and user's behaviour. This separation makes websites more accessible to users and more visible for bots of search engines. These are issues located between creative thinking and social practices connected with technology standards. It is a vast territory for quality research on humans in cyberspace.

### 3.    Knowledge Transfer and Interface Design

According to the tradition of technological determinism a state of civilisation depends on a predominant medium. From the perspective of culture it is important how data transmission is performed. However, paradigms of knowledge transfer are far more important. From this point of view even such a traditional form of organising data as a book is a kind of interface. This interface has produced certain forms of perception connected with the educational system and knowledge processing. It resulted in the appearance of specific cultural modes of thinking, restructured perceptual and cognitive processes. Simultaneously, the art of typesetting and theory of book design was developed. From the times of Gutenberg and his battle for perfect typesetting, which ruined him, the question of balance between the form and the meaning of the text has been a main issue in typographers' efforts.

However, more than 500 years of typographic tradition is also the history of inaccessibility for blind users. The real change in the development of book interface came with modernism. The idea of readability and usability prevailed in 20th century discourse on book design. But modernism did not raise the discussion to the aspect of accessibility of a book as an interface. Inaccessibility is a general problem connected with analogue interfaces, which usually enable only one-channel communication whereas digital ones often include built-in multi-channel possibilities of perception. In case of analogue interfaces it was necessary to construct alternative means of perception (i.a. visual, voice and tactile). Digital channels have potential interoperability, which means using the same data in different ways connected with a type of perception. Theory of accessibility is thus connected with digital media.

Another issue is usability as a standard of communication. It is neither readability nor accessibility. Usability was actually born in Bauhaus as a mental concept for modernist humankind. It shifted from habitat architecture to architecture of information but it still means functionality of design. We can trace this idea in Marcel Breuer's concept of the ideal of a chair, when he was saying: 'In the end we will sit on resilient columns of air'[6]. This metaphor reveals designer's consciousness of the body of the user of a piece of furniture. It also suggests the need to reduce an interface to those features that are necessary for its functionality, arguing with the idea that form is the main problem of design. The comfort understood as user's experience becomes the leading interest of a designer. As we know, an ideal chair is the one that our bodies wouldn't feel at all, the one that is invisible, untouchable and non-existing. The important task for a designer is approaching to such an ideal in the process of designing.

New media art searches for new opportunities to diagnose abilities of human body and mind in the context of machines. This basic assumption leads to the conclusion that a technology user is also a participant and this is a new perceptual paradigm. Creative process becomes an interaction design area where the needs of various social groups are transformed into artistic objects.

The prehistory of HCI can be traced back not only in engineering but also in artistic works of Nam June Paik, Bill Viola, Christa Sommerer, Laurent Mignonneau and others. The good example here is David Rokeby's work, *Very Nervous System*, which was described as adding new meaning to the term 'interactivity'.

> The active ingredient of the work is its interface. The interface is unusual because it is invisible and very diffuse, occupying a large volume of space, whereas most interfaces are focused and definite. Though diffuse, the interface is vital and strongly textured through time and space. The interface becomes a zone of experience, of multi-dimensional encounter. The language of encounter is initially unclear, but evolves as one explores and experiences. The installation is a complex but quick feedback loop. The feedback is not simply 'negative' or 'positive', inhibitory or reinforcing; the loop is subject to constant transformation as the elements, human and computer, change in response to each other. The two interpenetrate, until the notion of control is lost and the relationship becomes encounter and involvement. [...] The installation could be described as a sort of instrument that you play with your body but that implies a level of control, which I am not particularly interested in. I am interested in creating a complex and resonant relationship between the interactor and the system.[7]

*Very Nervous System* is the interactive circuit, which may be seen as a beyond-language conversation of human and computer. It is very similar to contemporary systems, which enable controlling computer with the eye movement or body gestures without VR equipment. Various inventions concerning the use of brain waves to control interfaces, even 3D virtual environment of Second Life, have been developed for several years in multiple research centres (e.g. Keio University).[8]

Such technologies can serve Internet users with movement disabilities helping them to control computer and interact with other Internet users. But what is also important is the social networking of people with disabilities. These are two main aspects of accessibility. They concern different communication obstacles - the first refers to the use of technology, the second to social exclusion.

## 4. Selected Examples of User-oriented Design

It is worth to mention here several selected examples of user-oriented design which designate positive directions. Projects described below are both of artistic and scientific nature; some are experiments in mediated social interaction, some - explore the possibilities of new assistive technologies and propose new ways of inclusion of users with various disabilities (physical, sensory and cognitive).

Antoni Abad, a Spanish artist, founded Zexe.net website. It is an artistic project connecting various groups of marginalised people from different cities, e.g. Gypsies, prostitutes, taxi drivers, etc. One part of the website, called *Canal Accessible, serves people with movement disabilities who create their own wikimap of Barcelona where they mark all places in the city space which are not accessible for people on wheel chairs[9]. The users are documenting their work with photographs taken with mobile phone cameras.

In fact, this is not only the common map of physical obstacles in their daily life, but also a communication canal for discussions on various themes and a kind of exhibition area showing their problems to other Internet users. This work can be defined as a space for creating the discourse of marginalised groups. Such wikimap, being the user-generated content service, is not only the interface of HCI, but also of social symbolic relations helping to redefine the meaning of the real space.

WinkBall is a videochat system allowing users to communicate in a most natural way, using facial expressions, natural language and video recording or video streaming. The target user is described as a user of all ages - which means that system is user-friendly, easy to operate and encouraging also for older persons to use it. What is more important, WinkBall is actually a tool designed for deaf users, allowing them social networking. This system was developed as cooperation project of Goldsmiths University in London by Assistive Technologies Group at IT Department, Deaf@x and WinkBall.

WinkBall allows deaf users to create signed videos, signed blogs and signed forums, which means that it allows for a full social networking activity, with no need of simplification of facial expression and signed language to symbols or alphabet. James Ohene-Djan, leading designer, researcher and founder of WinkBall, concludes that the main aim was to create the situation, when 'people within deaf community can communicate with each other online, using their native languages'[10]. The interface is very easy. It also has *push to talk* function, which means that during a conversation the person who is signing is automatically detected as a speaker and shown on the screen without interrupting the conversation. This allows users to follow the conversation naturally, without a need to stop it, and without misunderstandings, which could be provoked by the fact that interactors do not hear each other.

The interesting aspect of interaction via WinkBall appeared in the phase of introducing the tool to potential users at schools for deaf children. Teachers and students realised that video chat increased their abilities in facial self-expression and in signing and thus expanded their possibilities of communicative interaction with other people. This is an interesting situation when mediated communication teaches people to understand each other better in situations of interpersonal not-mediated communication. Thus, a computer becomes a mirror, enabling people to talk with each other. User-oriented design in this case results in a paradoxical situation, which was not predicted by a designer. A user, being the first subject and the cause of a tool design, starts to find himself/herself in this tool. The design is such a perfect image of the user that he or she starts to learn from this mirror how to communicate with other persons similar to him/her. Design is thus a reflection of the user.

On the other hand, the computer - which is here only a medium, is also a basic tool for social communication, and the possibility to communicate via WinkBall is only one of its multiple functionalities. All this means that a communicative situation being the embodiment of Narcissus story, is at the same time paradoxically opposite to what Marshall McLuhan said about it:

> For if Narcissus is numbed by his self-amputated image, there is a very good reason for the numbness. There is a close parallel of response between the patterns of physical and psychic trauma or shock (...) Any invention of technology is an extension or self-amputation of our physical bodies, and such extension also demands new ratios of new equilibriums among the other organs and extensions of the body.[11]

On the contrary, via WinkBall a user does not experience the self-amputation of the body. He/she starts to learn his/her body from the beginning. He learns his face and gestures in the process of confrontation with computer. This opposition may be a result of the fact that computer-mediated interaction is actually social, and computer itself forwards us to the others. But McLuhan is not wrong about the electronic media - his assumptions about media as 'the extensions of man' has just been proved by recent neurophysiologist research conducted by Erica Michael and Marcel Just from Carnegie Mellon University. Researchers have scanned brains while using various media. The results are astonishingly in accordance with McLuhan's 'the medium is the message' - in example, listening and reading of the same text cause completely different mental reactions and memory effects.[12]

## 5.    Selected Examples of Assistive Technologies, Systems and Devices

HCI is connected strongly with researches on the perceptual apparatus and cognitive process. It results in the emergence of completely new ideas concerning possible ways of perceiving. New inventions and interfaces of totally new types have been created for people with sight or hearing impairment. Some of such interfaces are based on the idea of the replacement of senses.

The vOICe is Peter Meijer's project stemming from the concept of 'seeing with ears'. Device consists of a camera mounted in spectacles, connected with headphones and completed by the software processing the optical signals and changing them into the soundscape. It means that the process of seeing is exchanged for hearing. The video image is analysed by the device as the stream of visual data and transformed into a stream of audial data. The vOICe recognises obstacles located close to the user and warns him by emitting sound representation of objects. This is the process of scanning space and creating a soundscape. The volume represents the brightness of objects with continuous monitoring of the close environment[13]. It should be noticed that this process is highly abstract and does not let the user operate the device in an intuitive way. It demands at least three months of specialised training and there is no evidence that the results will lead to full success in every case.

Technically, The vOICe sensory substitution and synthetic vision approach provides access to any visual information through an auditory display. A theoretical possibility is that it can not only be used for practical purposes in various visual tasks, but that it may - through education and extensive immersive use with conscious and subconscious visual processing - also lead to vivid and truly visual sensations, a 'visual awakening', by exploiting the neural plasticity of the human brain. However, very little is known about the prospects, and learning to see requires much effort on behalf of the blind user, possibly comparable to mastering a foreign language, and without guarantees for worthwhile results.[14]

The perceptual apparatus needs to be prepared and taught to understand the stream of audial data but the problem lies in the physical properties of audio channel perceived by humans which has low information capacity in comparison to visual channel. This kind of sensorial substitution can be seen as a process of translation of the visual in order to build alternative experience for the blind users.

The necessity of this kind of translation opens new demands for interface design and engineering. The process of design is therefore closely interconnected with the quickly developing state-of-art in neurophysiology, psychology and electronics. HCI has to turn towards both anthropology and electronics. Whereas anthropology analyses patterns of culture, electronics aims at constructing databases of the patterns of perception. Assistive technologies are created on the crossing of the patterns of perception embedded in machines and patterns of cultures embedded in human cognition.

The vOICe requires constructing databases of 3D objects with all possible perspectives from the most probable points of view of a potential user. This modelling includes the 'use cases' which depict scenario of users' communication activities with total surrounding. In this way, location and detection mean also cognition and interpretation of environment. It is a new dimension of accessibility of the world to the blind. This is a new type of communication situations, which is only possible with the mediation of technology.

The problem of 'the extensions of man' is also concerned today with new senses that have never been discussed earlier in the context of technology. The mediation between environment and body often shifts to the body itself. Runner Oscar Pistorius is an example of the analogue cyborgisation of human being and extended possibilities of the body. His case provoked a discussion on the subject of human body extensions and their influence on sport results. Today, assistive technologies and prosthetics come to the point where disabled body equipped with prosthesis gains better results than abled-body. But prostheses are the solution only to the problem of the lack of certain part of body: an arm, a hand or a leg, they can not solve the problem of the lack of a certain sense: sight or hearing. On the other hand, assistive technologies are focused first of all on developing 'prostheses' of senses by sensorial substitution.

However, AT design may also mean creating totally new paths for sensing the environment via media. This is the case of Cabboots, a project developed by Martin Frey from Academy of Fine Arts in Berlin. The device consists of shoes whose soles are equipped with infrared sensors and electromechanical elements changing the angulations of the shoe while using it. Cabboots create an intuitive interface to the environment on the level of mediated touch of the ground (a certain path that can be programmed). The change in surface (real or simulated) is represented as a change of angulation of the shoe which causes a natural effect of changing the angulation of the foot (which means that a user is turning).

The device is therefore using the sense of touch, the sense of balance and it is also extending the idea of a shoe as an extension of our perception. But in this case a shoe is not a kind of a barrier, protecting a foot from the environment. In Cabboots a shoe is also a connector to the environment, it is a tool of interaction, a tool of communication with the path, a tool for seeing. It is because of the infrared sensor that is actually a kind of eye. On the other hand Cabboots animate our tactility, and thanks to that the whole body becomes a sensible sensor, and the user becomes a sensitive self.

The design of this device is intuitive, and thus it can be used both by people with memory problems (in Alzheimer disease) or by people with vision impairment. The prototypes of the device become more and more mobile and functional. They let users program the device to remember a specific track, i.e. a route back home. Cabboots are therefore paradoxically both the metaphor of 'seven mile shoes' and let the user quite safely 'lose his head' as they are leading him to the programmed location. They see and they remember - so the users do not have to do it by themselves.

This device raises the question of intelligent objects and the limits of their influence on future life of people. Shoes are directly controlling movements of the user. Thus using Cabboots means being controlled by one's own shoes. The question is what would happen if such smart devices are managed by a wearable personal computer connected to the Internet and opened for hacking. But the fact that objects are gaining intelligence does not necessarily mean that people have to lose it. However, it is clear that analogue high-end prostheses (like Pistorius' ones) are fully controlled by the user and digital ones (like Cabboots) - are not.

Regarding the aspect of Cabboots design, there are several additional remarks, which should be done here. While the technological aspect of controlling the device seems to be complex, the perceptual and cognitive aspect of its usage is simple. The designer's idea was to give a kind of intuitive interface, which can be operated by anyone, without a long training. The goal has been reached as the use of Cabboots demands only a natural use of body balance, which reminds walking on a well-trodden path whose borders are felt by the foot because of its slightly different angulation. In other words, the idea of simplicity of use and natural interaction was reached here by the designer employing complex technologies, which are not noticed by the device user.

Finally, it is worth to shortly mention Roberto Manduchi who develops similar but still completely different project. His 'electronic cane' is a kind of assistive technology device, which uses laser beam and spatial sensors. It finds obstacles in space, measures the distance, depth and size of objects and informs the user about it via the sound interface. The prototype tester, Lucia Florez, confirms the invention being intuitive and compares it to 'skin perception'[15].

Electronic cane as well as The vOICe and Cabboots are inventions based on sensory substitution but perform it differently. It should be noticed here that the ideas are simple but to reach this simplicity the technology needs to be complex. Therefore, the design for people with visual impairments needs to blend both, complexity and simplicity - the previously mentioned simplexity.

## 6.    Conclusion

Concluding, the result of the process of interfaces design for people without disabilities is augmented perception, even if we think only about the level of symbolic communication and the extensions of body and mind. But the final effect of designing interfaces for people with disabilities is first and foremost the process of reducing perceptual deficiency and sensory substitution. This can be regarded as a process parallel to media convergence - sensorial convergence. Derrick de Kerckhove, rethinking Marshall McLuhan, concludes:

> There is clearly more to design than containment and seduction. In a very large sense, design plays a metaphorical role, translating functional benefits into sensory and cognitive modalities. Design finds its shape and its place as a kind of overtone, as an echo of technology. Design often echoes the specific character of technology and corresponds to its basic pulse. Being the visible, audible or textural outer shape of cultural artifacts, design emerges as what can be called the 'skin of culture'.[16]

The contemporary 'skin of culture' seems to be hybrid: design means at the same time screenology, projecting interactions and augmenting perception. The design, which Derrick de Kerckhove was writing about in middle 90's, was concentrated on the shape and appearance of things and objects. Today, design is mainly projecting a user's experience, behaviours and feelings. It is closer to body and mind, develops cognitive processes and, in fact, programs a new user. Thus, it can be called the 'skin of a user' - which is taking us back to Marshall McLuhan thought[17], but in the completely new cultural context.

# Notes

[1] J Maeda, *The Laws of Simplicity: Design, Technology, Business, Life*, MIT, Massachusetts, 2006, pp. 17-18.

[2] M McLuhan, *Understanding Media: The Extensions of Man*, MIT Press, Massachusetts CA, 1994.

[3] M Wesch's personal website, [viewed on 3rd November 2008]. URL: <http://www.ksu.edu/sasw/anthro/wesch.htm>. M. Wesch: 'The Machine is US/ing US' in YouTube, [viewed on 3rd November 2008]. URL: <http://www.youtube.com/watch?v=6gmP4nk0EOE>.

[4] S Jones, S. Fox, 'Generations Online in 2009', Pew Internet Project Data Memo [report], Pew Internet and American Life Project, 28th January 2009 [viewed on 13th February 2009], p. 2-3, URL: <http://www.pewinternet. org/Reports/2009/Generations-Online-in-2009.aspx?r=1>.

[5] P Lipiński, 'Milioner z Naszej Klasy', ['A Millioner from Our Class']. Interview with Maciej Popowicz, the creator of Nasza-Klasa website. *Duży Format: Dodatek do Gazety Wyborczej* [online]. 20th May 2008, URL: <http://wyborcza.pl/1,75480,5222854,Milioner_z_Naszej_Klasy.html>.

[6] Bauhaus, 1919-1928. H Bayer, W Gropius, I Gropius (eds), Museum of Modern Art [New York 1938], Arno Press, New York 1972, p. 130.

[7] D Rokeby, 'Installations: Very Nervous System (1986-1990)' *in David Rokeby Website*, 12 November 2000 [viewed on 14th February 2009], URL: <http://homepage.mac.com/davidrokeby/vns.html>.

[8] 'Using Brainwaves To Chat And Stroll Through Second Life: World's First', in *Science Daily*, 16th June 2008 [viewed 14th February 2009], URL: <http://www.sciencedaily.com/releases/2008/06/080613163213.htm>.

[9] Canal *Accessible, URL: <http://www.zexe.net/BARCELONA>.

[10] J Ohene-Djan from WinkBall on SEE HEAR, Wednesday 20th January 1pm, BBC2 [viewed on 20th January 2010]. In: YouTube: <http://www.youtube.com/watch?v=xAWddylqPpg&feature=autofb>.

[11] M McLuhan, *Understanding Media: The Extensions of Man*. MIT Press, Massachusetts CA 1994, pp. 44-45.

[12] D Tapscott, *Grown up Digital: How the Net Generation is Changing Your World,* McGraw-Hill, New York, 2009, p. 104.

[13] Vision Technology for the Totally Blind [project website], 7th February 2009 [viewed on 14th February 2009], URL: <http://www.Seeingwith sound. com>.

[14] P B L Meijer, 'VOICE. Self-Training Paradigm for the vOICe. Training' [viewed on 10th March 2009]. URL: <http://www.seeingwithsound. com/training.htm>.

[15] A Coombs, 'Researchers engineering better Technologies for the Blind' in *San Francisco Chronicle* [online], 27th November 2005 [viewed on 14th

February 2009], URL: <http://www.sfgate.com/cgi-bin/article.cgi?f=/c/a/ 2005/ 11/27/ING3TFS91M1.DTL>.

[16] D de Kerckhove, *The Skin of Culture: Investigating the New Electronic Reality*, Ch Dewdney (ed), Somerville House Publishing, Toronto, 1995, p. 154.

[17] McLuhan, op. cit., p. 47.

# Bibliography

*Bauhaus, 1919-1928*. H. Bayer, W. Gropius and I. Gropius (eds). Museum of Modern Art [New York, 1938], Arno Press, New York, 1972.

Canal *Accessible, [viewed 14th February 2009], URL: <http://www.zexe.net/BARCELONA>.

Coombs, A., 'Researchers engineering better Technologies for the Blind'. *San Francisco Chronicle* [online], 27th November 2005 [viewed on 14th February 2009], URL: <http://www.sfgate.com/cgi-bin/article.cgi?f=/c/a/ 2005/11/27/ING3TFS91M1.DTL>.

*Gadżety popkultury: Społeczne życie przedmiotów. [Pop-Culture Gadgets: The Social Life of Things]*. W. Godzic and M. Żakowski (eds). Wydawnictwa Akademickie i Profesjonalne, Warszawa, 2007.

Jones, S. and S. Fox, 'Generations Online in 2009', *Pew Internet Project Data Memo* [report], Pew Internet and American Life Project, 28th January 2009 [viewed on 13th February 2009], URL: <http://www.pew internet.org/Reports/2009/Generations-Online-in-2009.aspx?r=1>.

Kerckhove de, D., *Connected Intelligence: The Arrival of the Web Society*. W. Rowland (ed). Somerville House, Toronto, 1997.

———, *The Skin of Culture: Investigating the New Electronic Reality*, Ch. Dewdney (ed), Somerville House Publishing, Toronto, 1995.

*Kody McLuhana: Topografia nowych mediów. [McLuhan's Codes: Topography of New Media]*. A. Maj and M. Derda-Nowakowski (eds), with Derrick de Kerckhove's participation. Wydawnictwo Naukowe ExMachina, Katowice, 2009.

Levine, F., Locke, Ch., Searls, D. and D. Weinberger, *Cluetrain Manifesto: The End of Business as Usual.* Perseus Pub., Cambridge, MA, 2001.

Lipiński, P., 'Milioner z Naszej Klasy' ['A Millioner from Our Class']. Interview with Maciej Popowicz, the creator of Nasza-Klasa web site. *Duży Format. Dodatek do Gazety Wyborczej* [online]. 20th May 2008, URL:<http://wyborcza.pl/1,75480,5222854,Milioner_z_Naszej_Klasy.html>.

Maeda, J., *The Laws of Simplicity: Design, Technology, Business, Life.* MIT, Massachusetts, 2006.

Maj, A., *Media w podrozy* [*Media in Travel*]. Wydawnictwo Naukowe ExMachina, Katowice, 2008.

Manovich, L., *The Language of New Media.* MIT Press, Cambridge, MA, 2001.

Meijer, P.B.L.: 'VOICE. Self-Training Paradigm for the vOICe Training'. [viewed on 10th March 2009]. URL: <http://www.seeingwithsound.com/training.htm>.

McLuhan, M., *Understanding Media: The Extensions of Man.* MIT Press, Massachusetts CA, 1994.

Nielsen, J., *Designing Web Usability: The Practice of Simplicity.* New Riders Publishing, Indianapolis, 1999.

*James Ohene-Djan from WinkBall on SEE HEAR*, Wednesday 20th January 1pm, BBC2 [viewed on 20th January 2010]. In: YouTube: <http://www.youtube.com/watch?v=xAWddylqPpg&feature=autofb>.

Rokeby, D., 'Installations: Very Nervous System (1986-1990)' *in David Rokeby website*, 12th November 2000 [viewed on 14th February 2009], URL: <http://homepage.mac.com/davidrokeby/vns.html>.

Stallman, R., 'The GNU Operating System and the Free Software Movement', in *Open Sources: Voices from the Open Source Revolution.* Ch. Di Bona, S. Ockman and M. Stone (eds). O'Reilly Media, Sebastopol, 1999.

Tapscott, D. and Williams, A. D., *Wikinomics: How Mass Collaboration Changes Everything.* Atlantic Books, New York, 2007.

Tapscott, D., *Grown up Digita:. How the Net Generation is Changing Your World.* McGraw-Hill, New York, 2009.

Tufte, E.R., *The Visual Display of Quantitative Information.* (2nd ed.). Graphics Press, Cheshire, 2001.

——, *Envisioning Information.* Graphics Press, Cheshire, 1990.

'Using Brainwaves To Chat And Stroll Through Second Life: World's First', in *Science Daily*, 16th June 2008 [viewed 14th February 2009], URL: <http://www.sciencedaily.com/releases/2008/06/080613163213.htm>.

Vision Technology for the Totally Blind [project website], 7th February 2009, [viewed on 14th February 2009], URL: <http://www.seeingwithsound.com>.

Wesch, M., 'The Machine is US/ing US' in YouTube, URL: <http://www.youtube.com/watch?v=6gmP4nk0EOE>, Michael Wesch website, URL: <http://www.ksu.edu/sasw/anthro/wesch.htm>.

Zeldman, J., *Designing with Web Standards.* (2nd ed.) Peachpit Press, Berkeley, CA, 2006.

**Anna Maj**, Ph.D., is an assistant professor in the Institute of Cultural Communication, University of Silesia, Katowice, Poland. Interested in media anthropology and theory of perception; currently her research and writing is devoted to the issues of travel and mobility in the context of new technologies. Her research and participation in the *Cyberculture* conference was supported by The Foundation for Polish Science (FNP) with the grant for young researchers.

**Michal Derda-Nowakowski**, Ph.D., is an assistant professor in the Department of Electronic Media, University of Lodz, Poland. He is also the founder and editor-in-chief of ExMachina Academic Press. Interested in web anthropology, design and typography; currently his research and writing is devoted to the issues of HCI and perception.

# Politics and Social Software: Recommendations for Inclusive ICTs

## *Christina Neumayer, Celina Raffl and Robert M. Bichler*

**Abstract**
The emergence of social software and the new perception and use of the Internet promise to enable decentralized actions, a range of possibilities to share and exchange information open and free of charge, to collaborate equally, and to foster intercultural understanding and participation. These new possibilities have the potential to lay the foundation for a new way of political participation and social movements to emerge, but there are also limits because of existing social structures and increasing commercialisation of the Internet. In this chapter we discuss theoretical concepts that we currently observe as characteristics of political activism and the Internet in general, and of social software in particular: [1] the foundation for community building, [2] the interrelation of the real and the virtual space, [3] digital divide and social inequalities, and [4] the influence of globalisation. The Internet provides the foundation for communities to emerge and to shape society, for both social benefits (e.g. empowerment of citizens, ecological conservation, democratisation and participation) as well as negative consequences (e.g. social inequalities, knowledge gaps). Based on these four concepts we outline recommendations for inclusive Information and Communication Technologies (ICTs), i.e. possibilities social software theoretically offers for social movements, political activism and participation.

**Key Words:** Communities, Cooperation, Cyberspace, Information and Communication Technologies (ICTs), Social Inclusion.

*****

## 1.     Introduction

The Internet changes politics, not only from a governmental and parliamentarian perspective but also on the individual level. Social software in particular promises to enable decentralised actions, a range of possibilities to share and exchange information open and often free of charge, to collaborate equally and to foster intercultural understanding and participation. These new possibilities have the potential to lay the foundation for new ways of political participation and social movements to emerge. '[T]he role of information and communication technologies had a significant impact on the form and function of political mobilization.'[1] ICTs provide the infrastructure for diverse groups or people to engage in a common cause within weak-tie networks. Some claim that a virtual public sphere emerges by political online

interaction and that online communities provide opportunities for
participation and engagement.[2]

The virtual space is not only a big marketplace, it is also a space of
political interaction and moreover a central resource of information.[3]
'Networks include nodes and links, use many possible paths to distribute
information from any link to any other, and are self-regulated through flat
governance hierarchies and distributed power.'[4] Flat hierarchies are essential
for political processes since they foster grassroots activities and give civil
society the opportunity to engage into political participation without guidance
of institutions or organisations. Blogs, wikis, and social networking sites
provide a technological basis for grassroots action to coordinate and for
activists to communicate. The Internet can support the organisation of topic-
oriented pressure groups, protest organisations, and ideological movements
outside the mainstream. Participation, discussion, the active role of users,
organisational and social benefits by using the global infrastructure for
creating networks are important elements for political participation and
activism. As Bradley argues: 'Our citizen's role can be empowered with IT
support in the home – there are opportunities to widen and strengthen
democracy.'[5] Political leaders, commercial global players and international
institutions have an enormous influence on the structure and the design of the
web as infrastructure, the commodification of information goods and web
services, on power relations, and contents. According to Howard Rheingold
social software allows network-structured interactions that 'have real
potential for enabling democratic forms of decision-making and beneficial
instances of collective action' but, he continues, 'that doesn't mean that the
transition to networked forms of social organization will be a pleasant one
[...]'[6]

Communities that emerge in cyberspace can lead to enhancement of
political activities, but there are certain disadvantages as well, that are
inherent in the technology. The outcome, political orientation, and methods
for online political activism and participation are dependent on the users,
developers and producers of social software. Although the Internet can
potentially connect people all over the world, limitation in Internet access,
lack in computer skills and literacy make the political forum it offers less
inclusive - not only, but especially in the developing world.[7] Cultural
differences can lead to misinterpretations when political mobilisation enters a
global arena through digital social networks.

In the following we discuss theoretical concepts that we currently
observe as characteristics of political activism and ICTs, in particular of
social software: [1] the foundation for community building, [2] the
interrelation of the real and the virtual space, [3] digital divide and social
inequalities, and [4] the influence of globalisation.[8] Based on these concepts
we develop guidelines to enhance political engagement and grassroots

activism that lead to a more inclusive society. This requires cooperation among citizens, their willingness and possibilities for participation. Freedom, openness and transparency, access to information and education are key principles for the emergence of an inclusive society.

## 2.      Cybercommunities and Politics

The heterarchical, decentralised and likewise open architecture of the Internet provides the necessary precondition for virtual communities and hence for participation, new social movements and grassroots activism to emerge. Cyberspace is understood according to Pierre Lévy's definition of a space that enables social movements, i.e. grassroots democracy, and political participation.[9] Common history, knowledge, and practices foster the strength of a community. Natalia Waechter (see this volume) argues that studying the nature of online networks helps us to understand how online communication is related to young people's development. The web enhances networking of people from different backgrounds, histories and experiences to share interests and aspirations.[10] As Wellman argues, we find community in networks, not groups, since a community does not only share a common interest, but is based on interaction, communication, discussion and relationships that networks provide.[11] Social software has the potential to enhance political participation and grassroots activism. In *Technologies of Cooperation* Saveri et al. refer to social software as a combination of tools that make the quick emergence of group-forming networks possible:

> It includes numerous media, utilities, and applications that empower individual efforts, link individuals together into larger aggregates, interconnect groups, provide metadata about network dynamics, flows, and traffic, allowing social networks to form, clump, become visible, and be measured, tracked, and interconnected.[12]

The Internet provides space to articulate group identity, e.g. by sharing a political cause.[13] As Anderson argued in the context of print media, a nation can be considered an imagined political community since it is impossible for all members to meet; but they all refer to a hypothetic commonality.[14] Anderson's *Imagined Communities* show the common ground by shared ideology or interests, a common discourse emerged, and people with different dialects understood the messages.[15] In the same way as print-media helped to distribute information for an imagined community within one nation, the Internet can have this functionality on a global scale.[16]

Online communities rather emerge from networks than groups. 'In networked societies, boundaries are permeable, interaction with diverse others, connections switch between multiple networks, and hierarchies can be flatter and recursive.'[17] Social software provides the potential for political actions, although commercial structures are inherent in most websites and thus create hierarchies that are in favour of some participants and oppressive for others. 'Smart-mobbing is about using the Internet and mobile communications to self-organize collective action'[18], thus we have to consider the role of engineers who created the websites and the underlying intention and purpose of their creation, i.e. usually to make profit, rather than enhancing political protest.

The so-called *information revolution* is carried out by 'literate and language related' [19] societies and is therefore a product of an elitist part of the world's population that does not include financially and educationally backward groups. Both, users as well as the design of social software, have an impact on defining the ideological colouring of the global outcome. As Rheingold puts it '[t]he impacts of smart mob technology already appear to be both beneficial and destructive, used by some of its earliest adopters to support democracy and by others to coordinate terrorist attacks.'[20] Online communities share different ideas, political causes, symbols, imaginary, and ideologies, which are dependent on the physical actors who discuss, exchange ideas, and participate by using digital ways of political expression. The use of social software for political protest or participation is dependent on the ideologies, as well as the cultural and political contexts of its users and developers.

## 3.    Between Real and Virtual

Social software has already changed the way we perceive, design, and (re-)use information and communication technologies. We claim that cyberspace is not a sphere of its own, distinct from real life, but an expression of social structures that are to some extent transferred to the virtual space and vice versa. Hence cyberspace is a social space, because it is created, shaped and (re-)designed by technicians, constructors, engineers.[21] Designing and structuring cyberspace is a social act and cyberspace is a product of human action and creativity. Referring to online communities Donata Marletta aims in her chapter in this volume to overcome online and offline dichotomies to make the distinction between real and virtual world obsolete. The real and the virtual sphere are closely related and interdependent. Social inequalities, power structures and ideologies existing in real space are therefore transferred to the virtual sphere. Already in the 1960s Marshall McLuhan referred to changes of spatial dimension due to new electronic mass media:

> Today, after more than a century of electric technology, we
> have extended our central nervous system itself in a global
> embrace, abolishing both space and time as far as our planet
> is concerned.[22]

The *Internet Galaxy* as Castells argues, influences a similar change as McLuhan has identified with the emergence of television and technical mass media in general.[23]

The perception of time and space has changed with the emergence of ICTs. New media and globalisation processes have a major impact on the structure and organisation of so-called *Global Cities*[24] as well as the individual and the social within this context:

> Information technologies are yet another factor contributing to the new logic for agglomeration. These technologies make possible the geographic dispersal and simultaneous integration of many activities.[25]

According to Castells the suspension of spatial and temporal distances is the dominant social logic of the *Network Society*. Since humans are living in real physical space - the space of places - this process brings along a loss of the self of individuals.[26] The transformation of space and time has an enormous impact on identity formation, especially the possibilities of self-representation in cyberspace by social software.

The vision that 'new communication technologies, decentrally employed, could just as easily lead to a cultural revolution in which the citizens take their problems into their own hands, defining and designing their needs, products and life forms for themselves'[27] is still present in discussions about political participation in the virtual space. Although the perception of space and time has changed through ICTs, there are still prevailing disadvantages in social structures that are transferred into the virtual space and influence online participation and political engagement. As Bell argues in reference to Castells' *Network Society*: 'The elites of self-programmable labour live exclusive lifestyles while social exclusion and poverty escalate around them.'[28]

Social structures are projected on the virtual space. This can be discussed in terms of Bourdieu's understanding of capital.[29] Economic, social, symbolic, and cultural capital, such as education, are important concepts regarding the use of web technologies and (inter)actions in the virtual space. Power relations are transferred as inequalities into the virtual space:

> Who owns access to your devices, either to push information at you or to pull information from you? Some of the answers will emerge from political processes, but many of them are sensitive to technical design decisions. In that regard, the designs that dominate early in the growth of a technology can have disproportionate power over the way

the technology will affect power structures and social lives.[30]

There are two extreme perspectives in terms of power relations: ICTs can be used to increase control over users, and to diminish privacy, but are also associated with a more powerful role of users and increasing self-determination regarding content. This leads to an enforcement of collaborative democratic possibilities and influence on design.

These two perspectives are based on two contrary policy making approaches. On the one hand, one can identify a top-down approach, which is characterised by mental disappropriation, loss of control, and surveillance. On the other hand a bottom-up approach enables the opportunity for self-determined life-styles, participation, and protection of personal rights. Current societies are based on many contradictions, e.g. between self-determination and heteronomy, or inclusion and exclusion. ICTs foster cooperation and competition for rationalising the accumulation of economic, political, and cultural capital. In the information society, or 'informational capitalism', social systems and structures are increasingly shaped by knowledge, and computer-mediated communication.[31] As a result the importance of network logic and globalisation, i.e. time-space-distanciation, of social relationships increases. ICTs do not follow predictable, mechanically determined and one-sided effects, but a set of multiple antagonistic economic, political, and cultural tendencies, and therefore cause both, opportunities and risks at the same time.

In *Technologies of Cooperation* Rheingold and his working group point out, that a 'cooperative strategy does not replace competitive strategy; the two are inter-related and co-evolve. A key challenge is learning to understand the dance between the two strategies, their respective range of choices [...].'[32] This 'dance' refers to the idea that the current technological infrastructure both enables and constrains cooperation, participation, and political activism. Cooperation requires public awareness and empowerment of people. Class becomes a political concept, because '[t]he task of a theory of class in this respect is to identify the existing conditions for potential collective struggle and express them as a political proposition.'[33] Hence a theory of class refers to necessary conditions for collective political struggle to foster grassroots activism.

Conflicts and struggles of current societies, i.e. property, power, and skills, have been transformed in the information age. Information and knowledge are central forces and became a strategic economic resource. Knowledge production is inherently social, cooperative, and historical. The creation of knowledge usually requires collective efforts, thus it becomes a public good. Knowledge production becomes more and more networked, interlinked, and collaborative. The Internet enables reproduction and free global distribution of information with the help of technologies. Information can be stored on physical carriers, it is a non-rival and intangible good. Information goods, in contrary to physical property, can be shared without loosing the possibility of re-using them.[34] Intellectual property rights artificially transform information into a scarce resource. A monopoly for selling and licensing information is established in favour of the information-owner. Intellectual property rights rather support private accumulation of profit than collaborative knowledge production and collective ownership. As Benkler argues strong intellectual property rights reduce the chance of cooperation, user integration, and user-generated content.[35]

Decentralized organisation of the Internet allows the emergence of direct-democratic grassroots communities that challenge the centralisation of power; hence a participatory society can be established. At the same time ICTs and social software in the global networked information space foster the rise of totalitarian forms of surveillance and control. ICTs have the potential to strengthen both, participation and surveillance. These are two tendencies that contradict each other, but both affect society. The inherent democratic potential of ICTs is often not realised because of asymmetrical distribution of power and resources in the real world.

## 4.    Digital Inequalities

Social patterns existing in real space, including social inequalities, have an impact on cyberspace communities. We assume that political activism via social software is in many cases initiated by an elite, representing their interests, and not necessarily those of the citizens. Those excluded from cyberspace thus depend on guidance of real-space-elites. Potential of access to the Internet and information and the disadvantages of exclusion were subsumed under the term 'digital divide', which was put on the agenda of political and public debate in the 1990's. The term describes the unequal access to new digital media, mainly to the Internet. Digital divide refers to two major phenomena: the gap between developed countries and developing countries and the dissimilar access to information technologies within certain societies.

Although simply providing access (i.e. the technological infrastructure) will not automatically lead to global activism, participation, or social equality, access is the necessary precondition to take benefit from the positive potentials of the Internet and related technologies.[36] Nils Gustafsson underlines in his chapter that digital social networks potentially provide space for 'post-organisational weak ties' that support global political problem solving by a global collective functioning as a collective gatekeeper and at the same time distributing information across the world. However, he argues, that these are possible developments that have to be nurtured in a positive way.

Participation, social movements, collective intelligence, collaborative knowledge production, citizen journalism, user generated content, etc. are new qualities of social software, but inequalities in social class, education, skills, and lack in capabilities influence the way technology is used and political engagement is perceived.[37] Although the Internet provides the potential for political engagement, activism, and social movements '[e]very new form of communication both heightens ties between those who already know one another, and raises the walls of exclusion for those lacking access to the new medium of communication.'[38] Those excluded from the virtual space thus have to depend on the real-space-elite.

Due to commodification of information and increasing commercialisation of the Internet the initial hopes of creating a free cyberspace away from social power structures, traditional hierarchies and inequalities, were replaced by profit-oriented realism. 'Beyond their scale, what is striking about today's patterns of communication and cultural globalization is that they are driven by companies, not by countries.'[39] Therefore what is needed, is governance of the Internet as a global virtual space. Melissa DeZwart and David Lindsay (see this volume) discuss concepts of legitimacy and governance in virtual worlds. They argue that an interaction between law, technology, markets, and norms is necessary to allow governance of the virtual world. Governance of the Internet therefore can help to ensure that the global virtual sphere is less determined by real world social inequalities. The form governance takes, as well as its direction, is depending on those who have the power to decide.

Increasing commercialisation of the Internet led to its control by elite that is able to restrict or enhance political protest and networks of critical voices across the world. The enthusiastic assumption that the Internet would lead to more profit in social, economic, and political terms is not accurate 'if viewed from the point of view of the shortfall in market growth represented by those who could afford a computer, modem, or even low cost of the local phone call that linked them to a server.'[40] Purchasing power and imbalanced power relations, as well as lack in cultural, economic, and social capital can restrict access to the political potential of social software.

The burst of the dot.com bubble at the turn of the millennium initiated a discussion about lack in grassroots democracy and collaboration by commodification of cyberspace. As Lessig argues, the Internet was created as a global space, controlled and regulated under the influence of commerce. Increasing commercialisation often leads to mainstreaming of ideas, values, and goods. Although theoretically offering enough space and capacity to serve the needs of disadvantaged and neglected groups and to fill niches, certain groups are still - either consciously or unintended - excluded from using the Internet. Hardware as well as software and web interfaces are often not designed in a way that certain people, e.g. elderly or those with disabilities can use them according to their needs, as Anna Maj and Michal Derda-Nowakowski criticise (see this volume). The authors seek to foster alternatives such as open source and open access that embody non-standardised solutions. The Internet itself is neither regulated nor controllable, but a combination of hardware, software, and of code, that can enhance freedom of their users or be an instrument of control.[41] 'The users are guests in the house of Social Media giants.'[42] Civil rights and political freedom cannot be guaranteed by a capitalist system that exclusively makes social actions possible if they are adjusted to their ideologies. Thus, Internet governance has to develop concepts that foster digital inclusion from a transdisciplinary perspective considering technology design and societal context.

## 5.     A Global Virtual Sphere

The global architecture of the virtual sphere is not restricted to local, e.g. national or geographical constraints. The network character of social software provides the potential to transform local political concerns into global issues by gaining attention from people all over the world.

> The conventional media are trapped in a technology of central production and mass distribution, which limits their ability to allow citizens to 'confer in an unrestricted fashion'. The internet is a technology designed for dialogic communication. The internet is global in design.[43]

As Rantanen suggests: 'different media are open to globalization in different ways. While old media [...] are often more national in their orientation, new media such as video or the Internet are much more global.'[44] Although global information distribution was possible by mass media as well, global visibility has increased through the Internet's possibilities for global networking and grassroots democracy. '[N]etworks play a mediating role by connecting prospective participants to an opportunity for mobilization and enabling them to convert their political consciousness into action.'[45] National political actions, causes, and decision-making processes can trespass national boundaries and rapidly acquire worldwide attention and support.

Information technologies and related to them changes in communication structures are amongst the deep drivers of globalisation. At the same time the expanding logic of capitalism and development of global market goods and services, worldwide distribution of information, new global division of labour driven by multinational corporations, the growth of migration and the movement of people foster global interconnectedness.[46] There is a difficult relationship between the 'global as the principle source of domination and the local as the principal source of resistance and emancipation.'[47] Local, national and global interaction is necessary for political activism and awareness by a global community.

> Networked, digitized information media cut across territorial boundaries of cultural groups. They juxtapose differences in a homogeneous medium. They bring together individuals with common interests but divergent nationalities and traditions.[48]

The global Diaspora and 'political narratives that govern communication between elites and following different parts of the world'[49] would need a careful translation from one context to another.

People act in local contexts, hence mobile, transboundary political practice is possible not only through institutional global spaces, but through powerful imaginaries, languages, and symbols that inspire global action. Places of political action and decision-making are linked by 'rapid communications into complex networks of political interaction.'[50] According to Appadurai we can assume that mass media in general and especially the Internet create a new kind of nationalism that is not restricted to national boundaries anymore.[51] Hence globality is a new resource for users who mix technical properties with local practices. The term *globalisation*[52] refers to the global outcome of a local protest, which can only function by the use of rhetorical aptitude and a political ideology supported by traditional local media, which is biased by the government in power.

The outcome of these technical properties depends on the users and their perception of a particular political problem, worldview or ideology, and the way they are able to use the technologies.[53] According to Giddens local action becomes action from a distance with impacts beyond national boundaries. Globalisation is characterised by intensification of international social relationships by the specifics of network structures with interdependencies and interactions with people who are not restricted to space and time.[54] The transformation of local social interrelationships with their traditions and values into the global sphere is what Giddens terms *embeddedness*. Globalisation therefore means disembedding from a local context and 'the 'lifting out' of social relations from local concepts to indefinite spans of spacetime.'[55]

As Poster argues:

> Global communication, one might say, signifies transcultural confusion. At the same time, the network creates conditions of intercultural exchange that render politically noxious any culture, which cannot decode the message of others.[56]

Although the Internet in general and social software in particular provides possibilities to enhance political engagement on a global scale, cultural misinterpretations, social inequalities, as well as commodification of information and web services are hindering factors that need to be overcome to foster global grassroots activism.

## 6.       Conclusion and Recommendations for Inclusive ICTs

Learning from theoretical concepts we conclude that ICTs provide the foundation for communities to emerge and to shape society, for both social benefits (e.g. empowerment of citizens, ecological conservation, democratisation and participation) as well as negative consequences (e.g. social inequalities, digital divide). Based on the four concepts mentioned above we outline recommendations for inclusive Information and Communication Technologies from a normative, social science perspective. We emphasise on the potentials and possibilities, which social software theoretically offers for social movements, political activism, participation and grassroots democracy to emerge.

[1] Community building in cyberspace requires an open, participatory framework. Following Jenkins we can define a participatory culture by following characteristics: 'relatively low barriers to artistic expression and civic engagement', 'strong support for creating and sharing one's creations with others', 'some type of informal mentorship whereby what is known by the most experienced is passed along to novices', 'members believe that their contributions matter', 'members feel some degree of social connection with one another.'[57] Birdsall describes a development from 'build it and they will come' to 'they will come and build it' focusing on the changing role of content consumption to content production by users, what underlines the concept of a participatory culture as an individual- and society-centred communication process.[58] To foster community building in cyberspace, technology design as well as social and political contexts, have to leave space for grassroots democracy, and political participation to overcome the heteronomy of contemporary politics and to move towards a more participatory virtual culture.

[2] Societal structures and political concepts are transferred from real world into the virtual space. Since cyberspace is a social space, the real and the virtual cannot be seen independently from each other. This also includes the design process. Technology design is a social act and technicians should be understood in their social role as experts, hackers, laymen, and common users that adapt to their technical needs. Constructing technology is per se a social act. Hence people have the ability to shape technologies. At the same time technologies influence society, they are both, enabling and constraining. The architecture of technology is designed by elite and by

private companies that usually do not consider grassroots activism as a desired goal. Very often people tend to arrange themselves with technologies, rather than changing or adapting them.[59] By including users in the design process, users' needs for political participation and grassroots democracy can be considered as a valuable design guideline.

Apart from a participatory technology design approach real world context has to enhance participation, the emergence of bottom-up discussion and social movements. Cultural, political and societal context have to be considered in Internet governance. An interrelationship between open content and open access, the assurance of respecting privacy, and avoidance of surveillance technologies especially in countries with restrictive governments, are preconditions for political engagement in real space and thus moreover in the virtual sphere.

[3] The digital divide still excludes many people especially in the developing world to use social software for political engagement. Considering the enormous part of the population that is currently excluded from the Internet we argue that social software, if not supported by traditional media or opinion leaders, cannot be the adequate tool for grassroots democracy to emerge, especially in countries with enormous inequalities and restrictive regimes. Universal access is the precondition for using ICTs for grassroots democracy, although lack in skills, education, motivation, and capabilities lead to exclusion as well. Imbalances in economic, social, symbolic, and cultural capital require an interdisciplinary approach to overcome inequalities in using social software for political engagement.

[4] Social software provides possibilities to enhance political engagement on a global scale, although cultural misinterpretations, social inequalities, and commodification of information and web services hinder global grassroots activism. The users and 'produsers' of social software can either enhance competition, or communication and collaboration in cyberspace. The possibilities of the technologies can be used in different ways and the future direction it takes depends upon its actors. Commodification of social software hinders grassroots activism which is not directed according the rules of the market and economic benefits. Thus, global use of ICTs for political participation, social movements and political activism needs alternative concepts that foster cooperation on a global scale, as well as empowered citizens in the real space.

# Notes

[1] W L Bennet & A Toft, 'Identity, Technology, and Narratives: Transnational Activism and Social Networks' in *Routledge Handbook of Internet Politics*,

A Chadwick & Ph N Howards (eds), Routledge, London, New York, 2009, pp. 146-260.

[2] N Negroponte, *Being Digital*. Coronet, London, 1995; H Rheingold, *The Virtual Community: Homesteading on the Electronic Frontier*. Addison-Wesley, Readgin, 1993;A Toffler & H Toffler, *Creating a New Civilization: The Politics of the Third Wave*, Turner Publications, Atlanta, 1995.

[3] Ch Fuchs, 'The Self-Organization of Cyberprotest' in *The Internet Society II: Advances in Education, Commerce & Governance*, K Morgan, C A Brebbia, & J M Spector, (eds), WIT Press, Southampton, Boston, 2006, pp. 275-295.

[4] H Rheingold, *Smart Mobs: The next Social Revolution*. Perseus Books Groups, Cambridge, 2002, p. 163.

[5] G Bradley, *Social and Community Informatics: Humans on the Net*. Routledge, New York, 2006, p. 100.

[6] Rheingold, *Smart Mobs: The next Social Revolution*, p. 163.

[7] S Buckler & D Dolowitz, *Politics on the Internet*. Routledge, Milton Park, 2005, p. 4f.

[8] Ch Neumayer & C Raffl, 'Facebook for Protest? The Value of Social Software for Political Activism in the Anti-FARC Rallies', in *DigiActive Research Series*, December 2008.

[9] P Lévy, *Collectice Intelligence: Mankind's Emerging World in Cyberspace*. Perseus Books, Cambridge, MA, 1997.

[10] G Bradley, *Social and Community Informatics: Humans on the Net*, p. 165.

[11] B Wellman, 'Physical Place and CyberPlace: The Rise of Personalized Networking'. *International Journal of Urban and Regional Research*, vol. 25, no. 8, 2001, pp. 227-252.

[12] A Saveri, H Rheingold & K Vian, *Technologies of Cooperation*, Institute for the Future, Palo Alto, 2005.

[13] Y-Ch Kim & S J Ball-Rokeach, 'New Immigrants, the Internet, and Civic Society' in *Routledge Handbook of Internet Politics*, A Chadwick & Ph N Howards (eds), Routledge, London, New York, 2009, p. 279.

[14] B Anderson, *Imagined Communities: Reflections on the Origin and Spread of Nationalism*. Verso, London, New York, 1983.

[15] Anderson, *Imagined Communities: Reflections on the Origin and Spread of Nationalism*.

[16] R J Holton, *Globalization and the Nation-State*. McMillan Press, London, 1998, p. 34.

[17] Wellman, *Physical Place and CyberPlace: The Rise of Personalized Networking*, p. 227.

[18] H Rheingold, 'From Facebook to the Streets of Colombia', in *SmartMobs: The next Social Revolution: Mobile Communication, Pervasive Computing,*

*Wireless Networks, Collective Action*, 2008, 22.05.2008, <http://www.smartmobs.com/2008/02/04/from-facebook-to-thestreets-of-colombia>.

[19] Ph Graham, 'Hypercapitalism', *New Media & Society*, vol. 2, no. 2, 2000, p. 132.

[20] H Rheingold, 'SmartMobs: The next Social Revolution: Book Summary', 2002, 10. 02. 2009, <http://www.smartmobs.com/book/book_summ.html>.

[21] C Raffl & R M Bichler, 'Vom Sozialen in den Virtuellen Raum. Ernst Blochs 'Konkrete Utopie' im Cyberspace?, in *Raumkonstruktion und Raumerfahrung. Jahrbuch 2007 der Ernst-Bloch-Assoziation, VorSchein Nr. 29*, D Zeilinger (ed), Antogo, Nürnberg, 2007, pp. 107-128.

[22] M McLuhan, 'The Medium is the Message', in *Media Studies*, P Marris & S Thornham (eds), University Press, New York, 1964, p. 43.

[23] M Castells, *The Internet Galaxy*. Oxford University Press, Oxford, 2001.

[24] S Sassen, *Metropolen des Weltmarkts: Die neue Rolle der Global Cities*, Campus Verlag, Frankfurt am Main, New York, 1997.

[25] S Sassen, 'Wirtschaft und Kultur in der globalen Stadt: Economy and Culture in the Global City', in *Die Zukunft des Raums: The Future of Space*, B Meurer (ed), Campus Verlag, Frankfurt, New York, 1994, p. 76.

[26] M Castells, *The Rise of the Network Society: Economy, Society and Culture, Vol. I*, Blackwell Publishers, Cambridge, Oxford, 1996.

[27] M Klar, 'Globale Information - ein Projekt. Global Information - a Project', in *Die Zukunft des Raums. The Future of Space*, B Meurer (ed), Campus Verlag, Frankfurt, New York, 1994, p. 169.

[28] D Bell, *Cyberculture Theorists: Manuel Castells and Donna Haraway*. Routledge Critical Thinkers, New York, 2007, p. 68.

[29] P Bourdieu, 'The Forms of Capital', in *Education: Culture, Economy and Society*, A H Halsey, H Lauder, P Brown & A Stuart Wells (eds), Oxford University Press, Oxford, 1997.

[30] Rheingold, *Smart Mobs: The next Social Revolution*, p. 96.

[31] R M Bichler, Ch Fuchs & C Raffl, 'Perspectives of Cyberethics in the Information Society', in *Framing Evil: Portraits of Terror & the Imagination*, N Billias & A B Curry (eds), Interdisciplinary-Press, Oxford, 2008, p. 158.

[32] Saveri, Rheingold & Vian, *Technologies of Cooperation*, p. 30.

[33] M Hardt & A Negri, *Multitude: War and Democracy in the Age of Empire*, Penguin Books, London, 2004, p. 104.

[34] R M Stallman, 'The GNU operating System and the Free Software Movement', in *Open Sources: Voices from the Open Source Revolution*, C DiBona, S Ockman & M Stone (eds), O'Reilly, Sebastopol, CA, 1999.

R M Bichler, Ch Fuchs & C Raffl, 'Co-operative Cyberethics for a Sustainable Information Society', in *Proceedings of the 16th ISA World Congress of Sociology: The Quality of Social Existence in a Globalising World*, Durban, CD-ROM, 2006 p. 23.

[35]Y Benkler, 'Coase's Penguin, or Linux and the Nature of the Firm', in *Code. Collaborative Ownership and the Digital Economy*, R A Aiyer (ed), MIT-Press, Cambridge, MA, 2005, p. 197.

[36] G Aichholzer, *Vom 'Digital Divide' zur sozialen Inklusion als Herausforderung der Informationsgesellschaft.* Tagung 'Perspektiven der Informationsgesellschaft - Technische und gesellschaftliche Entwicklungen', Bundesministerium für auswärtige Angelegenheiten, Vienna, 2002.

N Couldry, 'Communicative Entitlements and Democracy: The Future of the Digital Divide', in *The Oxford Handbook of Information and Communication Technologies*, R Mansell, Ch Avgerou, D Quah & R Silverstone (eds), Oxford University Press, Oxford, 2007, pp. 383-403.

N Selwyn, 'Reconsidering Political and Polular Understandings of the Digital Divide'. *New Media and Society*, vol. 6, no. 3, 2004, pp. 341-362.

J v Dijk, *The Deepening Divide. Inequality in the Information Society*, Sage, Thousand Oaks, London, New Delhi, 2005.

[37] Ph Tichenor, G Donohue & C Olien, 'Mass Media Flow and Differential Growth in Knowledge'. *Public Opinion Quarterly*, vol. 34, 1970, pp. 159-170.

[38] D Della Porta & S Tarrow, 'Transnational Process and Social Activism: An Introduction', in *Transnational Processes and Social Activism*, D Della Porta & S Tarrow (eds), Rowman & Littlefield Publishers, Lanham, Boulder, New York, Toronto, Oxford, 2005, p. 4.

[39] D Held & A McGrew, *Globalization/Anti-Globalization: Beyond the Great Divide*, Polity Press Cambridge, Malden, 2007, p. 39.

[40] N Couldry, 'The Forgotten Digital Divide: Researching Social Exclusion/Inclusion in the Age of Personalised Media', *To be presented at: Globalisation and Convergence Conference*, MIT, May 10-12.2004, 23.05.2008, <http://cms.mit.edu/conf/mit2/Abstrracts/NickCouldry.pdf>.

[41] L Lessig, *Code. And Other Laws of Cyberspace. Version 2.0*, Basic, London, 2007.

[42] T Scholz, 'Market Ideology and the Myths of Web 2.0'. *First Monday*, vol. 13, no. 3, 2008, online.

[43] C Sparks, 'Media and the Global Public Sphere: An Evaluative Approach', in *Global Activism Global Media*, W de Jong, M Shaw & N Stammers (eds), Pluto Press, London, 2005, p. 43.

[44] T Rantanen, *The Media and Globalization.* Sage, London, Thousand Oaks, New Delhi, 2005, p. 95.

[45] F Passy, 'Social Networks Matter. But How?', in *Relational Approaches to Collective Action*, M Diani & D McAdam, (eds), Oxford University Press, Oxford, 2003, p. 24.

[46] D Held & A McGrew, *Globalization/Anti-Globalization: Beyond the Great Divide*. Polity Press, Cambridge, Malden, 2007, p. 9.

[47] Held & McGrew, *Globalization/Anti-Globalization: Beyond the Great Divide*, p. 168.

[48] M Poster, *Information Please: Culture and Politics in the Age of Digital Machines*. Duke University Press, Durham, London, 2006, p. 159.

[49] A Appadurai, 'Disjuncture and Difference in the Global Cultural Economy', in *Global Culture. Nationalism, Globalization, and Modernity*, M Featherstone (ed), Sage, London, 1990, p. 300.

[50] Held & McGrew, *Globalization/Anti-Globalization: Beyond the Great Divide*, p. 20.

[51] Appadurai, *Disjuncture and Difference in the Global Cultural Economy*, p. 296.

[52] R Robertson, 'Glocalization: Time-Space and Homogeneity-Heterogeneity` in *Global Modernities*, M Featherstone, S Lash & R Robertson (eds), Sage, London, 1995, pp. 25-44.

[53] S Sassen, 'Electronic Networks, Power, and Democracy', in *The Oxford Handbook of New Media*, R Mansell, Ch Avgerou, D Quah & R Silverstone (eds), Oxford University Press, Oxford, 2007, pp. 349ff.

[54] A Giddens, *The Consequences of Modernity*, Stanford University Press, Stanford, CA, 1990.

[55] Giddens, *The Consequences of Modernity*, p. 21.

[56] Poster, *Information Please: Culture and Politics in the Age of Digital Machines*, p. 12.

[57] H Jenkins, *Confronting the Challenges of Participatory Culture: Media Education for the 21st Century*, The MacArthur Foundation, Chicago, 2006, p. 7.

[58] W F Birdsall, 'Web 2.0 as a Social Movement', *Webology*, vol. 4, no. 2, 2007.

[59] C Raffl, 'Assessing the Impact of Open Content Knowledge Production in Web 2.0'. *The International Journal of Technology, Knowledge and Society*, vol. 4, no. 3, 2008, pp. 85-92.

# Bibliography

Aichholzer, G., *Vom 'Digital Divide' zur sozialen Inklusion als Herausforderung der Informationsgesellschaft*. Tagung 'Perspektiven der

Informationsgesellschaft - Technische und gesellschaftliche Entwicklungen'. Bundesministerium für auswärtige Angelegenheiten, Vienna, 2002.

Anderson, B., *Imagined Communities: Reflections on the Origin and Spread of Nationalism.* Verso, London, New York, 1983.

Appadurai, A., 'Disjuncture and Difference in the Global Cultural Economy', in *Global Culture. Nationalism, Globalization, and Modernity.* Featherstone, M. (ed), Sage, London, 1990, pp. 295-310.

Bell, D., *Cyberculture Theorists. Manuel Castells and Donna Haraway.* Routledge Critical Thinkers, New York, 2007.

Bennet, W. L & A. Toft, 'Identity, Technology, and Narratives. Transnational Activism and Social Networks' in *Routledge Handbook of Internet Politics.* Chadwick, A. & Howards, Ph. N. (eds), Routledge, London, New York, 2009, pp. 146-260.

Benkler, Y., 'Coase's Penguin, or Linux and the Nature of the Firm', in *Code. Collaborative Ownership and the Digital Economy.* Aiyer, R A (ed), MIT-Press, Cambridge, MA, 2005, pp. 169-206.

Bichler, R. M., Fuchs, Ch. & C. Raffl, 'Perspectives of Cyberethics in the Information Society', in *Framing Evil. Portraits of Terror & the Imagination.* Billias, N. & Curry A. B. (eds), Interdisciplinary-Press, Oxford, 2008, pp. 153-162.

Bichler, R. M., Fuchs, Ch. & C. Raffl, 'Co-operative Cyberethics for a Sustainable Information Society', in *Proceedings of the 16th ISA World Congress of Sociology. The Quality of Social Existence in a Globalising World.* Durban, CD-ROM, 2006.

Birdsall, W. F., 'Web 2.0 as a Social Movement'. *Webology*, vol. 4, no. 2, 2007.

Bourdieu, P., 'The Forms of Capital', in *Education: Culture, Economy and Society.* Halsey, A. H., Lauder, H., Brown, P. & Stuart Wells, A. (eds), Oxford University Press, Oxford, 1997, pp. 46–58.

Bradley, G., *Social and Community Informatics: Humans on the Net.* Routledge, New York, 2006.

Buckler, S. & D. Dolowitz, *Politics on the Internet*. Routledge, Milton Park, 2005.

Castells, M., *The Internet Galaxy*. Oxford University Press, Oxford, 2001.

Castells, M., *The Rise of the Network Society: Economy, Society and Culture, Vol. I*. Blackwell Publishers, Cambridge, Oxford, 1996.

Couldry, N., 'The Forgotten Digital Divide: Researching Social Exclusion/Inclusion in the Age of Personalised Media', *To be presented at: Globalisation and Convergence Conference*. MIT, May 10-12.2004, 23.05.2008, <http://cms.mit.edu/conf/mit2/Abstrracts/NickCouldry.pdf>.

Couldry, N., 'Communicative Entitlements and Democracy: The Future of the DigitalDivide', in *The Oxford Handbook of Information and Communication Technologies*. Mansell, R., Avgerou, Ch., Quah, D. & Silverstone, R. (eds), Oxford University Press, Oxford, 2007, pp. 383-403.

Della Porta, D. & S. Tarrow, 'Transnational Process and Social Activism: An Introduction', in *Transnational Processes and Social Activism*. Della Porta, D. & Tarrow, S. (eds), Rowman & Littlefield Publishers, Lanham, Boulder, New York, Toronto, Oxford, 2005, pp. 1-19.

Dijk, J. v., *The Deepening Divide: Inequality in the Information Society*. Sage, Thousand Oaks, London, New Delhi, 2005.

Fuchs, Ch., 'The Self-Organization of Cyberprotest' in *The Internet Society II: Advances in Education, Commerce & Governance*. Morgan, K., Brebbia, C. A. & Spector, J. M. (eds), WIT Press, Southampton, Boston, 2006, pp. 275-295.

Giddens, A., *The Consequences of Modernity*. Stanford University Press, Stanford, CA, 1990.

Graham, Ph., 'Hypercapitalism'. *New Media & Society*, vol. 2, no. 2, 2000, p. 131-156.

Hardt, M. & A. Negri, *Multitude: War and Democracy in the Age of Empire*. Penguin Books, London, 2004.

Held, D. & A. McGrew, *Globalization/Anti-Globalization: Beyond the Great Divide*. Polity Press Cambridge, Malden, 2007.

Holton, R. J., *Globalization and the Nation-State*. McMillan Press, London, 1998.

Jenkins, H., *Confronting the Challenges of Participatory Culture: Media Education for the 21st Century*. The MacArthur Foundation, Chicago, 2006.

Kim, Y-Ch. & S. J. Ball-Rokeach, 'New Immigrants, the Internet, and Civic Society' in *Routledge Handbook of Internet Politics*. Chadwick, A. & Howards, Ph. N. (eds), Routledge, London, New York, 2009, pp. 275-287.

Klar, M., 'Globale Information - ein Projekt. Global Information - a Project', in Die Zukunft des Raums: The Future of Space. Meurer, B. (ed), Campus Verlag, Frankfurt, New York, 1994, pp. 165-172.

Lamla, J., Anthony Giddens. Campus Verlag, Frankfurt, New York, 2003.

Lessig, L., Code. And Other Laws of Cyberspace. Version 2.0. Basic, London, 2007.

Lévy, P,, Collectice Intelligence: Mankind's Emerging World in Cyberspace. Perseus Books, Cambridge, MA, 1997.

McLuhan, M., 'The Medium is the Message', in Media Studies. Marris, P. & Thornham, S. (eds), University Press, New York, 1964.

Negroponte, N., *Being Digital*. Coronet, London, 1995.

Neumayer, Ch. & C. Raffl, 'Facebook for Protest?: The Value of Social Software for Political Activism in the Anti-FARC Rallies', in DigiActive Research Series. December 2008.

Passy, F., 'Social Networks Matter: But How?', in Relational Approaches to Collective Action. Diani, M. & McAdam, D. (eds), Oxford University Press, Oxford, 2003, p. 21-48.

Poster, M., *Information Please: Culture and Politics in the Age of Digital Machines*. Duke University Press, Durham, London, 2006.

Raffl, C., 'Assessing the Impact of Open Content Knowledge Production in Web 2.0'. *The International Journal of Technology, Knowledge and Society*, vol. 4, no. 3, 2008, pp. 85-92.

Raffl, C. & R. M. Bichler, 'Vom Sozialen in den Virtuellen Raum. Ernst Blochs 'Konkrete Utopie' im Cyberspace?, in *Raumkonstruktion und Raumerfahrung. Jahrbuch 2007 der Ernst-Bloch-Assoziation, VorSchein Nr. 29*. Zeilinger, D. (ed), Antogo Verlag, Nürnberg, 2007, pp. 107-128.

Rantanen, T., *The Media and Globalization*. Sage, London, Thousand Oaks, New Delhi, 2005.

Rheingold, H., 'From Facebook to the Streets of Colombia', in *SmartMobs. The next Social Revolution: Mobile Communication, Pervasive Computing, Wireless Networks, Collective Action*. 2008, 22.05.2008.

Rheingold, H., *Smart Mobs: The next Social Revolution*. Perseus Books Groups, Cambridge, 2002.

Rheingold, H., 'SmartMobs: The next Social Revolution: Book summary', 2002, 10.02.2009, <http://www.smartmobs.com/book/book_summ.html>.

Rheingold, H., *The Virtual Community: Homesteading on the Electronic Frontier*. Addison-Wesley, Readgin, 1993.

Robertson, R., 'Glocalization: Time-Space and Homogeneity-Heterogeneity' in *Global Modernities*. Featherstone, M., Lash, S. & Robertson, R. (eds), Sage, London, 1995, pp. 25-44.

Sassen, S., 'Electronic Networks, Power, and Democracy', in *The Oxford Handbook of New Media*. Mansell, R., Avgerou, Ch., Quah, D. & Silverstone, R. (eds), Oxford University Press, Oxford, 2007, pp. 339-361.

Sassen, S., *Metropolen des Weltmarkts: Die neue Rolle der Global Cities*. Campus Verlag, Frankfurt am Main, New York, 1997.

Sassen, S., 'Wirtschaft und Kultur in der globalen Stadt: Economy and Culture in the Global City', in *Die Zukunft des Raums. The Future of Space*. Meurer, B. (ed), Campus Verlag, Frankfurt, New York, 1994, pp. 71-90.

Saveri, A., Rheingold, H. & K. Vian, *Technologies of Cooperation*. Institute for the Future, Palo Alto, 2005.

Schiller, H. I., *Information Inequality. The Deepening Social Crisis in America*. Routledge, New York, London, 1996.

Scholz, T., 'Market Ideology and the Myths of Web 2.0'. *First Monday*, vol. 13, no. 3, 2008, online.

Selwyn, N., 'Reconsidering Political and Polular Understandings of the Digital Divide'. *New Media and Society*, vol. 6, no. 3, 2004, pp. 341-362.

Sparks, C., 'Media and the Global Public Sphere: An Evaluative Approach', in *Global Activism Global Media*. Jong, W de, Shaw, M. & Stammers, N. (eds), Pluto Press, London, 2005, pp. 34-49.

Stallman, R. M., 'The GNU operating System and the Free Software Movement', in *Open Sources: Voices from the Open Source Revolution*. C DiBona, S Ockman & M Stone (eds), O'Reilly, Sebastopol, CA, 1999, pp. 53-70.

Tichenor, Ph., Donohue, G. & C. Olien, 'Mass Media Flow and Differential Growth in Knowledge'. *Public Opinion Quarterly*, vol. 34, 1970, pp. 159-170.

Toffler, A. & H. Toffler, *Creating a New Civilization: The Politics of the Third Wave*. Turner Publications, Atlanta, 1995.

Wellman, B., 'Physical Place and CyberPlace: The Rise of Personalized Networking'. *International Journal of Urban and Regional Research*, vol. 25, no. 8, 2001, pp. 227-252.

**Christina Neumayer** recently joined the IT-University of Copenhagen as a PhD fellow. Prior, she was a research fellow at the ICT&S Center at the University of Salzburg.

**Celina Raffl** is PhD fellow at the ICT&S Center and lecturer at the Department of Communication Studies at the University of Salzburg.

**Robert M. Bichler** is currently a lecturer at the Shanghai International Studies University. Prior, he was a research fellow and lecturer at the ICT&S Center at the University of Salzburg.

# PART II

## Cyber-Governance, Cyber-Communities, Cyber-Bodies

# Governance and the Global Metaverse

*Melissa de Zwart and David Lindsay*

**Abstract**
The governance of emerging global online communities such as MMORPGs, virtual worlds and social networking sites, raises fundamental issues concerning the legitimacy of rule-making, including problems such as the applicability of democracy and the rule of law, issues of consent and accountability, public versus private rule making and the application of national laws to global virtual communities. This chapter will consider questions regarding the legitimacy of decisions made by private entities, especially service providers, the relevance of applying territorial national laws to global technological spaces and the rights of citizens of virtual communities. It will also consider the role of the networked 'dividual' within these communities and consider the relationship between the dividual and regulation and control. It concludes that governance of virtual spaces must reflect the networked nature of the global metaverse that gives effect to individual choices regarding social actions.

**Key Words**: Virtual worlds, internet, governance, regulation, Deleuze, control.

****

## 1. Introduction

This chapter examines the complexity of governance issues arising in the context of virtual worlds. It identifies various levels of governance operating upon and within virtual worlds and considers the legitimacy of current forms of rule-making. It considers the governance issues that are particular to the virtual world environment and asks whether the debates concerning Internet governance generally contribute to or merely confuse the identification of a suitable governance model for virtual worlds. The purpose of the study is to demonstrate that issues of governance affecting virtual communities are different from those relevant to the Internet generally, and involve a complex network of overlapping interests. It concludes that key issues arising from virtual world governance, such as protection of identity and transparency of rule making, will increasingly have relevance for local governments and rule makers, as their citizens interact with one another and with government more frequently online. Thus, rather than seeking to impose existing laws wholesale upon virtual communities, law makers may be better advised to determine what lessons can be learnt from these communities.

## 2.    Virtual Worlds

Before we consider the application of governance mechanisms to virtual worlds, it is important to identify the nature of the environments captured within this term. It is now reasonably well recognised that not all virtual worlds are the same. Some are text based, others highly graphical, some open and others highly regulated. Some of the most successful worlds are aimed at children and young teens, such as *Club Penguin*, *Neo Pets* and *Habbo*, and hence are highly moderated in terms of content, language and access. Others are deliberately created to facilitate and encourage player-driven competition, with little regulation beyond enforcement of the Terms of Service. The space-themed environment of *EVE* consciously encourages players to behave like pirates, *Second Life* adopts a hands-off policy towards content creation to encourage commerce in virtual goods and services, and environments such as *LiveJournal* have many thriving self-regulating communities. However, the danger is that regulators, seeking to simplify the regulatory environment may wish to lump them in together, leading to inappropriate forms of regulatory control.[1] This chapter will focus upon massively multiplayer online role-playing games (MMORPGs) such as *World of Warcraft* and *EverQuest*, and social virtual worlds, such as *Second Life*, as they currently attract the highest number of users and demonstrate the range of issues to which virtual communities give rise.[2] The key attributes of these environments is that participants interact in a shared, persistent environment, in real time, through an avatar and that the data creating the environment is hosted on a central server (or servers) controlled by the service provider.[3] MMORPGs generally have a game object, requiring players to adopt a character from a predetermined set of characteristics and to level up through a series of challenges and tasks, whereas as social virtual worlds may have no object other than socialising. However, many spaces within social virtual worlds are dedicated to role-play and prescribe their own rules and objects, further muddying any attempts to clearly categorise such environments.

It should also be recognised that it is no longer possible to draw neat boundaries around such communities. Increasingly, participants in environments such as *World of Warcraft* maintain their own web sites dedicated to WoW, hosting machinima, images, blogs and detailed wikis and explanations of the game and the gaming backstory. They meet up at conventions and gatherings to discuss the game and role-play. They video conference, read and write fan fiction and use their avatars in other contexts. So online communities do not remain solely online for all of their inhabitants.

## 3.    Governance Issues

As the number of people participating in virtual worlds increases, along with the amount of money invested in and circulated through virtual worlds, increasing demands will be made by national governments to control the activities that occur within them. Key governance issues identified by virtual worlds stakeholders at *Virtual Policy 08* (UK) as requiring further exploration included:

- The complex nature of governance of virtual worlds which consists of a mix of self-regulation, End User Licence Agreements ('EULAs'), national regulation and codes of conduct;
- The applicability of classifying virtual worlds as a separate classification for regulatory purposes (as distinct from broader regulation of the Internet);
- The perceived lack of lobbying power/ cohesive interests amongst service providers;
- The question of whether national laws should apply to virtual worlds, or whether they should be recognised as a separate place, and the related matter of determination and enforcement of jurisdiction with respect to applicable laws;
- The nature and quality of consent provided by users;
- Clarification of the question of whose interests should be protected pursuant to regulatory intervention (i.e. children or adults);
- Recognition that enforcement procedures are a necessary aspect of effective regulation;
- Recognition of the variety of models of virtual worlds;
- The need for clearer induction procedures and education of users; and
- The identification of an appropriate legal model for participation in virtual worlds.[4]

As can be seen from this list, these are fundamental issues in need of resolution. There is a danger that if such questions are not meaningfully resolved by the service providers and key stakeholders, governments will move to regulate virtual worlds without fully understanding the nature of such environments. This is particularly the case given concerns frequently expressed by the mainstream media about the dangers of such environments, ranging from violence and pornography to paedophilia.

Virtual world creators and inhabitants alike have thus far resisted calls for greater regulation on the basis that they are artificial spaces and hence protected by 'the Magic Circle'. The concept of the magic circle is derived from Johan Huizinga's discussion of play spaces and identifies the game space, in which players are separated from the real world and agree to abide by the applicable game rules whilst they are in that space, as being outside the application of 'real world' laws.[5] Virtual world pioneer Richard Bartle describes this as a willingness to forgo certain freedoms so that certain benefits and freedoms of the virtual world may be experienced during the time in-world.[6]

However, this concept is under attack from many quarters, including national regulators, on the basis that many of these in-world actions have impacts upon people outside of the 'game'. Media reports of fraud, sexual grooming, money laundering and terrorism have led to greater scrutiny from domestic governments, particularly with respect to threats posed to children.

Joshua Fairfield has recently argued that the magic circle distinction between in game and out of game activities is not helpful in determining when real world laws should apply to in-world events.[7] Fairfield argues that drawing a boundary on the basis of what occurs in the game and what occurs outside it, should be replaced with the recognition that virtual worlds should be permitted to create their own rules, acknowledged and accepted by members in their consent to the terms of service ('ToS') and community norms. When a dispute arises, these rules should be respected and in most cases enforced by domestic courts as reflecting the community norms to which all members of that community have consented. This proposal acknowledges the relationship between in and out of world activities and has precedents, for example, in the approach of the law of torts to sport, recognising consent to injuries fairly incurred within the rules of the game.

We will return to the question of whether there is any need for increased regulation and governance of virtual worlds, but first we will identify current sources of governance in virtual worlds.

## 4.      Current Sources of Governance

The sources of law (rules) which may currently be identified in virtual worlds are:

- The EULA/ToS: the contractual terms accepted by the end user, albeit frequently without reading them;
- The community rules or acceptable use guidelines;
- The code: the underlying physics of the world which determines what the avatar can (or cannot) do;
- The general law applicable to the end user and/or the service provider; and
- Possibly, the specific norms or rules that apply to the particular environment, such as rules regarding speech, conduct and appearance, for example, the steampunk sim of Caledon (and surrounding sims) in *Second Life*.

Grimes, Jaeger and Fleischmann further simplify this down to two forms of governance, being the underlying source code of the program and the civil code of rules.[8]

Even with these multiple layers of control, there remains within the virtual world some gaps or capacity for change and uncertainty. In some environments this gap may be left deliberately to facilitate expansion of the world through user creation of new content. As Humphreys observes MMORPGs (and by analogy social virtual worlds) continue to evolve and grow after launch, with input from both service provider and users.[9] In other cases, the gaps may simply be a consequence of the service provider not anticipating and coding for all contingencies in the game. For example, the code may allow or enable some particular activity that may be prohibited by the game rules or community norms. These gaps therefore leave room for exploits of the code, modification, hacking or other behaviour which is at odds with the articulated rules of the game. A question then arises as to whether an exercise of this power is 'cheating' or merely exploiting an aspect of the world's functionality.[10] Your point of view on this would be dictated by both the nature of the world and your attitude as a member of that world.

Castells has identified four layers of cultural attitudes underpinning the Internet being the techno-meritocratic, the hacker, the virtual communitarian and the entrepreneurial.[11] The hacker, representing a 'culture of convergence between humans and their machines in a process of unfettered interaction', may regard such actions merely as a potential waiting to be fulfilled.[12] The virtual communitarian, on the other hand, may place a higher value on mutual respect for community norms.

As Grimes et al. observe, there are multiple forms of governing documents in virtual worlds, however there is no fixed or common terminology regarding what terms such documents should contain, nor any commonality of language or structure.[13] A key aspect of such documents is the software licence agreement that permits the user to use the underlying computer software subject to the terms of use dictated by the service provider. As the recent litigation involving Blizzard, the owners of *World of Warcraft*, and MDY, the creators of Glider, a program that facilitates automated play, demonstrates, this structure represents an extremely powerful form of control. Blizzard has alleged that end users of WoW, who have paid their subscription fee and are otherwise legitimate authorised users of the WoW software, are in breach of the software licence when they use Glider in conjunction with WoW. Thus this use of the unauthorised program places them in breach of the contract and transforms them into copyright infringers. MDY they claim is then liable for inducing end users to breach contract and copyright. This claim has been upheld by the District Court of Arizona, with the judge finding on summary judgment that MDY was liable for tortious interference with contract and contributory and vicarious copyright infringement.[14] On a further hearing the Court concluded that MDY is also liable under the Digital Millennium Copyright Act provisions relating to trafficking in technological products designed to circumvent technological measures that control access to a protected work and that protect a right of the copyright owner; that Donnelly, the president and day to day manager of MDY, was personally liable for the tortious interference, copyright infringement and DMCA violations and that Blizzard is entitled to a permanent injunction against the continued sale and distribution of Glider.[15] The key interest of this case from a governance perspective is the finding of the Court that the grant of the limited license to use the game software is expressly made subject to the user's 'agreement to and continuing compliance with this License Agreement.' Further, the licence agreement provides that '[a]ll use of the Game Client is subject to' the EULA and the ToU. This strict enforcement of the copyright licence ignores the fact that modifications (or 'mods') of game software, despite being explicitly prohibited by the Licence Agreement and ToU, are frequently made by gamers and are seen as part of the gaming culture.[16] There are thousands of mods available on the Internet and Blizzard provides some support to the modder community. Hence there is ambivalence and tension in the relationship between the service provider and users, reflecting fear, respect and resistance at the same time.[17]

In fact it is in the lowest level of sources of law identified above that the most effective level of governance has emerged. Users appear to be most content to abide by the rules of their community, where those rules reflect the norms embodied by the community, thus reinforcing the point made by Fairfield above. This level of consent is however very difficult to scale up to large communities. An attempt to provide some structure for this type of approach is provided by the *MetaPlace* terms of service, which are based upon the concepts articulated by Raph Koster in his 'Declaration on the Rights of Avatars'.[18] Koster's Declaration explicitly recognises, for example, that every member of the virtual community has the right to contribute to the shaping of the community's code of conduct 'as the culture of the virtual space evolves, particularly as it evolves in directions that the administrator did not predict.' Further, the administrator has a duty 'to work with the community to arrive at a code of conduct that is shaped by the input of the community.' Koster has put these rights into practice in the Terms of Service of *MetaPlace*.[19] These provide users with rights including freedom of speech, reasonable processes to resolve grievances and ownership of their intellectual property. However, even this model recognises that these TOS do not suit all environments and a context-specific assessment must be made regarding the appropriateness of granting such rights to users. Whilst greeted with enthusiasm by the virtual world community, there appear to be some inconsistencies in the terms as they attempt to serve the needs of users, creators and platform provider.[20]

## 5.      The Nature of Control

Service providers are both creator and controller of the virtual world. As Sal Humphreys asserts, in developing the code that generates the virtual world service providers do not merely launch a completed environment, but from that time forth must also take responsibility for civic control as the 'manager of communities'.[21] This may be a role that the developer neither understands nor wants. On the other hand, as Bartle has argued it may be a deliberate strategy, actively wanted by developer and players alike.[22]

Linden Lab, the developers of *Second Life*, have had a troubled relationship with their users ('residents'), at times asserting control in the guise of the benevolent dictator and at others seeking to shelter behind the mantle of service provider. As the discussion of the Glider case demonstrates, the relationship between the service provider and community involves elements of devotion and resistance and, as each community has unique attributes and aspirations, that relationship requires more constant maintenance than the service provider may have anticipated. The players are dedicated to supporting and nurturing their virtual worlds, through fan forums, blogging and conventions. However, where interests of players or citizens and the service provider diverge, there can be serious dissent, for example the ban on 'broadly offensive content' in *Second Life*. Bartle's description of the game providers as 'gods' does not apply so directly to worlds such as *Second Life*, where so much control is granted to citizens through allowing them to create content and acquire a sense of ownership.[23] However, even the attempts by Linden to grant ownership over intellectual property to its users have come under attack. One of the most successful in-world content vendors in *Second Life*, Stroker Serpentine, has, through his offline identity Kevin Alderman, recently initiated a class action claim against Linden with respect to copyright and trade mark infringement. The claim states that Linden has failed to take available steps to detect and prevent infringement of Alderman's creations by other *Second Life* vendors as Linden itself benefits from trade in infringing content.[24] The filing of the action reflects Alderman's frustration at having brought two copyright infringement actions against other *Second Life* participants with respect to copying of his *Second Life* sex products, with little practical outcome. The frustration results from the difficulty of identifying infringers and enforcing judgment against them, as the Complaint states: 'A Second Life pirate who becomes subject to a DMCA takedown notice will usually not challenge it, but rather will simply create a new free account and re-upload the content, employing the tried and true whack-a-mole approach.'[25]

In his short essay 'Postscript on the Societies of Control', published in 1990, Gilles Deleuze discusses the passing of Foucault's disciplinary societies of the eighteenth and nineteenth centuries and the emergence of 'societies of control'.[26] This is reflected in attitudes to and institutions of work, education, finance and leisure and in that society's machines: old societies made use of levers, pulleys and clocks, disciplinary societies used machines involving energy (with its attendant dangers) and societies of control use computers. Importantly, Deleuze observed that 'the man of control is undulatory, in orbit, in a continuous network. Everywhere *surfing* has already replaced the older *sports*.'[27] The technologies of control make it possible for the modern 'dividual' to be monitored and regulated at all points within society, for the embodied individual of Foucault's disciplinary society has become the divisible human subject reducible to various data representations ('masses, samples, data, markets, or *'banks'*') via computing technology.[28] Deleuze uses the example of an electronic security card which can allow a person to move freely throughout a building or city but which could just as easily be programmed to prevent that person's entry to certain areas at particular times or on designated days, legitimately or illegitimately.[29] Deleuze observes that this reflects 'the progressive and dispersed installation of a new system of domination.'[30] Thus technology, and in particular networked computer technology, is an essential element of control societies.

Building upon Deleuze's analysis of control societies, Alexander Galloway has considered the manifestation of control in distributed computer networks. In his book *Protocol: How Control Exists After Decentralization*, Galloway argues that despite the typical characterisation of the Internet as 'rhizomatic and lacking central organization', the protocols necessary to facilitate communication between linked networks of differing nature and configuration reflect a new mechanism that facilitates both distributed control, such as the need to comply with TCP/IP protocols, and rigid hierarchies, such as the operation of the Domain Name System.[31] Those wishing to join the network must abide by and implement these protocols. Thus Galloway contradicts Lawrence Lessig's arguments, made in both *Code and Other Laws of Cyberspace* and *The Future of Ideas: The Fate of the Commons in a Connected World* that the Internet essentially started off 'free' and lacking any form of control and has been subjected increasingly to control by the law and commercial interests.[32] Rather, Galloway claims: 'the founding principle of the Net is control, not freedom. *Control has existed from the beginning.*'[33] Of course, this is a protocological or technical form of control that, as Deleuze's example of the swipe card demonstrates, is neither good nor bad, but is capable of being put to either use.

Virtual communities are clear manifestations of Deleuze's societies of control, regulated by technological protocols, which define what you can and cannot do. As Galloway observes in his book on videogames *Gaming: Essays on Algorithmic Culture*, such games represent a clear manifestation of informatic control: 'to play the game means to play the code of the game. To win means to know the system.'[34] Videogames (and by extension virtual game worlds such as MMORPGs) thus represent a uniquely transparent example of the political structures of the information age. In order to win, the player must internalise the algorithm and play in accordance with its rules.[35]

Having attempted to relinquish a level of protocological control over *Second Life* in order to foster commerce, Linden is being pushed by some of its more successful developers to reinstate it. How this dispute is ultimately resolved will provide interesting insights into the balance of control in *Second Life*.

## 6.      Consent

So, reflecting upon these competing and conflicting needs, does the EULA provide the most effective form of governance?

The development of the ability to transmit content electronically, and hence to monitor, charge for and potentially restrict the use, reuse, modification and further transfer of that content, has led to a shift from the regulation of distribution of such content from general laws such as copyright to the private ordering of rights through contract. On the one hand, proponents of greater control over such uses, headed up by the US content industries, have argued for greater control over access and re-use through the legal enforcement of technological protection mechanisms and contractual waiver of exceptions existing under the copyright law. On the other hand, advocates of greater rights of access and manipulation, such as the Creative Commons movement, have bemoaned the overly restrictive nature of the copyright law and created suites of 'copyleft' licences to be attached to new works, flagging the rights of re-use and attribution to be accorded to a work. In this climate, private ordering through contract has been advocated as a superior form of rights management, albeit for very different reasoning.[36]

This thinking has of course influenced issues of governance of virtual worlds, the worlds themselves being creative manifestations of the service provider, assisted in most cases by user created content. Therefore the trend has been to regard the best way to regulate such worlds as to leave it up to service providers to enter into a contract with users.

However, this model has many flaws, not the least of which is the fact that most users do not read the EULA, and even if they did there is no scope for them to negotiate its terms. Membership of the world is offered solely on a take it or leave it basis. Further, citizens entering a virtual world will carry with them a belief that they carry with them certain entrenched values or norms, which may be legally enforced in that virtual world. As

noted above, citizens also acquire a sense of ownership over the virtual world
when they engage in creation of content.

Further, when disputes emerge between members of the virtual
community, the contract between the member and the service provider
seldom provides an effective mechanism for resolution of such disputes. As
the *Second Life* example discussed above illustrates, Alderman's attempts to
enforce his intellectual property rights against other users in the absence of
Linden's co-operation or enforcement, have proved almost worthless.

## 7.     Internet Governance

Does the Internet governance debate provide any guidance on
effective governance of virtual worlds? Internet mythology provides us with
two stories regarding the governance and control of the Internet. One
approach, taken from the stories told by the cyberlibertarians such as John
Perry Barlow, tell us that the Internet is not susceptible to control. As an end
to end network, connected by users' adoption of the TCP/IP protocol and
operating on a distributed network, offering redundant links, these
commentators tell us that: 'You can't stop the signal'.[37] On the other hand the
cyberpaternalists conclude that the architecture of the Internet can be used to
determine and dictate and therefore effectively control behaviour.

In his recent work on Internet governance and regulation, Andrew
Murray draws upon these two opposing views of Internet control and
concludes that neither is accurate.[38] Building on Castells' concept of network
individualism, Murray argues that the key to understanding regulatory
challenges is to be found in network individualism or weak collectivism.[39] He
states:

> Network individualism or weak collectivism is an effect of
> modern communications cultures and is particularly strong
> in the decentred network that is the internet. With no single
> point of control, as is found in other media carriers, the
> opportunity for regulation through law or code is
> diminished and the opportunity for communities to set
> standards and values (short of norms) which challenge
> regulatory communications from regulatory bodies is
> enhanced.[40]

This leads to the development of a broader network of networks as
communities gravitate towards other communities that share similar values.
In linking together and sharing their cultures each community affects and
influences the others, the points of contact being individuals who are
members of multiple communities. This means that any attempt to intervene
in one part of the network will have unanticipated consequences for other

parts of the network. Murray concludes: 'This makes traditional command and control regulation highly disruptive.'[41]

Therefore regulation of this network of communities is not merely a question of identifying and imposing the 'correct' existing laws on virtual worlds, but to ask as Poster did with respect to the broader Internet in 1995: 'are there new kinds of relations occurring within it which suggests new forms of power configurations between communicating individuals?'[42] Poster concludes: 'Internet communities function as places of difference from and resistance to modern society. In a sense, they serve the function of a Habermasian public sphere without intentionally being one.'[43] However, as danah boyd has recently warned us, the promise of the Internet, and online communities in particular, bringing to us the 'next generation public sphere' brings with it the risks of 'next generation divides'. She argues:

> The public sphere was never accessible to everyone. There's a reason that the scholar Habermas talked about it as the bourgeois public sphere. The public sphere was historically the domain of educated, wealthy, white, straight men. The digital public sphere may make certain aspects of public life more accessible to some, but this is not a given. And if the ways in which we construct the digital public sphere reinforce the divisions that we've been trying to break down, we've got a problem.[44]

Further, as virtual communities provide multiple and different public spheres, people may choose to represent themselves differently with respect to each particular community in which they are engaged. Thus a person's rights to protect their various identities through which they interact with various communities, and thus truly embrace the advantages of being Deleuze's dividual, may become paramount.[45]

As Donata Marletta has observed elsewhere in this volume, it appears inevitable that the contacts made in these online communities will spill out into the offline community as increasingly, online connections are extended by face-to-face meetings, fan conventions, video links and networking, as she says 'building bridges between physical and virtual spaces.'[46] Therefore, it becomes difficult to determine whether issues such as protection of the dividual's many identities (and their vast array of personal data and information generated both knowingly and unknowingly during their online interactions) is a matter for on or offline regulation. Umut Burcu Tasa presents us with an optimistic approach to this dilemma, stating that 'the interconnected, collaborative and rhizomatic nature of Cyberspace... implies a huge potential for creating new holistic visions of existence.'[47]

Thus a networked model of interconnected public spheres may provide some guidance regarding governance of virtual worlds.

## 8.          Conclusions: Governance of the Global Metaverse?

Can it be said then that there is justification for a blanket approach to governance of virtual worlds? There is a diversity of environments that may satisfy the definition of a virtual world, yet each represents and reflects the interests and expectations of a diversity of users. The value of such worlds lies in this very diversity, which should be respected and encouraged. Therefore any governance model adopted should reflect the importance of the network as the organising agency, respecting the need of the individual, or perhaps, more accurately in this environment, Deleuze's 'dividual', to participate in a range of interconnected experiences, which should not be fragmented or interrupted by the interference of inconsistent domestic laws. This analysis still reflects the choice between control by national governments or control by service providers, there is little reflection of control by the citizens of virtual worlds. National governments can best support the development of virtual worlds by creating consistent supportive and facilitative frameworks, which respect the needs of users and service providers rather than imposing external controls. However, it is also desirable to clarify the relationship between the service provider and the citizen regarding important matters such as privacy, surveillance, ownership of intellectual property, transparency of terms and age appropriate content. This approach would be most likely to facilitate the development of productive, vibrant virtual communities embodying values of the public sphere.

We have already become accustomed to living in the society of control:

> Formatted by code, harmonised with the language of machines, our life history, tastes, preferences and personal details become profiles, mailing lists, data and ultimately markets. Societies of control regulate their population by ensuring their knowing and unknowing participation in the marketplace through enforced compatibility with code.[48]

What we now need to learn is to leverage the positive opportunities that this presents to assert control over the technology. Virtual communities represent the opportunity and potential for greater control and greater freedom. The technology underpinning the Internet may embody the technologies and protocols of control but users are learning how to question and resist this dominant model, thus governance models should provide space to reflect the needs of both owners and users to explore these new freedoms.

# Notes

[1] 'Virtual worlds are not all the same, and the law should therefore be careful about treating them as if they were all the same.' R Bartle 'Why Governments aren't Gods and Gods aren't Governments' *First Monday*, Special issue number 7 (September 2006), <http://firstmonday.org/issues/issue11_9/bartle/index.html>, accessed 9 September 2008, fn. 11.

[2] For further discussion of the classes of virtual worlds see ENISA Position Paper: *Virtual Worlds, Real Money, Security and Privacy in Massively-Multiplayer Online Games and Social and Corporate Virtual Worlds*, November 2008, p 8 and R Reynolds 'The Four Worlds Theory', *Terra Nova Blog*, 28 August 2005, <http://terranova.blogs.com/terra_nova /2005/08 /the_four_worlds.html>, accessed 18 December 2008. Although this paper refers exclusively to Western world MMORPGs, it is acknowledged that the MMORPGs based in Asia, particularly in China and South Korea, have attracted even larger numbers of active subscribers.

[3] ENISA Position Paper, above, p. 8.

[4] Virtual Policy '08 - Summary of Policy Discussions, available from: <http://www.virtualpolicy.net/VP08.html, accessed 4 February 2009>.

[5] Johan Huizinga, *Homo Ludens*, 1938, trans. 1971, see discussion in R Bartle 'Virtual Worldliness: What the Imaginary Asks of the Real' (2004) 49 *New York Law School Law Review* 19 at pp. 23-27.

[6] Bartle, 'Virtual Worldliness', above p. 23.

[7] J Fairfield, 'The Magic Circle', *Vanderbilt Journal of Entertainment and Technology Law* (forthcoming 2009).

[8] J Grimes, P Jaeger and K Fleischmann 'Obfuscatocracy: A Stakeholder Analysis of Governing Documents for Virtual Worlds' *First Monday*, Volume 13 Number 9 - 1 September 2008, <http://www.uic.edu/htbin/cgiwrap/bin/ojs/index.php/fm/article/viewArticle/2153/2029>, accessed 9 September 2008. See also S Humphreys 'Ruling the Virtual World: Governance in Massively Multiplayer Online Games' (2008) 11(2) *European Journal of Cultural Studies* 149, pp. 153-154.

[9] Humphreys, above, p. 150.

[10] See the discussion of software coded rules in Norrath (*EverQuest*) in G Lastowka, 'Planes of Power: EverQuest as Text, Game and Community', *The International Journal of Computer Game Research*, 9.1, 2009, <http://gamestudies.org/0901/articles/lastowka>.

[11] M Castells, *The Internet Galaxy: Reflections on the Internet, Business, and Society*, Oxford, Oxford University Press, 2001, pp. 37- 61.

[12] Castells, above, p. 50.

[13] Grimes, Jaeger and Fleischmann, above, p. 10.

[14] *Blizzard Entertainment, Inc and Vivendi Games, Inc v MDY Industries, LLC,* 14 July 2008, Arizona District Court, Judge David Campbell.

[15] *MDY Industries, LLC v Blizzard Entertainment, Inc and Vivendi Games, Inc and Blizzard Entertainment, Inc and Vivendi Games, Inc v Michael Donnelly,* No CV-06-2555-PHX-DGC, Order, Arizona District Court, Judge David Campbell, 28 January 2009. The decision is currently the subject of an appeal.

[16] H Postigo, 'Video Game Appropriation through Modifications: Attitudes Concerning Intellectual Property among Modders and Fans', *Convergence* 59, 14, 2008.

[17] See, for example, the official Blizzard post on the outcome of the Glider litigation, <http://forums.worldofwarcraft.com/thread.html?topicId=1491000 2728 &sid=1>, accessed 6 February 2009, and the cautious response of the modder community: Mike Schramm, 'Blizzard Responds to the Glider Decision', *WoW Insider,* 5 February 2009, <http://www.wowinsider.com/ 2009/02/05/blizzard-responds-to-the-glider-decision/>, accessed 6 February 2009.

[18] R Koster, 'Declaration of the Rights of Avatars', 26 January 2000, <http://www.raphkoster.com/gaming/playerrights.shtml>, accessed 22 September 2009. Note that MetaPlace is not a virtual world itself, but rather a platform for creating a range of virtual spaces.

[19] MetaPlace, <http://www.metaplace.com/>, accessed 22 September 2009. See further R Koster, 'Declaring the Rights of Metaplace Users', 15 September 2009, <http://www.raphkoster.com/2008/09/15/declaring-the-rights-of-metaplace-users/>, accessed 22 September 2009.

[20] See S Axon, 'Picking Apart the MetaPlace Bill of Rights', *Massively,* <http://www.massively.com/2008/09/18/picking-apart-the-metaplace-bill-of-rights/>, accessed 22 September 2009.

[21] Humphreys, above, p. 151.

[22] Bartle, 'Virtual Worldliness', above, p 30.

[23] T Malaby, 'Coding Control: Governance and Contingency in the Production of Online Worlds', *First Monday,* Special issue number 7 (September 2006), http://firstmonday.org/issues/special11_9/malaby/ index.html , accessed 9 September 2008.

[24] T Nino, 'Class Action Lawsuit levelled against Second Life's Linden Lab', <http://www.metaversejournal.com/2009/09/16/class-action-lawsuit-leveled-against-second-lifes-linden-lab/>, 16 September 2009, accessed 22 September 2009.

[25] *Eros LLC v Linden Research Inc,* Complaint, filed 15 September 2009, para. 30.

[26] G Deleuze, 'Postscript on the Societies of Control', no. 59, *October* 3, 1992, p. 4.

[27] Deleuze, 'Societies of Control', above, p 6 (emphasis in original).

[28] Deleuze, 'Societies of Control', above, p. 5. See further, R Williams 'Politics and Self in the Age of Digital Re(pro)ducibility',1.1, *Fast Capitalism*, 2005http://www.uta.edu/huma/agger/fastcapitalism/1_1/will ia ms.html, accessed 22 September 2009.

[29] Deleuze, 'Societies of control', above, p. 7.

[30] Deleuze, 'Societies of control', above, p. 7.

[31] A Galloway, *Protocol: How Control Exists After Decentralization*, The MIT Press, Cambridge, Massachusetts, 2004, at p. 8.

[32] Galloway, *Protocol*, above, at p. 141. See Lawrence Lessig *Code and Other Laws of Cyberspace*, New York Basic Books, 1999 and Lawrence Lessig, *The Future of Ideas: The Fate of the Commons in a Connected World*, New York, Random House, 2001.

[33] Galloway, *Protocol*, above, p. 142.

[34] A Galloway *Gaming: Essays on Algorithmic Culture*, Minneapolis, University of Minnesota Press, 2006, p. 90.

[35] Galloway, *Gaming*, above, p. 91.

[36] N Elkin-Koren 'Governing Access to Users-Generated-Content: The Changing Nature of Private Ordering in Digital Networks' in E Brousseau, M Marzouki & C Meadel (eds) ·*Governance, Regulations and Powers on the Internet*, Cambridge University Press, 2009.

[37] <http://www.serenitymovie.com/>, accessed 4 February 2009>. Mr Universe: 'There is only the truth of the signal. Everything goes somewhere and I go everywhere'.

[38] A Murray, 'Symbiotic Regulation', 2008, ExpressO, <http://works.bepress.com/andrew_murray/1>, accessed 6 February 2009. See also A Murray, *The Regulation of Cyberspace: Control in the Online Environment*, Oxford, Routledge, 2006.

[39] M Castells, *The Internet Galaxy*, above, pp. 129-133.

[40] Murray, 'Symbiotic Regulation', above, p. 14-15.

[41] Murray, 'Symbiotic Regulation', above, p. 16.

[42] M Poster, 'CyberDemocracy: Internet and the Public Sphere' 1995, <http://www.hnet.uci.edu/mposter/writings/democ.html>, accessed 4 February 2009. See also P Boeder, 'Habermas' Heritage: The Future of the Public Sphere in the Network Society', *First Monday*, volume 10, number 9, September 2005. http://firstmonday.org/issues/issue10_9/boeder/index.html, accessed 4 February 2009.

[43] Poster, above.

[44] d boyd 'The Not-So-Hidden Politics of Class Online', *Personal Democracy Forum*, New York, 30 June 2009, <http://www.danah. org/papers/talks/PDF2009.html>, accessed 24 July 2009.

[45] See further N Moore 'Icons of Control: Deleuze, Signs, Law' (2007) 20 *International Journal for the Semiotics of Law* 20, p 50. See further, for a practical example of the issues that this generates for governments, the work of the Australian Government 2.0 Taskforce, <http://gov2.net.au/about/>, accessed 22 September 2009.

[46] D Marletta 'Hybrid Communities to Digital Arts Festivals: From Online Discussions to Offline Gatherings'.

[47] U Tasa 'Redefining the Body in Cyberspace: Art's Contribution to a New Understanding of Embodiment', in this volume.

[48] D Berry and J Pawlick 'What is Code? A Conversation with Deleuze, Guattari and Code' (2005) 2 *Kritikos*, <http://intertheory.org/berry.htm>, accessed 4 September 2009.

## Bibliography

Bartle, R., 'Why Governments aren't Gods and Gods aren't Governments'. *First Monday*, Special issue number 7, September 2006, <http://firtmonday.org/issues/issue11_9/bartle/index.html>.

——, 'Virtual Worldliness: What the Imaginary Asks of the Real'. *New York Law School Law Review* 19, 2004, pp. 23-27.

Berry, D. and J. Pawlick, 'What is Code?: A Conversation with Deleuze, Guattari and Code'. *Kritikos*, no. 2, 2005, <http://intertheory.org/berry.htm>, accessed 4 September 2009.

Boeder, P., 'Habermas' Heritage: The Future of the Public Sphere in the Network Society'. *First Monday*, volume 10, number 9, September 2005. <http://firstmonday.org/issues/issue10_9/boeder/index.html>, accessed 4 February 2009.

Castells, M., *The Internet Galaxy: Reflections on the Internet, Business, and Society*. Oxford, Oxford University Press, 2001, pp 37- 61.

Deleuze, G., 'Postscript on the Societies of Control'. *October* 3. 59, 1992.

Elkin-Koren, N., 'Governing Access to Users-Generated-Content: The Changing Nature of Private Ordering in Digital Networks' in *Governance, Regulations and Powers on the Internet*. E. Brousseau, M. Marzouki & C. Meadel (eds), Cambridge University Press, 2009.

ENISA Position Paper: *Virtual Worlds, Real Money, Security and Privacy in Massively-Multiplayer Online Games and Social and Corporate Virtual Worlds*, November 2008.

Fairfield, J., 'The Magic Circle'. *Vanderbilt Journal of Entertainment and Technology Law*, 2009.

Galloway, A., *Protocol: How Control Exists after Decentralization*. The MIT Press, Cambridge, Massachusetts, 2004.

——, *Gaming: Essays on Algorithmic Culture*. University of Minnesota Press, Minneapolis, 2006.

Grimes, J., P. Jaeger and K. Fleischmann, 'Obfuscatocracy: A Stakeholder Analysis of Governing Documents for Virtual Worlds'. *First Monday*, Volume 13 Number 9 - 1 September 2008, <http://www.uic. edu/htbin/cgiwrap/bin/ojs/index.php/fm/article/viewArticle/2153/2029>.

Humphreys, S., 'Ruling the Virtual World: Governance in Massively Multiplayer Online Games'. *European Journal of Cultural Studies* 149, 11(2), 2008, pp. 153-154.

Lastowka, G., 'Planes of Power: EverQuest as Text, Game and Community'. *The International Journal of Computer Game Research*, 9.1, 2009, <http://gamestudies.org/0901/articles/lastowka>.

Malaby, T., 'Coding Control: Governance and Contingency in the Production of Online Worlds'. *First Monday*, Special issue number 7 (September 2006), <http://firstmonday.org/issues/special11_9/malaby/index.html>.

Moore, N., 'Icons of Control: Deleuze, Signs, Law'. *International Journal for the Semiotics of Law*, 20, 2007.

Murray, A., *The Regulation of Cyberspace: Control in the Online Environment*. Routledge, Oxford, 2006.

———, 'Symbiotic Regulation'. ExpressO, 2008,http://works.bepress.com/andrew_murray/1, accessed 6 February 2009>.

Poster, M., 'CyberDemocracy: Internet and the Public Sphere', 1995, <http://www.hnet.uci.edu/mposter/writings/democ.html>,          accessed          4 February 2009.

Postigo, H., 'Video Game Appropriation through Modifications: Attitudes Concerning Intellectual Property among Modders and Fans'. *Convergence* 59, 14, 2008.

Williams, R., 'Politics and Self in the Age of Digital Re(pro)ducibility' in 1.1 *Fast Capitalism*, 2005,<http://www.uta.edu/huma/agger/fastcapitalism /1_1/ williams.html>., accessed 22 September 2009.

**Melissa de Zwart,** PhD., is an Associate Professor in the School of Law, University of South Australia.

**David Lindsay,** PhD., is a Senior Lecturer, Faculty of Law, Monash University.

# Hybrid Communities to Digital Arts Festivals:
## From Online Discussions to Offline Gatherings

*Donata Marletta*

**Abstract**
The aim of this chapter is to contribute to blurring the gap between virtual communities and communities based on face-to-face embodied interaction, trying to deconstruct the obsolete online/offline dichotomy. Since the 1990s the concept of virtual community has changed and has been substituted by a fluid perception, where informational and physical contacts co-exist. Computer networks allow people to create a whole range of new social spaces in which they interact with one another. Through the use of interaction media people have formed thousands of groups to discuss different topics, create knowledge, and share mutual interests. Virtual community represents a form of post-modern community, characterised by the liberation of the individual from social constraints such as identity, ethnicity, social status and geographical space. In order to reinforce the disembodied relations built around the Internet discussions, members of virtual communities feel the need to meet during more embodied face-to-face gatherings. In such a context of continuous change and innovation, I am following digital arts communities, which make use of both cyberspace and physical space as places for interaction, collaboration, and connectivity. Global gatherings such as festivals devoted to art and technology play a critical role in the maintenance and nourishment of these social groups. International events such as Ars Electronica, Elektra and Transmediale draw people from all over the world; they represent both valuable forums and platforms for artists and intellectuals, and a unique chance for the participants to migrate from the cyberspace to a physical space.

**Key Words:** Community, Online, Offline, Cyberspace, Festival, Digital Art.

*****

The terrific development of new technologies has led to an acceleration of information flows and allowed people to connect through 'one click'. Boundaries of time and space are rapidly collapsing, creating opportunities for new forms of social ties and connections between people to happen. The Internet has been studied as a social immersive space in which users develop communities and construct imaginary worlds. Multiuser environments, constructed metaphorically as public social places, have attracted many people willing to socialise with others outside their situated geographical boundaries. The affirmation of the Internet as a new social space raises the question of what today constitutes a community.

In order to gain a wider overview of the concept of community, I believe that it is crucial to go back and re-discover the genesis and the evolution of this notion, and how it has been conceptualised within the literature among scholars from different disciplines.

Historically the notion of community has been associated with the notion of geographical place. In his seminal work *Gemeinschaft und Gesellschaft* the German sociologist Tönnies was one of the first authors who conceptualised community and its characteristics. According to the transformations in the organisation of social life that emerged as a consequence of the ascendancy of modernity, Tönnies makes a clear distinction between two types of social groups: Gemeinschaft (Community) and Gesellschaft (Society). Gemeinschaft is characterised by natural will, and an organic sense of community, and Gesellschaft is characterised by rational will, and by a sense of individualism rather than communal. Tönnies is very critical towards Gesellschaft, in which he sees a form of social organisation based on hyper-individualism, which causes abandonment of collective memory, instinct, and habits.[1]

Within the anthropological literature it is worthy of note the notion of community developed by Turner. The anthropologist differentiates between society and community, the two main models for human interrelatedness. Society, or *societas*, is a highly structured and hierarchical system; community, on the other hand, is an unstructured and heterogeneous group of equal individuals, however soon it develops a structure. Turner looks at community within the wider context of the 'rites of passage', previously developed by Arnold Van Gennep, and claims that during these rites a particular kind of comradeship emerges as a product of interstructural liminality. This group is a community or comity of comrades, and Turner uses the Latin noun *communitas* to identify such a group, which is characterised by absence of hierarchical structure, transcending any distinctions of status, age and kinship position. Members of *communitas* are linked together by special bonds that persist during the years, after the rites of passage are over.[2] A distinctive characteristic of this group is its transitory existence; paradoxically *communitas* soon looses its spontaneity and becomes institutionalised developing a structure, and converting the free relationships into norm-governed relationships. Turner claims that existential or spontaneous *communitas* exist not only in preliterate and preindustrial societies, but also in complex modern societies, where the values of *communitas* are present within groups such as the beat generation and the hippies. Members of these groups stress personal relationships rather than social obligations, and emphasise spontaneity and immediacy.[3]

community the author uses the concept of social networks primarily because such definition is mainly based on social interaction, shifting the focus away from place.[17] These new social groups represent a form of post-modern community characterised by the liberation of the individual from social constraints such as identity and geographical space. It should be noted that within these groups participants promote a sense of brotherhood among each other, and in order to fortify the disembodied and abstract relations, and to help participants to stay in touch, members of virtual communities feel the need to meet, sporadically or on a regular basis, during physical face-to-face gatherings.

In the article 'The Anthropology of Online Communities', anthropologists Wilson and Peterson claim that in analysing on line groups the main problem is that there is no agreement among scholars in considering these groups as real or imagined communities. The difficulty derives from the ephemeral nature of the media, the Internet, the definition of community itself, and from rapidly obsolescing technologies. The authors suggest that a rigid distinction between online and offline communities is not helpful. Instead, they claim, it is more useful to see communities as a continuum that exists regardless of the ways in which community members interrelate.[18] In the same vein, Wellman and Gulia criticise those researchers who treat the Internet as an isolated social phenomenon, without taking into account how interactions on the Net coexist together with other aspects of people's lives. The Net then is not a separate reality, but is only one of many ways in which the same people may interact.[19]

In the introduction to the special thematic section of the *Journal of Computer-Mediated-Communication* dedicated to Online Communities, authors Preece and Maloney-Krichmar claim that among researchers interested in studying CMC it is progressively accepted to consider online communities as the result of a blend between online and offline elements, presenting some physical components. These groups can start as a face-to-face communities and then move to the digital media within the realm of cyberspace. Alternatively, members of an online community decide to meet during scheduled face-to-face settings.[20] Thus, one dimension does not necessarily exclude the other.

A common thread emerges within the above reviewed literature on online communities; it is the clear need among participants to meet face-to-face, during scheduled or more spontaneous meetings. For this reason, I am looking at digital arts festivals as events that create and promote social connectivity. I have carried out my fieldwork both offline and online, in the sense that through an ethnographic approach I have observed festivals dedicated to contemporary art and digital culture. Concurrently I have monitored and followed, giving also my contribute to online discussions of two mailing lists, Rhizome and <nettime>, in which participants discuss and share information about digital art, festivals, and net culture in general. These online communities nurture both digital art festivals and the digital art movement, and offer their participants the opportunity to critically share knowledge and keep experimental culture alive.

Established in 1996, Rhizome has played a fundamental role in the history, promotion and development of the link between art, Internet and new technologies. Rhizome, which since 2003 is affiliated with the New Museum of Contemporary Art in New York, is a web site, a digital art archive, and an open forum for issues related to the creation, support and critique of emerging artistic practices engaged with technology. The <nettime> group was founded in 1995, and since then it represents a valuable international forum for discourses about all aspects of net culture and new media, from art to politics. The contents of the forums are all archived in the web site, and freely accessible. Leading figures in the net culture's scene like authors Bruce Sterling and Peter Lunenfeld, or Geert Loving, independent media theorist and founder of <nettime>, and Felix Stalder who is both an academic and the current <nettime> moderator, are among the authors who regularly post texts on <nettime>. In addition I have joined the online network Digicult, which through the web site and the monthly e-magazine 'Digimag' contributes with articles, reviews and reports to the distribution of critical knowledge around new media and digital culture.

In the relatively short time span of one year I attended five of the major electronic and new media arts festivals worldwide, namely Mutek and Elektra (Montréal, Canada, May 08, May 09), Ars Electronica (Linz, Austria, September 08), and Transmediale and ClubTransmediale (Berlin, Germany, January 09). These festivals made me aware that there are people who regularly meet over the year in different locations around the world, to experience in a single time and space frame what can be seen as a ritual with its own rhythms and characteristics. In such a context the relation between online and offline communities becomes tangible. Here, at these events, people who were previously in contact through Computer Mediated Communication (CMC) meet face-to-face, and at the same time they keep updating their blogs and web sites, communicating in real time with other people located in different parts of the world, sharing their experiences and spreading the news through their networks. The planet could be seen as simultaneously connected through wires and through people: here both the physical and the virtual are intrinsically tied together, forming a new hybrid space.

The common denominator between most of digital arts festivals worldwide is that through performances and installations they offer to festival goers augmented sensorial experiences, aiming to integrate the spectators into the machinery of the artworks, engaging them in a form of emotive dialogue. A remarkable example of direct involvement of the audience into the work of art is the immersive performance *Feed*, which I had the chance to attend in May 2009 during the tenth edition of Elektra festival in Montréal. *Feed*, by Austrian artist Kurt Hentschläger, pioneer of aesthetic and sensorial exploration on the interrelation between sounds and visions, is a sensorial experience that challenges the limits of the human body through the use of low frequency sound modulations, 3D projections, thick artificial smoke, and flickering stroboscopic lights, bringing the spectators at the very core of the artistic creation, and wrapping the audience in an overload of sensorial stimuli. The piece is divided into two parts; the first is a non-narrative cinematic experience, displaying an uncanny ballet of 3D created characters. In the second part the perception of space evaporates, wiped out by a massive injection of artificial fog. The intense use of stroboscopic flicker and pulse lights provokes the collapse of any conventional perception of time and space, and the audience experience a sense of loss, completely overwhelmed by sensorial stimuli. Interestingly, this second part of the performance is not documentable because of the presence of the thick artificial smoke and the stroboscopic lights; therefore the performance is absolutely ephemeral, representing a unique event to be experienced in person.

Another prominent example of strong emotional involvement occurred during the 2008 edition of Ars Electronica Festival in Linz. In that occasion, in fact, I had the chance to experience another tremendous and extremely touching performance: *Bleu Remix* by Yann Marussich. Under the assistance of physicians and chemists, a mysterious substance, injected in the artist's body, influenced his system and became visible in blue traces that appeared on his skin. Arguably, this substance represents the tangible vector through which inner mobility is connected with outer immobility. The artist was sitting motionless in a glass shrine placed in a white art gallery room, which was illuminated by spot lights, pointing at his body. The audience, gathered on the floor around the glass box, was staring at the artist, and waiting for something to happen.

After a while, when the atmosphere was overloaded by tension and pathos, a blue fluid started oozing from Marussich's eyes: he was crying blue tears. The performance lasted for one hour, during which we witnessed to the tribulation of Marussich's body; the blue liquid poured from his mouth, nose, and skin pores, provoking a state of internal pain, which was reflected in his staring, powerful gaze. The inner sounds of his body remixed live by a DJ, enhanced the dramatic atmosphere of the performance.

Within this contemporary scenario both digital art festivals and online art communities form a new social space. This new space, which is to be found at the intersection between the material and the immaterial, is linked with the notion of *liminal* space - Latin for threshold, as formulated by the anthropologist Turner. According to him some ritual performances occur in physically detached places, away from the flow of the everyday routine; in this sense ritual action is out of the ordinary. Following Van Gennep's rites of passage model, Turner argues that a ritual exemplifies the transition of an individual from one state to another. Between the states the ritual subjects are set to spend some time in an interstructural or liminal situation; liminality is a state of being in between phases. During this phase of transition the liminal subjects are, in Turner's words, 'betwixt and between'. The subjects are all treated equally and constitute a community without status and hierarchies, the *communitas*. Turner herewith extends the liminal concept to modern societies in his study of 'liminoid phenomena'. The term 'liminoid' refers to experiences that have characteristics of liminal experiences, but if the liminal predominates in tribal societies, the *liminoid* - liminal-like, flourishes in modern industrialised societies, that are characterised by the emergence of technical innovations. The liminoid is a break from society, is play, is leisure, and allows people to express themselves through free and spontaneous experimentations and performances.[21] It is arguably in this space, a grey indefinite area that virtual and non-virtual realities merge together.

In this chapter I have predominantly reviewed a relevant segment of the existing literature on the concept of communities, both within the traditional studies from various disciplines, and from the more contemporary literature on communities that emerge from cyberspace. Discussions around the blurred boundaries between the online and the offline continue to be on the agenda of many researchers, and although some progress has been achieved, the path is still long. New issues will arguably arise; new technologies and new modes of interaction will be created. We will moreover have to continue to reflect critically on these constant changes and contribute to their discourse. This perpetuation is enclosed and encouraged in the following quote from the philosopher and theorist of digital culture Pierre Lévy, with which I would like to end this chapter:

> The contemporary multiplication of spaces makes us nomads again...we leap from network to network [...] spaces metamorphose and bifurcate beneath our feet, forcing us to undergo a process of heterogenesis.[22]

## Notes

[1] F Tönnies, *Gemeinschaft und Gesellschaft*, 8th edition, Buske, Leipzig, 1935, translated by C P Loomis, *Community and Society*, The Mitchigan State University Press, 1957
[2] V Turner, *The Forest of Symbols: Aspects of Ndembu Ritual*, Cornell University Press, London, 1967.

[3] V Turner, *The Ritual Process: Structure and Anti-Structure*, Aldine Transaction, Chicago, 1969.

[4] M Maffesoli, *The Time of the Tribes: The Decline of Individualism in Mass Society*, SAGE, London, 1996

[5] B Anderson, *Imagined Communities*, Verso, London, 1991, p. 5.

[6] H Rheingold, *The Virtual Community: Homesteading of the Electronic Frontier*, MIT Press, Cambridge MA, 1994, p.5.

[7] A Fung, *Bridging Cyberlife and Real Life: A Study of Online Communities in Hong Kong*, in Critical Cyberculture Studies, edited by D Silver and A Massanari, New York University Press, New York, 2006, pp. 129-139.

[8] A J Kim, *Community Building on the Web*, Pachpit Press, Berkeley, CA, 2000

[9] N K Baym, *Finding the Quality in Qualitative Research*, in Critical Cyberculture Studies, edited by D Silver and A Massanari, New York University Press, New York, 2006, pp.79-87.

[10] A De Souza e Silva, *From Cyber to Hybrid: Mobile Technologies as Interfaces of Hybrid Spaces*, Space and Culture, Vol. 9, No. 3, August 2006, pp. 261-278

[11] W Gibson, *Neuromancer*, Harper-Collins, London. 1994

[12] W Mitchell, *City of Bits: Space, Place and the Infoban*, MIT Press, Cambridge MA, 1995.

[13] M Crang, 'Public Space, Urban Space and Electronic Space: Would the Real City Please Stand Up?', *Urban Studies Journal*, Vol. 37, No. 2, 2000, pp. 301-317.

[14] M Ostwald, *Virtual Urban Futures*, in Virtual Politics: Identity and Community in Cyberspace, edited by D Holmes, SAGE, London, 1997.

[15] N Watson, *Why We Argue About Virtual Community: A Case Study of the Phish.net Fan Community*, in Virtual Culture: Identity and Communication in Cyberspace, edited by S Jones, SAGE, London, 1997, pp. 102-132.

[16] B Wellman, M Gulia, *Net Surfers Don't Ride Alone: Virtual Communities as Communities*, in Communities in Cyberspace, edited by P Kollock and M E Smith, Routledge, New York, 1999.

[17] S Jones, *Cybersociety 2.0: Revisiting Computer-Mediated-Communication and Community*, SAGE, London, 1998.

[18] S M Wilson, L C Peterson, 'The Anthropology of Online Communities', *Annual Review of Anthropology*, Vol. 31, No. 1, 2002, pp. 449-467.

[19] B Wellman, M Gulia, *Net Surfers Don't Ride Alone: Virtual Communities as Communities*, in Communities in Cyberspace, edited by P Kollock and M E Smith, Routledge, New York, 1999.

[20] J Preece, D Maloney-Krichmar, 'Online Communities: Design, Theory, and Practice', *Journal of Computer-Mediated-Communication*, Vol. 10, No. 4, 2005, pp. 00-00.
[21] V Turner, *Celebration, Studies in Festivity and Ritual*, Victor Turner Editor, Washington DC, 1982
[22] P Lévy, *Becoming Virtual: Reality and the Digital Age*, Plenum, New York, 1988, p.31

## Bibliography

Anderson, B., *Imagined Communities*. Verso, London, 1991, p. 5.

Baym, N. K., 'Finding the Quality in Qualitative Research', in *Critical Cyberculture Studies*. D. Silver and A. Massanari (eds), New York University Press, New York, 2006, pp.79-87.

Crang, M., 'Public Space, Urban Space and Electronic Space: Would the Real City Please Stand Up?'. *Urban Studies Journal*, Vol. 37, No. 2, 2000, pp. 301-317.

De Souza e Silva, A., 'From Cyber to Hybrid: Mobile Technologies as Interfaces of Hybrid Spaces'. *Space and Culture*, Vol. 9, No. 3, August 2006, pp. 261-278

Fung, A., 'Bridging Cyberlife and Real Life: A Study of Online Communities in Hong Kong', in *Critical Cyberculture Studies*. D. Silver and A. Massanari (eds), New York University Press, New York, 2006, pp. 129-139.

Gibson, W., *Neuromancer*. Harper-Collins, London, 1994.

Jones, J., *Cybersociety 2.0: Revisiting Computer-Mediated-Communication and Community*. SAGE, London, 1998.

Kim, A. J., *Community Building on the Web*. Pachpit Press, Berkeley, CA, 2000

Lévy, P., *Becoming Virtual: Reality and the Digital Age*. Plenum, New York, 1988

Maffesoli, M., *The Time of the Tribes: The Decline of Individualism in Mass Society*. SAGE, London, 1996

Mitchell, W., *City of Bits: Space, Place and the Infoban*. MIT Press, Cambridge MA, 1995.

Ostwald, M., 'Virtual Urban Futures', in *Virtual Politics: Identity and Community in Cyberspace*. D. Holmes (ed), SAGE, London, 1997.

Preece, J. and D. Maloney-Krichmar, 'Online Communities: Design, Theory, and Practice'. *Journal of Computer-Mediated-Communication*, Vol. 10, No. 4, 2005, pp. 00-00.

Rheingold, H., *The Virtual Community: Homesteading of the Electronic Frontier*. MIT Press, Cambridge MA, 1994.

Tönnies, F., *Gemeinschaft und Gesellschaft*. 8th edition, Buske, Leipzig, 1935, C. P. Loomis (transl). *Community and Society*, The Mitchigan State University Press, 1957.

Turner, V., *The Forest of Symbols: Aspects of Ndembu Ritual*. Cornell University Press, London, 1967.

———, *The Ritual Process: Structure and Anti-Structure*. Aldine Transaction, Chicago, 1969.

———, *Celebration, Studies in Festivity and Ritual*. Victor Turner Editor, Washington DC, 1982.

Watson, N., 'Why We Argue About Virtual Community: A Case Study of the Phish.net Fan Community', in *Virtual Culture: Identity and Communication in Cyberspace*. S. Jones (ed), SAGE, London, 1997, pp. 102-132.

Wellman, B., Gulia, M., 'Net Surfers Don't Ride Alone: Virtual Communities as Communities', in *Communities in Cyberspace*. P. Kollock and M. E. Smith (eds), Routledge, New York, 1999.

Wilson, S. M. and L. C. Peterson, 'The Anthropology of Online Communities'. *Annual Review of Anthropology*, Vol. 31, No. 1, 2002, pp. 449-467.

**Donata Marletta** is an Italian researcher. In 2007 she started a PhD programme at the Centre for Tourism and Cultural Change, Leeds Metropolitan University in the United Kingdom. Her research project and main interest focus on the relationship between art and technology, critical cyberculture studies, and on the emergence of new social spaces - online and offline, created by digital art festivals.

# PART III

# New Concepts in Education and Entertainment

# Playing Games as an Art Experience:
## How Videogames Produce Meaning through Narrative and Play

*Jef Folkerts*

**Abstract**

Occasionally it can be quite rewarding to look at cultural phenomena from a different or unusual perspective. Exactly this inquisitive scientific attitude marks a major similarity between the contributors in this section. The exploration of concepts and applications, originally intended for entertainment use in cyberculture, can lead to new ways of thinking and to novel applications in sometimes-unexpected fields and disciplines. While the other authors[1] beforehand seemed to have a specific goal in mind, adapting existing 3D virtual worlds for specific educational purposes, my approach is more conceptual in nature. My aim is to explore in which ways videogames (featuring explorative 3D virtual worlds: another analogy with my fellow authors) could induce an artistic experience with their players. I approach videogames as a common cultural product, understood as an artefact from which we can draw meaning. In that way games are not unlike other cultural phenomena like magazines, art, films, books, fashion, architecture and design. Without exception they all are products of the imagination, and as cultural artefacts an expression *of*, and a reflection *on* the culture they emerge from. On the other side they all, one way or another, arouse imagination among their users. I am particularly interested in the artistic and aesthetic nature of games. My hypothesis is that signification processes - especially artistic interpretation - in videogames are comparable to those in literature and film. These processes are nonetheless of a different nature, producing different effects - which is mainly due to the gamer's *prosuming* mental and physical input. In this chapter I argue that a key aspect of the artistic experience is to be found in the way recipients get involved with a specific meta-cognitive perspective on what is displayed in the artwork. My final intention is to explore and analyse such mental activities in gameplay.

**Key Words**: Videogames, Art, Representation, Semiotics, Imagination, Identification, Consciousness, Metacognition, Constructing Meaning.

\*\*\*\*\*

## 1.     About the Artfulness of Videogames

I start off with the assumption that we deal with art only when it seduces us to get involved with a consciousness that reveals a particular perspective on its content, in our strive for adequate interpretation.

Additionally I claim that this kind of involvement can occur in the gameplay of (some) videogames. Afterwards I will explain in greater detail what exactly I mean here, since I suspect some critical reader may doubt my intentions already: why would anyone want to engage in this subject, why would anyone want to approach videogames as art? Videogames are entertainment, and not intended as art. To begin with I agree with this objection completely, but I still think there are reasons to look at games in another, unusual way. While reading interviews with, and texts of game designers, game critics and game study scholars like Warren Robinett, Chris Crawford, Tim Schafer, Peter Molyneux, Raph Koster, Clive Barker, Ian Bogost and Henry Jenkins, I often encounter art related intuitions and convictions about games. Hardly ever videogames are being compared to science, politics or religion: no, games are an art form[2]. But are they really? In what capacity then? And what do promoters of this view mean by art exactly?

It seems to me that the notions art, aesthetic and artistic often are wrongly used synonymously. On top of that there seems to be a sort of general agreement about the matter, as if it is perfectly clear to anyone what we mean by the term *art*. When a game designer or game critic claims that a game is art, she usually states something like *it is about creatively expressing thoughts or emotions*, that *traditional art forms are uniquely tied together by interactivity* (and hence games are art), that games *trigger strong emotional responses* (just like art does), or that the virtual environments provide us with profound *aesthetic experiences*. But art does not have to be beautiful at all - an acknowledged viewpoint since modernism and postmodernism: it is more often primarily about power of expression. By which statement I by no means claim that art *cannot* be beautiful. On the contrary, there is a lot of art that interlinks a marvellous visual representation with an intrusive and urgent message. My concern in this matter is that there seems to be no general agreement between game designers, game critics, philosophers of art and cultural scholars about what we mean by art and the art experience. I daresay the label *art* is altogether granted too easily regarding videogames. Of course this leaves me with the task on hand to explore what we actually do understand by the notion art nowadays.

## 2.      Evolution in Art Theories

A short review of two thousand years Aesthetics and Philosophy of Art clarifies that conceptions of art always depend on the perspective that someone, a society, or the art world holds concerning art. Does an author in his definition want to stress the *intrinsic properties* of art, the *individual expression* of an artist, the *instrumental socio-cultural or economic functions* of art, or the *emotional and cognitive features of the art experience*? These various perspectives were conceived under what philosopher of art Stephen

Davies identified as the three main theoretical approaches of art: functionalism, proceduralism (and within that institutionalism) and the intentional approach. Followers of functionalism believe that art wields one or more specific, truly unique and distinctive effects on society. Proceduralism is based on the idea that the creation (and reception and valuation) of an artwork necessarily has to occur under specific rules and procedures. The institutional conception - being a subclass of proceduralism - contains that we may call something a work of art only if some person (or a group of people), who is respected and empowered by the art world, labels it as such. The intentional approach finally, argues that the artist's intention should be decisive for the reception, classification and interpretation of art works, as well as the determination of what should be acknowledged as the most important aesthetic features. I will not elaborate in detail on these conceptions. However, I would like to underline and support Davies' favour for the procedural/institutional approach here, because I share his conviction that the ever-changing art world always respects and answers appropriately to socio-cultural evolution. The proper approach to art and how it should provide aesthetic enjoyment and artistic significance is governed by interpersonal conventions of the art world, conventions that evidently can be changed, and in fact do change from time to time.[3]

Whatever may change in art or our conception of it, one representational phenomenon seems to exist in practically all viewpoints: *mimesis*, which treats art as a kind of imitation - roughly spoken either of nature (Plato) or of culture (Aristotle). Philosopher of art Van den Braembussche shows that we encounter this particular concept of art contemplation - conceived more than two thousand years ago - in almost all subsequent artistic or aesthetic conceptions. Until, not so long ago in the twentieth century, post-structuralism finally banned all mimetic concepts from theory of art: representations are not grounded on similarity or identity, but refer to (their differences with) other representations and have no foundation in social reality whatsoever. In order to escape this postmodern arbitrariness the French philosopher Jean-François Lyotard in his later work conceptualised the so-called Kantian Turn - inspired by the 18th century philosopher Immanuel Kant. This seemed a resolute departure from the postmodern perspective by the way, which he himself - of all people - had developed not long before, among others in his influential *The Postmodern Condition*.[4] As a matter of fact both the famous Austrian art historian Sir Ernst Gombrich and the equally influential philosopher Nelson Goodman were tributary to Kant as well, in their formerly conceived criticism on the predominant mimetic theories. Their criticism was more or less inspired by Kant's fundamental question marks about the always presupposed passive nature of our perception: does our mind record reality merely through empirical perception, or do we add something ourselves to be able to know reality?

In his new approach (around 1990) Lyotard attributes substantial significance to our reflective judgement, which is grounded on emotion, imagination and the Idea for which no concept is in reach yet. He transforms this reflective judgement to a definition of aesthetic judgement in which the Sublime has to play a leading role. Because imagination, emotion and reason are incompatible at first, this experience of the Sublime initially arouses feelings of unease or crisis. In other words, we do not know exactly how to link form and content of what we perceive to our existing mental patterns and this can be rather discomforting. Eventually however, it will very likely make intelligible what transcends our imagination, and inspire to new (moral) ideas.[5]

It seems pretty obvious that contemporary approaches of art ascribe an essential role to the *experience* of art. The artistic is not necessarily an intrinsic property of an artefact, but is defined by conventional conceptions in our mind that we link to an object (Kant), and/or in the symbolic value we assign to it (Goodman), in short, in the experience itself and the interpretive process involved. When we both read William Gibson's *Neuromancer* I have a different reading experience than you have. On the basis of my specific cultural baggage and personal experiences I make it my story, with my individual imagery, identifications and interpretations. All things considered I read a different book. This point of view is moreover confirmed and illustrated by contemporary literary theories. After structuralism and post-structuralism the post-classical narratology - initiated among others by Monika Fludernik and David Herman - strives after a more cognitive approach of narrative and literature: the role of the reader and the reading process are assigned an essential function in the 'production' of meaning.

## 3.      The Artistic-Aesthetic Distinction

In my strive for transparency in the artistic-aesthetic confusion - since these terms are often used arbitrarily as substitutes - I propose a slight adjustment or specification in terminology, in a way that in my opinion better connects to what people intuitively feel with these notions. While most people primarily identify aesthetics with beauty, we easily can determine that art does not have to be beautiful, that the *artistic experience* is not always enjoyable. I only have to refer to contemporary artists like Lucian Freud, Francis Bacon, Damien Hirst, Marina Abramović, Marlene Dumas, Erwin Olaf and Dolores Zorreguieta, whose creations often on first sight arouse disgust and repulsion in their beholders. Literature and film can produce similar reactions, as demonstrated by novels from Marquis de Sade, William S. Burroughs, Bret Easton Ellis, and films like Pasolini's *Salo, or the 120 Days of Sodom*, Kubrick's *A Clockwork Orange* or Haneke's *Funny Games*.

It seems not entirely implausible to cross out the term *aesthetic* for now, just like the notion *aesthetic experience,* to describe the essence of an art experience. Stephen Davies offers an in my view adequate distinction between what is aesthetic and what is artistic. He maintains that we generally describe *aesthetic* properties as objective features perceived in the object. 'Their recognition does not depend on information about the circumstances under which the item was made, or about its intended or possible functions.'[6]

*Artistic properties* mostly depend on the content, on messages and meaning artworks communicate, that however by no means can be separated from the *aesthetic properties*. Examining a Balinese (narrative) painting Davies creates a clear insight into this distinction. The depicted story takes no part in the *aesthetic* judgement, because we cannot follow or comprehend it without specific knowledge of the portrayed individuals and the conventions about how to 'read' the scenes. This particular painting not only represents symbolic functions, but expresses important moral values in Balinese culture and religion as well. Davies acknowledges the importance of the aesthetic qualities of the painting, but the main value unmistakably is embedded in the *artistic* properties. And in this regard this painting is not very different from any artwork in other cultures: everywhere the significance of artistic content will be appointed above the aesthetic properties.[7]

## 4.      First and Second-Order Representation

In my view it is safe to conclude that the artistic properties of art and literature relate to the *what* of the reference, and the aesthetic to the directly discernable *how*. All art refers in some way to something outside itself, to something in reality, and the meaning of that reference is created mainly in the experience, in the artistic interpretation. But did we in the introduction not establish that videogames are intended for our amusement? So, first of all we need to examine the main features that define entertainment, and subsequent in what way the artistic experience differs from the entertainment experience. An attractive and in my opinion plausible insight in this delicate subject is to be found in the conception that for instance in light reading, soap opera or mainstream Hollywood film we usually do not encounter anomalies that force us to meaning-making. To grasp my intention it is essential to acknowledge that there is a clear distinction between our *comprehension* of actions and motivations of characters to understand the story, and our *interpretation* of what the story *means*, to explore in what way it tries to reflect on the world. Because amusement formats not intentionally stimulate interpretation, they easily create an illusion of absorption in the action: we are completely captured by it, immersed in it - which can be a warm and excellent feeling - but their meaning is generally fixed. This first-order representation and our imagination both reach closure: what you see is what you get.

In literature, art film and art on the other hand, the evoked mental images force us frequently to look for meaning. This process is strongly encouraged by the mode the representation differs from the 'ordinary', from what we already know, and by the multiplicity of interpretational levels.[8] This broadly valued characteristic of layered meaning seems to be a contemporary criterion of art by the way, and not a universal quality by definition: it merely mirrors the way we look at the world in our present age, and that is exactly the perennial essence of what art does. Anyway, the main stimulus to look for meaning is caused by circumstances in which motivations and consequences of actions and occurrences in the artistic representation are unclear or even disturbed, and therefore offer insufficient explanation to interpret adequately. Hence it forces us - mentally, intellectually in a way - to imagine a consciousness of the occurrences. We have to get involved with a certain perspective on the occurrences - that of the artist - from where we actually witness the representation of a representation process (whether it involves the mind of a story character or that of the storyteller/creator). This is generally the only possible way to get engaged in a process of meaning-construction with the uncompleted - and most of the time multi-interpretable - representation. As a reader or spectator we always strive to obtain closure, to construct a coherent unity of meaning. Bear in mind that we speak of an artistic experience only if we are being confronted with the (metaphoric or symbolic) referential meaning of something. So what is the author or artist trying to say about reality through this representation? In our attempt to find out we (consciously or subconsciously) step into the mind of the author/artist, to discover her perspective on reality, to find out what she wants to express in this particular reflection on the world. But especially we get entangled in the subtle process in which she developed this particular vision, how all the steps, thoughts, mental leaps and intellectual, emotional and conceptual considerations finally lead to this particular expression. Grounded on this second-order representation, literature, art film and art are creating an illusion of absorption in a consciousness: illusion, because it concerns our representation, our mental image of a fictional mind.[9]

To illustrate the functioning of this signification process I refer to an exercise in observing by philosopher Mieke Boon and journalist Peter Henk Steenhuis. Dialectically thinking aloud they analyse the Picasso painting *Musketeer with Sword*. Boon firstly confesses that for a long time she could not cope with Picasso, because the comfortable notion *beautiful* is no longer a criterion in modern art. She stresses the abstract nature of this painting, which, as a deviation from the regular, forces beholders to a specific mode of interpretation. This disordered, deformed musketeer asks you to look in a different fashion, to step out of your familiar frame of reference. In this particular case one has to accept this is no imitation of a musketeer in reality, according to Boon. The abstraction of this painting facilitates the ability to see its separate parts in their own quality, and in that action we become aware of a certain perspective. We are now able to perceive what Picasso had in mind. With his particular style of painting he tries to express something that did not exist before: he clearly does not want to copy something, but to represent *the essence* of something with a few strokes. In order to achieve this, he attentively has to look at what he sees, and at what he wants to express. In this implied observation process Picasso draws us into his perspective, into his vision on reality. By means of exactly this form of expression he seems to delineate the contradictions and inconsistencies in human beings: we are not simple schematic creatures, acting in clearly defined patterns. Simultaneously he provokes us to reflect on our actual viewpoints on vitality, as Boon concludes. This musketeer does not match our image - or schema, or frame, as cognitivists would say - of the manly, vital musketeer, due to his multitude of facial expressions, in which we perceive sadness, strength, pride and old age at once. Moreover Picasso's perspective stimulates reflection on what old age implies and what strength, on what it is to decline, to suffer, to be vulnerable, to be tough.[10]

Observing this painting initially engages us in first-order representation. While we perceive the concrete pictorial image, we try to find similarities with reality. Due to an obvious lack of this mimetic quality (the representation differs from the ordinary) we are pulled to a meta-level, into second-order representation in our quest for meaning. We assume a consciousness, a perspective on what is represented, which supports and intensifies our signification. Especially in this case it is evident that aesthetic and artistic properties are merged and intertwined: Picasso's painting style directs us to this particular mode of interpretation. In a sense it invites beholders to identify not so much with the painter, but with his *perspective* - a thought that maybe we should hold on to for a while, in regard to our coming analysis of game identity.

The assumed distinction in first and second-order representation appears to be very similar, by the way, to what cognitive psychologist Jerome Bruner already expressed in 1986 as the *dual landscape view,* in this case concerning literature. This twofold perspective allows readers to penetrate the lives and minds of characters, whose consciousness operates as an empathy magnet, according to Bruner.[11] Conceived this way, artistic engagement with a consciousness entails much more than just knowing and imagining what goes around in characters (and their creator), it provokes emotional identification as well.

## 5.      Meta-Cognitive Artistic Play

Our inclination to fill in gaps, to complete the openness in literature and art seems to be a partly evolutionary determined, partly acquired cognitive capacity, as literary scholar Shirley Brice Heath makes apparent. In a text on videogames I consider it noteworthy that she characterises art and the art experience as a specific type of game. This artistic 'play' offers us exercise in exactly those mental actions required to connect all things we perceive as incoherent to a unity. Discovery of deviations and incongruities is only possible due to the presence of a huge collection of harmonious 'units' in our minds (cf. schemas: a structural system of concepts - of objects, occurrences, situations and action patterns - stored in our mind). Art prompts us to detect differences between what we think we know and what we really see while reassembling the jigsaw puzzle. Brice Heath underscores our previous assumption that we need to step outside the frame of what is portrayed, to imagine what the artist herself saw or thought in the art creating - meaning making - process. Such artistic play offers the opportunity to lift the represented actions and intentions above the moment to transform them in multiple versions of something else. In her view this meta-cognitive process is play in more than one way, for it is exactly from this meta-level that we are able to observe ourselves as performer, and to get grip on the scene, and in this very process we learn to improve subsequent mental acts.[12] Did it strike you as well how closely this description resembles the observation of a third-person videogame?

Cognitivist Merlin Donald identifies *objects of art* in themselves also as a *cognitive construct*, in the sense that they are representations that influence the way not only artists, but art recipients as well perceive the world. Art is always aimed at a cognitive outcome, designed to engineer a particular state of mind in the beholder. Just like Brice Heath's, Donald's principles of metacognition connect remarkably well to our concept of second-order representation. For metacognition, he claims, is pre-eminently self-reflection, and art self-reflective: the artistic object challenges to reflect on the very process that created it. And that is on the mind of the artist, and therefore on society she emerged from.[13] In the meantime we can hardly deny that *representation of meaning construction* and *meta-cognitive reflection on reality* are significant aspects of the artistic experience.

**6.      Games as Sign Systems**

We acknowledged the cognitive, meta-reflexive nature of the artistic experience. However, we do not know in detail yet how this process operates in art and literature; especially concerning the way we perceive, identify and interpret symbolic or metaphoric references to reality. Although the artistic experience in its constructive nature is mainly situated in the beholder, I nevertheless want to try to pinpoint some media transcending features in art, literature and videogames. What are the typical attributes that somehow shape and direct our cognitive and meta-reflexive signification process? At the base of this inquiry lies the assumption that culture products like literature and art are better understood with the use of a proper theory of symbols, as Goodman demonstrated plainly in his groundbreaking *Languages of Art*.[14] As another cultural artefact a videogame as well refers to reality in some way, and we can treat it as a sign system accordingly, in order to comprehend the fashion in which it shapes a signification process. When we deal with a representation (something that stands for something else) without exception we use our imagination, in our strive to comprehend their meaning. That is to say, we make our own individual representation. This occurs when we read literature, watch a movie or play a game. While reading we construct a mental picture of the occurrences, the situations and the characters presented in the text, if we watch a movie we imagine the back-story of characters and possible plot turns, if we play a game we not only transfer ourselves into the virtual world, but also into our game character, the avatar: we imagine being somewhere else and someone else.

At least for now, in this text, I assume that mainly the narrative capacity of videogames is responsible for mimetic imagination. By which I definitely do not claim that ludic or play elements lack this ability. We can identify a lot of different genres and game types, where some games scarcely hold any embedded, scripted story elements, like in *Tetris, Pac-man, Pong, The Sims, SimCity*. Other videogames however, entangle gameplay and narrative to such an extent that one aspect cannot exist without the other: without narrativity there is no game, like in *Fable, Bioshock, Prince of Persia, The Elder Scrolls IV: Oblivion*, or *Uncharted: Drake's Fortune*. In our engagement with representations, that is to say, with all kinds of imaginations or imitations of events in reality, we are constantly engaged in assigning meaning to what is presented. In this signification process we unconsciously use the sign-functions icon, symbol and index. These sign-categories, originated from Peirce's semiotics, offer a system that delicately distinguishes specific modes in which representations refer to something else. Is the reference established by pictorial similarity or identity (icon), by convention or agreement (symbol), or by resemblance with a structural coherence or causality, in short, with a theory (index)? A common definition - conceived by Peirce - states that a sign is 'something which stands to somebody for something else in some respect or capacity'. Therefore, an arbitrary object, like a letter, a road sign, an index finger or a photograph, is no sign in itself. Furthermore a sign is not a thing, but an occurrence: something becomes a sign when somebody assigns meaning to it on account of a recognised difference with previous representations.[15] Analysis of semiosis, of sign usage, offers a sensitive methodology to comprehend the exact nature of these differences, to lay bare subtle nuances in our meaning-making process. We must bear in mind however, that our identification and signification of icons, symbols and indices in a videogame does not necessarily lead to an artistic experience. Previously I have demonstrated that there are some other elements involved to achieve this. Nevertheless, for a better understanding I will explain the function of sign usage by means of an inevitably concise analysis of the role playing game (RPG) *Fable, The Lost Chapters.*

## 7.     Meaning-Making in *Fable*

Right after start up an introduction commences where image fragments of the game world alternate with credits of the game producer, accompanied by increasingly pompous and emotive orchestral sounds. Unmistakably this refers to conventions from the motion-picture industry with the symbolic notion: attention, in a moment a thrilling story begins. After shooting some vague and diffuse images the camera focuses on an impressively armoured warrior who is engaged in serious combat training, swaying a huge sword. As a connoisseur of this game genre (the RPG-genre as symbolic sign, with its specific attributes and idiom) you know by convention that in a moment you step into the shoes of this protagonist, or as we say in Dutch, you slip into his skin: even before the real game starts it anticipates an identification process. Then we enter the game world, facing adventure. Static, two-dimensional wall paintings pass by, while a voice-over narrates about the village of Oakvale in the woods of Albion, where time seems to stand still. In semiotic terms we can mark this as dual iconicity: 1. as icons the wall paintings offer a tangible visual representation of the game space; 2. the narrator's story as an icon enables us to construct an even more extensive mental image of the environment and circumstances in Oakvale. Based on the text as iconic sign we are able to construct a concrete mental representation: we visualise it, as if we see a film in our mind. In this particular case we imagine nothing else than what paintings and narrator show us: in an icon the sign and its meaning coincide.

## 8.     Symbolic and Indexical References in *Fable*

A symbol refers to something else by convention: the idea that a white pigeon refers to peace we only know by agreement, just like we have agreements about language signs. Likewise in such symbols there is no natural similitude between form and meaning. We learn this conventional relation in our childhood from our parents and at school: this letter as signifier refers to that sound as signified, this word as signifier to that semantic meaning as signified. The name *Fable* even on itself functions as a symbolic sign, due to its obvious connotation with fairy tales, their idiom and structure.[16] Once we have acknowledged this, we realise it can hardly fail to occur that the hero will meet hardship and evil. Our alter ego - little Hero - just finished his mission to earn his sister Theresa a birthday present, as mischief strikes their village. Even before they see the merciless gang itself, Hero and Theresa witness a fellow villager crashing to the ground in front of them, an arrow in his back. Obviously the iconical represented dwellings and clothing refer to a past era, inducing a symbolic meaning that is even more intensified through the use of this particular weapon. Symbolic, because somehow we have learned (we have accepted and assimilated the conventional signification) to identify that the appearance of this game world indicates historical events in an age quite different from our own. It can be symbolic furthermore because it triggers associations with, and (iconic) mental images of medieval customs and practices - which only can occur because they are familiar to us through acquired conventions. We have seen it before in films or paintings, or read about it in books.

Did you notice, by the way, that one sign category can enclose another? Umberto Eco already identified more than once that the different sign functions, as conceived among others by De Saussure and Peirce, interlink somehow.[17] More recently semiotician and culture scholar Van Heusden developed this conception into an all-inclusive theory that in my view answers quite adequately to the capacity that one single representation can produce different sign functions.[18] An icon as a concrete representation can also symbolically stand for something else, and furthermore it can refer indexically to theoretical structures or models in reality as well. The triadic *index* (as opposed to the undivided *icon* and the dualistic *symbol*), shows us a structure, often understood as a certain causal or physical connection between the three elements of that sign: our mental representation of smoke as iconic sign bearer (*representamen*) (1) refers through the conventional or symbolic interpretation, or even more accurate, via the mental effect of this sign (*interpretant*) (2) to a fire (*object*) (3). We know that fire is the physical cause of smoke. Although this is one of the possible interpretations of this type of sign usage, it is not the essence of it. It is important to acknowledge that the index is not exclusively about indicating causal or physical relations between entities, it is especially about identifying essential, structural relations between phenomena: indexical sign usage offers logical or theoretical knowledge.

On a micro-level we distinguish a lot of indices in *Fable*. The distant sounds of villagers screaming during the raid can hardly refer to something else than to the violence inflicted by the bandits. A more interesting index on a meso-level we discern during Hero's first quest for good deeds, and is related to some non-playable characters (NPCs) and their role in the story. On the hill he encounters a little kid whose physical posture iconically displays fear and submission. As the cause of his anxious behaviour we hardly can interpret something else than the big lad in front of him. We see a causal relation here, but it offers a pattern, a theoretical model as well. The sign-effect in our mind might stimulate and enforce our view that in general (in this game as well in real life) somebody seems to behave submissively if he is intimidated by a stronger person. On the other hand we could conclude that there are physically strong human beings who mentally degrade themselves by torment the small and weak. In whatever way you conceive this sign: helping the kid earns you a gold piece. The indexical relation seems to be here: a good deed leads to profit. In addition, while you cross the village square several villagers address you and each other admiringly and approvingly: 'His mother will be pleased with his behaviour', 'Isn't he just adorable?' And in collecting your reward your dad speaks to you full of praise with the payoff: 'well done boy, take this gold piece for those good deeds', which completes this index. The mechanism in *Fable* is rather unambiguous: a good deed is repeatedly rewarded with gold, money, goods and compliments, and a bad one with scorn, disapproval and evasive conduct of others. On top of that by the way, once chosen the evil path, you will develop a demonic appearance. Putting all indices on a meso-level with a moral meaning structure side by side, we end up with a game that, on a macro-level, seems to aim almost exclusively on the ethical domain. This videogame is evidently encouraging a stronger awareness of moral and immoral action. But does mere ethical reflection by itself make it art?

## 9.       Involvement with a Consciousness in Gameplay

We saw that playing a game like *Fable* can trigger meaning-making on different levels. But can we label this process as artistic? I feel that the main question is still not quite answered: in what capacity could playing a game become an artistic experience? Previously I acknowledged the meta-cognitive nature of the artistic experience: a property that is mainly defined by involvement with a consciousness and an iconic representation of a signification process. Besides, in its openness and its layered or multidimensional constitution a work of art preferably encourages multiple interpretations. A videogame mostly concerns action, performance and movement within the boundaries of the game story, and we perceive these occurrences mainly as iconic *first-order* representation: as a gamer we are mentally and physically engaged in the *actions*, in the *events*. If for some reason the gameplay urges us to engage in *second-order* representation, to get involved with a consciousness, to create a mental picture of the designer's perspective on a meaning-making process, then initially I would assume that both its cause and its effect are of a different quality than in literature and art. But that is probably only true for the effect it renders - the motivations or triggers can be quite similar.

As I have demonstrated before, in order to provoke meaning-construction, the representation has to offer a disturbance or deviation from the ordinary, from what is obvious or apparent to us. Of course the threshold for what exactly we recognise as a deviation that requires an interpretation differs from person to person: a specific game situation might be quite obvious to you, but questionable to me on a semiotic level of which you maybe did not think of in the heat of the game. The *Fable* analysis, particularly the identification and interpretation of indexical signs (the threatened kid), was just one example of this. While playing you could stop and think about it, you could examine the reason for this specific problem to happen in exactly this stage of the game, and furthermore you could try to oversee the consequence of your choice in this particular situation, and especially what the designer possibly is trying to express with just these options provided: do you hit the annoying guy, and help the kid - hence applying violence while you do not want to be violent at all; or - quite the opposite - are you inclined to hit the little kid instead, being annoyed by his nagging and complaining, and pleasing the big guy at the same time; or do you just walk away - why bother your head about it at all?

We may assume that our choices and subsequent actions in a game are always linked to specific consequences, thoroughly considered and intended with specific goals in mind, and this betrays almost certainly something of the world-view of the designer, her specific perspective on reality, including ideas, reflections and signification processes she went through while conceiving this game, its story, its characters and its rules. Just playing the game in a regular fashion, executing the missions and quests while being totally immersed in the game world and the story (first-order representation) would render it as pure entertainment. But you could accidentally bump into something that draws you out and above the action in search for maybe a sharp-witted, socially critical or otherwise profound meaning. During this quest you could acquire and interpret the initially not so apparent (symbolic or indexical) references in order to signify what a particular game situation or an entire game is about. And moreover you could be inclined to mirror the discovered meaning with your own, possibly dissimilar opinions on the issues at hand. All in all this seems not very unlike a genuine artistic experience to me.

## 10.     Constructing Identities
It is obvious we can identify meta-cognitive processes in the previous description, and this is by definition self-reflection, which becomes almost visible and tangible here. It brings to mind again Donald's supposition, as he nominates meta-cognition an essential property of art, because it forces us to reflect upon the process it is created in, and therefore ultimately upon society. Playing (some) videogames also involves playing with meaning and meaning construction, and forces us to look at ourselves. It puts a mirror in front of us, which not only *shows* our own identity, in a certain way we can even get *to shape it*. Some concepts of James Paul Gee I find rather demonstrative and clarifying in this matter. He approaches videogames specifically as entertainment artefacts that possess quite interesting intrinsic capacities for learning, which I consider a pre-eminently

cognitive and meta-cognitive activity, but evidently not art. Gee distinguishes three identities within the gamer that exchange knowledge about the regular codes, common in the different semiotic domains that they usually attend: 1. the virtual character in the game: Hero in *Fable*; 2. the non-virtual, real world-identity of the gamer: Jef Folkerts playing a game, but who is also a lecturer on communication and media, a motorcyclist, an amateur photographer and a guitar player. This particular identity brings along a large and varied volume of expertise about common codes (sign systems) and conventions in these domains; 3. the *projective identity* of the gamer, implying two different meanings of the word *project*: a. to project one's values and desires on the virtual character; b. the project of the making of that character, of a creature that through a certain trajectory in time, defined by the gamers aspirations, gets shaped and moulded to the particular character he wants it to become. According to Gee this desire and strive for identity projection is so much forceful that gamers regularly redo a given fight scene, because they feel they 'have let their character down'. This responsible or loyal conduct seems to occur even in first-person shooters (FPS) like *Halo*, *Doom, Quake, Unreal*, in which the gamer usually cannot choose nor influence his avatar.[19] Interesting in Gee's account, and confirmed by personal experience, is the notion that even if we are not able to construct the 'personality' of our avatar, like we use to do in RPGs, we still seem to hold mental representations, convictions and intuitions about our alter ego. And even if we are not forced to meaning-making, due to the lack of anomalies in the mostly straightforward FPS-stories, we nonetheless seem to construct a personal reality in our imagination. In our private mental space the protagonist very much owns projected personality traits, including a moral and reflexive consciousness.

The concept of *ludic identity formation* from philosopher Jos de Mul adds a somewhat similar, but in one aspect substantially different perspective to the former. Ludic identity plays an essential role in the formation of human identity in real life, similar to the function of narrative identity. The main difference with previously mentioned concepts of identity I distinguish in what De Mul calls the third stage of ludic identity formation. De Mul adopts philosopher Paul Ricoeur's *narrative identity* concept, and substitutes Ricoeur's term *mimesis* with the notion *play*. In *Play3* the gamer identifies with the literal and metaphorical space of possibilities the game offers. While gaming he gradually embodies this *infinity of possibilities* as well as the essential key rules, and in this very process the gamer's own identity changes as well. The most important artistic reference in his argument is applicable to the tendency in recently developed videogames of what he calls discordance and the absence of closure. We already identified similar traits as fundamental in art and literature, but they become more and more approved and desired in games as well, which is confirmed by the success of widely acclaimed sandbox or open world games like the *Grand Theft Auto* series, *Assassins Creed*, *SimCity* and *Shadow of the Colossus*.

In De Mul's perception games not only structure (our concept of) the world, but (our concept of) ourselves as well. Gaming is therefore a meta-cognitive, meta-reflexive process that, due to our stronger emotional engagement is even more thorough and fundamental than in stories.[20] An in my point of view substantial difference with stories, film, literature and art however, is the fact that in these art forms we experience aberrations and multiple meaning-construction only mentally, while games actually enable us to *perform* a creative equivalent of this process. As an author/director/actor we are free to literally perform extensive experiments on character traits and moral attitudes, and furthermore by our own choices we are able to create deviations that possibly provoke new and unexpected - that is, not necessarily fixed in the game as it is purchased in the store - signification processes. Aside from this it is not improper to assume that the powerful and tight identification with our game character, cognitively as well as emotionally, renders a more intimate, more intense involvement with a consciousness than what literature or art film are capable of, if ever it comes to an artistic signification process. The mental representation of our avatar is after all an active and conscious bilateral construction of both the gamer and the game designer.

## 11.    Conclusion

We can reasonably conclude that it is not the *aesthetic* appearance, in the form of the iconical, visual imagery, which defines the artfulness of videogames. In fact, I suspect it is exactly this wrongfully conceived aesthetic preoccupation that causes the most common reason to credit games their assumed artistic qualities. Actually the artfulness of games seems closely related to the various modes in which the game story refers to reality, and prompts meta-reflection. We define the artistic nature by its content and by what it refers to, which we determine partly ourselves. While in literary texts we are being forced to meaning-making and meta-reflection by unusual occurrences, in games we are able to produce such anomalies ourselves by way of our own choices and subsequent actions. We continually signify the consequence of a decision after solving a quest or puzzle, and compare this particular outcome to other imaginable alternatives. Moreover games offer the opportunity to repeat the same challenge over and over again, which enables us to freely examine and consider the intrinsic or implied possibilities and outcomes. Did we choose well here? Does this outcome lead to the imagined course of the story, or to a desired state of our avatar? And, even more important for artistic meta-reflexive contemplation: what does the designer want to express about reality by connecting *this* choice to *that* particular outcome? Which steps in his meaning-making process have lead to this specific choice of alternatives, which eventually forces me to choose between only *this* violent action and *that* nonsensical one? From a meta-level we are able to observe ourselves as performer, and it is actually in the mirrored or adopted mental action of the game designer that we discover the particular (ethical, ideological, conceptual) issues to reflect on. Moreover we can witness the psychological process in which they originated, which is accessible only through the designer's consciousness, through her perspective, her intriguing or provocative view on reality. In this very process we also seem to shape ourselves in the mirror our avatar is holding out in front of us. It somehow appears to me this is not miles away from what art and literature are aiming at. In the end it will nevertheless always depend on the eagerness and imaginative urge and aptitude of gamers to engage in this kind of artistic, meta-reflexive thinking. This is admittedly not self-evident. We have to bear in mind that we are dealing with videogames here, intended and appreciated in the first place for the sheer fun they provide.

## Notes

[1] D Riha and T Thomas in this volume.

[2] With which I by no means claim that there are no politics, science or religion involved in videogames.

[3] S Davies, *Definitions of Art*. Cornell University Press, Ithaca, N.Y., 1991.

[4] J F Lyotard, *The Postmodern Condition: A Report in Knowledge*. University of Minnesota Press, Minneapolis, 1985.

[5] A A v d Braembussche, *Denken over kunst- een inleiding in de kunstfilosofie*. 3rd. ed., Coutinho, Bussum, 2000.

[6] S Davies, *The Philosophy of Art*. Blackwell Pub, Malden Mass, 2006, p. 53.

[7] Davies, pp. 52-58.

[8] I recall Lyotard's reinterpretation of Kant's Aesthetic Judgement and the Sublime, in which initially we fail to grasp the meaning of what we perceive, which is discomforting.

[9] B van Heusden, *Literaire cultuur – Handboek*. (1st ed.) OUNL / SUN, Heerlen / Nijmegen, 2001.

[10] M Boon and P H Steenhuis, 'Een ballet van zwart en wit'(A ballet of black and white), in *Trouw*, PCM Uitgevers, Amsterdam, 31-01-2009, pp. 30-31.

[11] J S Bruner, *Actual Minds, Possible Worlds*. Harvard University Press, Cambridge Mass, 1986.

[12] S Brice Heath, 'Dynamics of Completion', in *The Artful Mind: Cognitive Science and the Riddle of Human Creativity*. M. Turner (ed.), Oxford University Press, New York, 2006, pp. 133-150.

[13] M Donald, 'Art and Cognitive Evolution', in *The Artful Mind: Cognitive Science and the Riddle of Human Creativity*. M. Turner (ed.), Oxford University Press, New York, 2006, pp. 3-20.

[14] Goodman used the term symbol in a broad and general sense, to indicate representations like letters, words, texts, pictures, diagrams, maps, models and more, and their modes and means of reference. Hence Goodman's symbols are not to be understood in the contemporary semiotic sense. N Goodman, *Languages of Art: An Approach to a Theory of Symbols*. Hacket Publishing Company, Inc., Indianapolis, 1968.

[15] U Eco, *A Theory of Semiotics*. Indiana University Press, Bloomington, 1976.

P Cobley & L Jansz, *Introducing Semiotics*. Icon, Cambridge, 1999. Van Heusden, pp. 27-46.

[16] In the twenties of the 20th century Vladimir Propp examined the morphology of the Russian folk tale, which he divided in the smallest possible units, and identified a number of invariable action elements and characters (narratemes). All tales he analysed appeared to have almost the same structure, in which all occurring elements even had their own specific, conventional function. V Propp, *Morphology of the folktale*. (10 ed.) Research Center, Indiana University, Bloomington, Ind, 1958.

[17] U Eco, 'Producing Signs', In *On Signs*. M. Blonsky (ed.), Basil Blackwell Ltd, Oxford, 1985, pp. 176-183.

[18] Van Heusden, 2001.

[19] J P Gee, *What Video Games have to teach us about Learning and Literacy*. (1st Palgrave Macmillan pbk. ed.) Palgrave Macmillan, New York, 2004.

[20] J de Mul, 'The Game of Life: Narrative and Ludic Identity Formation in Computer Games', in *Handbook of Computer Game Studies,* MIT Press, Cambridge Mass, 2005, pp. 251-266.

## Bibliography

Boon, M. and P. H. Steenhuis, 'Een ballet van zwart en wit' (A ballet of black and white), in *Trouw*, PCM Uitgevers, Amsterdam, 31-01-2009, pp. 30-31.

Braembussche, A. A. van den, *Denken over kunst: een inleiding in de kunstfilosofie*. (3rd. ed.) Coutinho, Bussum, 2000.

Brice Heath, S., 'Dynamics of Completion', in *The Artful Mind: Cognitive Science and the Riddle of Human Creativity.* M. Turner (ed.), Oxford University Press, New York, 2006, pp. 133-150.

Bruner, J. S., *Actual Minds, Possible Worlds*. Harvard University Press, Cambridge Mass, 1986.

———, *Acts of Meaning*. Harvard University Press, Cambridge Mass., 1990.

Cobley, P. & L. Jansz, *Introducing Semiotics*. Icon, Cambridge, 1999.

Davies, S., *Definitions of Art*. Cornell University Press, Ithaca, N.Y., 1991.

———, *The Philosophy of Art*. Blackwell Pub, Malden Mass, 2006.

Donald, M., 'Art and Cognitive Evolution', in *The Artful Mind: Cognitive Science and the Riddle of Human Creativity,* M. Turner (ed.). Oxford University Press, New York, 2006, pp. 3-20.

Eco, U., *A Theory of Semiotics*. Indiana University Press, Bloomington, 1976.

Eco, U., 'Producing Signs', in *On Signs*. M. Blonsky (ed.), Basil Blackwell Ltd, Oxford, 1985, pp. 176-183.

Gee, J. P., *What Video Games have to teach us about Learning and Literacy*. (1st Palgrave Macmillan pbk. ed.) Palgrave Macmillan, New York, 2004.

Goodman, N., *Languages of Art: An Approach to a Theory of Symbols*. Hacket Publishing Company, Inc., Indianapolis, 1968.

Heusden, B. van, *Literaire cultuur: Handboek*. (1st ed.) OUNL / SUN, Heerlen / Nijmegen, 2001.

Lyotard, J. F., *The Postmodern Condition: A Report in Knowledge*. University of Minnesota Press, Minneapolis, 1985.

Mul, J. de, 'The Game of Life: Narrative and Ludic Identity Formation in Computer Games', in *Handbook of Computer Game Studies*. MIT Press, Cambridge Mass, 2005, pp. 251-266.

Propp, V., *Morphology of the Folktale*. (10 ed.) Research Center, Indiana University, Bloomington, Ind, 1958.

**Jef Folkerts** is a lecturer on Communication and Media at Hanze University Groningen / Applied Sciences in the Netherlands. He studied Arts, Culture and Media at the University of Groningen, and is currently engaged in Ph.D. research on the meaning-generating qualities of videogames.

# The 3-D Virtual Library as a Value-Added Library Service

## Daniel Riha

**Abstract**
Some of the most promising but least utilised online library channels on the Web are multi-user 3-D worlds. In the United States, after the success of Second Life (SL), Library 2.0 and other projects based on the SL platform, librarians share a conception that most existing web-based library services can be implemented in Second Life and that SL library user communities can flourish. The situation in Europe, in contrast, seems to be significantly more complicated. In Europe, multi-user 3-D worlds, and specifically the Second Life platform, have been utilised primarily for marketing purposes and have illustrated a lack of depth in understanding the actual opportunities presented by these new media. Although developments surrounding SL Library 2.0 seem to be promising in the American context, the history of online library services in the 3-D space reaches back to an era far before Second Life's development. The lessons learned in pioneering projects dating back as early as the late 1990s to the beginning of this decade might offer important lessons for avoiding future failures in the implementation of such library services.

**Key Words:** Virtual Library, 3-D Multi-User Environments, Active Worlds, Second Life, Virtual Community.

*****

.

## 1.     Introduction

This chapter describes the functionalities of 3-D library services and the necessary framework for establishing a long-term user community against a broad historical perspective. The concept of the 3-D Virtual Library, a winning concept developed in 2002 for the *Kunst am Bau* (Art on Construction) art competition and implemented in 2004 for the University of Constance Library (UCL) as the first of its kind in Germany, is compared with current 3-D library concepts. The 3-D Virtual Library is presented as a case study, laying out the issues surrounding its implementation, describing usage patterns and examining the potential value a multi-user 3-D interface might add to the online library user community in the European context.

## 2.     3-D Multi-user Virtual Library - The Concept

The widespread adoption of Internet technology induced a new communication paradigm for executing library services. Lévy already in 1997, identified the need for web-based online library services, presenting the concept of 'networked learner support'[1] as a new model for the practice of academic librarianship involving the creation, communication and utilisation of increasing amounts of traditional and new types of information resources.

The original proposal for the 3-D Multi-user Virtual Library for the *Kunst am Bau* competition in 2002 declared as its goal the design of a general 3-D space infrastructure for online user support and shared online communication. The 3-D Multi-user Virtual Library was built on the assumption that the web environment of an online library is less user-friendly compared to a real world library, and that the application of 3-D multi-user environments (MUVEs) might optimise computer-mediated communication (CMC) parameters for online library services. Other goals included increasing social awareness of online library users and creating an online social network of library users.

In this project, the project designer emphasised the increasing importance of two selected main functions of academic libraries - user education and reference services-as well as the need to implement these functions live and interactively in a shared online environment.

The virtual space of 3-D MUVL was intended to serve as a platform for user education. Maher, Simoff and Clark introduced the idea that a virtual learning environment could be designed according to a place metaphor, in which 'place [acts] as context for cooperation, access to other students, teachers and learning materials.'[2]

The 3-D MUVL space was designed as a constructivist online learning environment that would serve users with learning materials, social awareness and means for identifying colleagues with complementary expertise. The space was planned to be used for live training of library users and the empowerment of information literacy initiatives.

The assumption that 3-D multi-user environments may serve as ideal solutions for online information literacy courses, with their proven ability to establish and support different online communities, failed in the case of 3-D MUVL at UCL because 3-D live chat assistance became redundant when regular web services and parallel applied e-learning systems were implemented. The project offered browsing of library webpage content and links in the shared 3-D space, but these sub-features were not recognised as a valuable addition by the local student community.

UCL developed several information literacy courses in conjunction with the *Informations-Kompetenz I*[3] project. UCL's model consisted partly of web presentations, with major components residing in advanced e-learning modules produced using the open source e-learning system ILIAS. The courses were developed according to proven pedagogical methods and offered online users self-paced courses, tutorials and auto-evaluation tests, all of which did not require live human librarian assistance. Computer-mediated communication for learning and social awareness issues was not recognised as research issue during the IK project, and developers have not yet discovered any added value in live coaching of online users or course materials housed in the 3-D MUVL environment.

The U.S. ACRL Guidelines for Distance Learning Library Services state that:

> Access to adequate library services and resources is essential for the attainment of superior academic skills in post-secondary education, regardless of where students, faculty, and programs are located. Members of the distance learning community are entitled to library services and resources equivalent to those provided for students and faculty in traditional campus settings.[4]

The 3-D MUVL project partially examined the optimisation of virtual reference services (VRS). Web-based VRS are still not comparable with traditional library reference services. Distant users work online with open public access catalogues (OPAC) and search engines, but beginners often find such tools to be overly complicated. Users may value the assistance of library personnel present 'live' through an online library interface in a shared 3-D environment, where the librarian assists with navigation of online library information resources. This function could be important for users in avoiding information overload.

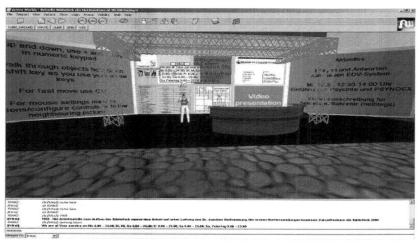

*Image 1*

For basic automated user support, 3-D MUVL utilised three types of bot scripts based on platform Xelagot[5] (Image 1) in four separate applications. These included an FAQ Answering Bot, Navigator Bot for introducing users to the virtual library units, a Quiz Bot for answering questions about the Lake Constance region as well as a Quiz Bot to which questions about the university could be addressed. These bots were not regularly used in operation at the 3-D MUVL interface, so data about user acceptance of this feature is not available.

3-D MUVL has not been operated as a VRS interface at UCL. Presumably, UCL does not have enough distance education users who might potentially profit from such an online coaching service.

Without a plan for integrating the 3-D MUVL into real library web services and without the regular live presence of library professionals devoted to online users, this interface was condemned from the outset to become a static repository for dated 3-D designs and information content.

Despite valuable attempts to organise student teams to update and revive the project, there was little chance that students could adequately serve online library users and fulfil the original 3-D MUVL project goals.

An additional 3-D MUVL feature was intended to support library marketing initiatives. Because the 3-D MUVL was located on an Active Worlds Educational Universe[6] (AWEDU) server, where over 60 international educational experiments were housed in 2007 (downscaled from over 100 projects in 2002), online visitors from other AWEDU sites could potentially have been attracted to UCL's presence and services.

However, the online population of AWEDU has been steadily decreasing since 2005. Academic users now prefer Second Life (SL) 3-D MUVE and its Virtual Campus. Second Life, with potentially millions of users and a growing community, may have a larger impact in relation to designed 3-D presentations today than was the case of the 2002 experiment in AWEDU.

The aforementioned results of 3-D MUVL usage patterns suggest a need for further research in order to answer the question of how to provide useful 3-D library services to today's users.

## 3.     The 3-D Multi-user Virtual Library - Technological Issues

The world of 3-D graphics is developing very quickly. Every year major technical improvements can be expected. The probability of a project to become technically and visually outdated is increasing each year. 3-D MUVL's implementation process took more than three years, starting in October 2002 and launching publicly in January 2006. Active Worlds' multi-user technology was utilized for this project, and it became outdated during the course of this project in the eyes of users and developers.

The decision to implement Active Worlds for the 3-D MUVL was influenced by number of factors:

> AW is a super-browser type application that integrates a web browser, a 3-D multi-user browser as well as text and voice chat interactive features.

> *Kunst am Bau's* competition rules set up a limiting condition that the project could not compete with any current library information system. Active Worlds' system fulfilled this condition.

> The shared 3-D interface enabled developers to easily update text, pictures, video and sound on a pre-made database consisting of objects and panels inside the environment.

> The 3-D MUVL was set up within the AWEDU Universe for 395 USD/year. This was, at that time, by far the most inexpensive 3-D solution available to academic developers.

> In 2002, Active Worlds was the leading multi-user system on the market and many successful online communities were based on AW and AW Educational Universe, which offered space for experimentation to more than 100 international academic teams.

The main disadvantage of Active Worlds is its Renderware 2.0 engine, which produces obsolete, low-end graphics. Other difficulties arise during the import and export of custom-made content.

Alternative solutions then available, such as Blaxxun Community Platform or game engines with multi-user capability, were considered, but the project manager had budget limitations in mind throughout the entire implementation. A non-Active Worlds solution would have required expensive new computer hardware, setting up of a multi-user software server and maintenance costs for both. The project budget did not allow for such contingencies. The 3-D MUVL project could not utilise game engine types of applications because of the following:

> Cost (professional game development environments typically cost more than 100,000 USD).

Community building (these applications are not focused on social networking and informal collaboration).

Complexity (the content produced with such software cannot be easily updated or re-designed by volunteer developers).

In 2002, Active Worlds seemed to provide a good value, balancing functionality requirements with limited budget requirements.

## 4.    Design Process

During the design process of the 3-D multi-user virtual library project, the author built upon Erickson's proven virtual space theory.[7] According to Erickson, many virtual worlds have applied various techniques for user interaction support. The primary effective technique recommended for 3-D virtual space designs is to organise repetitive events and construct spaces created for a given kind of interaction.

Activities in 3-D space such as navigation and object manipulation can increase levels of user participation and interaction in the virtual library environment. According to Erickson, many real spaces and social events have only one purpose: to support the interaction between people. This would indicate library services and spaces would be well-suited to the implementation of 3-D multi-user environments.

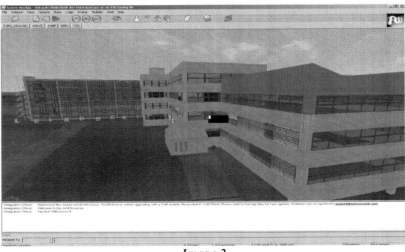

*Image 2*

Using this research as a premise, UCL's real world campus architecture served as the artistic inspiration for the 3-D multi-user virtual library (Image 2). The basic units of 3-D space were designed under following design labels:

(a)     Virtual Information Hall
(b)     Virtual Reference Desk
(c)     Virtual Lecture Rooms
(d)     Virtual Conference Space
(e)     Virtual Document Space
(f)     Virtual Media Lab
(g)     Virtual Gallery Space
(h)     Virtual Cafe

The design phase, based on the art competition proposal, focused primarily on building out these 3-D library spaces and executing the two aforementioned library services.

According to Boerner,[8] structural visualisations of the implicit relationships between hyperlinks and information resources on the Web might aid library users in understanding the relationships between digital artifacts and in reducing the potential for information overload of users.

The virtual library interface enabled browsing 3-D representations of documents, organised in the form of a document landscape (Image 3). These representations were used for visual browsing through documents 'on the fly,' allowing spatial navigation through clusters of documents.

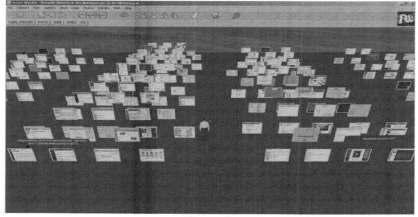

***Image 3***

The other 3-D MUVL units were designed to allow for any potential transformation into a virtual campus.

After 3-D MUVL Grande opened in January 2006, a group of interested students took care of project updating and management. During that year, they also, as a project extension, searched for new ways of creating a functioning online community in the local context.

In 2007, the 3-D MUVL project's objective was modified. The student team, in cooperation with the foreign exchange office of the university, attempted to focus on using the AWEDU virtual site as a mechanism for creating a virtual meeting point for foreign students coming to the University of Constance, offering them a videogame-like environment in which they might become familiar with the university campus and receive basic important information about their studies. A chat environment was envisioned as a channel for information exchange between newcomers and senior students. This idea was never realised, unfortunately. The student team stated the following reasons for failure to implement this phase in a project report:

> Although the Active Worlds Company started with the goal of delivering the 'the Web's most powerful Virtual Reality experience,' this promise is no longer valid in 2007. Four years after the 3-D MUVL concept proposal, this software is now outdated and cannot compete with current visual standards. Active Worlds impedes the integration of custom-made objects from other 3-D platforms and sets challenging hurdles that stop potential visitors from entering this virtual space.[9]

Another valuable attempt in reviving the project took place in summer 2007. A *REAL//VIRTUAL//ART* exhibition produced by the student team at *Gallery Turm* in Constance highlighted selected interactive 3-D features such as avatar-bots and introduced the concept of how virtual design might be applied by creating real copies of virtual objects in order to document the project's history.[10] Several terminals installed in the exhibit were equipped with an Active Worlds plug-in which enabled exhibition visitors to experience a 3-D interface. This helped increase the number of online visitors during the exhibition.

The project 3-D MUVL was in operation online in the AWEDU environment for almost three years (January 2006 until June 2008) with the original design and functionality delivered in 2004.

**5.     Current 3-D Virtual Library Concept Revival**
The latest developments surrounding Web 2.0 have implications for the academic library community. Library professionals intensively develop and discuss ideas about what services and functionalities Library 2.0 shall provide.

The buzz surrounding Library 2.0 is spreading out throughout the Second Life library community and the idea of a 3-D virtual library in 3-D social worlds has been resurrected. A major Second Life milestone took place on October 12, 2006, when the SL Library 2.0 opened its virtual door. SL Library 2.0, later renamed as in three components as the Alliance Virtual Library (AVL), the Alliance Library System (ALS) and Online Programming for All Libraries[11] (OPAL), existed by extending services currently offered online to librarians and library users into the Second Life environment. ALS and OPAL built the central library on the SL Info Island and began to offer virtual reference services utilising OCLCs QuestionPoint virtual reference service and traditional library services such as book discussions and research assistance. ALS offers instructional sessions on how to use and search databases and how to search and evaluate online information. ALS provides virtual tours of electronic resources as well. Another new feature provides instructional materials for information literacy instruction (Machinima).[12]

Thomas suggested that 'the process of Machinima-making proves to be an excellent tool to teach cyberculture.'[13] Second Life is an effective environment for educational Machinima production. According Swanson, Machinima offers librarians in Second Life 'a vehicle to work with library staff and library users (millenials and adults) to create a variety of content that can be used, shared or 'mashed up.''[14] She recommends using story-based Machinima instruction with 'Filmmaking group projects incorporating information literacy skills, active learning, critical thinking and use of technology.'[15] These classes are held at the Machinima Institute located on the ALA Arts Island in Second Life.

The AVL partner project, SL Medical Library (SLM), shares SL Library's mission statement, as well as its primary goals and objectives. The mission of the Second Life Library is to:

> Explore the issues of providing library services in a virtual world.

> Evaluate services currently offered by real world libraries in the light of features offered in virtual reality environments and the information needs of VR residents.

> Examine how libraries will remain relevant when more business and education activities take place virtually.

> Promote the real library and online library services to
> residents of Second Life.[16]

SLM's designers declared, 'in SLM, most existing web-based services in libraries can be implemented, but the main goal is to 'market' existing library services and resources in general. Special interest lies in exploring innovative ways of offering and distributing services.'[17]

In 2009, the Alliance Virtual Library created a pioneering new library service in Second Life. 'Info Island' now has over 50 library and partner islands. Info Island has become a base for various interactive library collections and exhibits. According to AVL, there are five 'core' library islands, including Info, Info International, Infotainment, Illumination and Imagination. They offer live reference services for more than 80 hours per week, with volunteers answering over 300 questions per week. AVL additionally started cooperation with the U.S. National Library of Medicine and has built Health InfoIsland together with medical and consumer health libraries, and now provides numerous exhibits and programs on how to locate accurate health information.[18]

AVL have succeeded in becoming one of the best virtual services offered in Second Life, proving this fact with its nomination for the Linden Prize (AVL became one of the prize finalists).[19]

Another major organisation active in Second Life is the American Library Association (ALA). Since 2008, ALA has operated ALA Island, an open-air campus including kiosks for ALA's divisions, offices, and round tables; two lounge areas; a publishing pavilion and a floating gallery that is dedicated to photographic exhibitions. This virtual space is used for various virtual professional meeting activities such as expert presentations on current librarianship topics as well as meetings of the Virtual Communities and Libraries Member Initiative Group (VCL MIG). In 2009, ALA presented this VCL MIG Statement of Purpose:

> To provide a group within ALA for members interested in
> fostering the practice of library work, the visibility of
> libraries and library workers, and the extension of library
> services within online social networks, virtual worlds, and
> other communities of intention.
>
> To provide a mechanism for sharing experiences and
> practices in-person or virtually through programming or
> asynchronous communications.
>
> To encourage wider participation by the profession and the
> association in virtual worlds.

> To establish a forum across all types of libraries and at all
> levels of library employment concerned with the
> development of library services in emerging social
> networks, virtual worlds, and other communities of
> intention.[20]

All of the 3-D library projects flourishing in Second Life are based in the United States. While Europe has taken a lead in the number of the active users in Second Life,[21] to date there is no comparable Second Life library service operating at the European level.

In 2007, the Amsterdam Public Library (APL) opened APL Island as a promising first Dutch library project in Second Life, stating the following goals:

> The library will initially be offering e-books, reservation
> facilities and will be promoting library membership. The
> virtual library will also be selling tickets in cooperation
> with AUB ticket points, an existing service of the real
> library. In addition live Amsterdam FM broadcasts will be
> produced. [...] The aim is to make the virtual library an
> experience library just like its counterpart in real life.[22]

According to APL Island's project leader, Delaney Haar, APL Island is used for conducting virtual experiments with possible new services since this is cheaper than experimenting in real life.

Another Second Life service provider, Talis, opened in February 2008 with the Alliance Library System. Talis Cybrary Island offers a free space allowing the design of virtual library branches in the hope of attracting some of the European SL users:

> The raison d'être behind Talis Cybrary City was to foster
> innovation within the library community. This it clearly
> did, with dozens of libraries taking advantage of the
> facilities to create their own Second Life library branch.
>
> Cybrary City, although open to all, did have a large
> majority of participants from North American libraries. We
> hope to gain a much larger representation from other
> continents among the residents of Cybrary Island.[23]

Kirriemuir points to the possible reasons for low adoption of Second Life service for libraries in Europe: 'Despite steady integration into a common European Union, each European nation retains certain individual elements of infrastructure. Libraries, for example, tend to follow different policies and systems in different countries.'[24] The fragmented European library infrastructure and different language base might help explain some of the reasons for why the Second Life platform has not become more popular in the provision of online library services in Europe, but a detailed analysis of this question is beyond the scope of this chapter.

The goals of the various 3-D virtual library projects based on the Second Life platform are very similar to the original goals proposed in the 3-D virtual library concept for *Kunst am Bau* in 2002. In the concluding section of this chapter will attempt to identify some possible limiting factors which inhibited wider utilisation of this 3-D virtual library project.

## 6.    Conclusion

Possible reasons for why users did not massively accept the 3-D interface and use the 3-D multi-user virtual library in AWEDU include:

Limited number of potential users

No integration with other library web services

No live user support in the AWEDU environment

No pre-designed goals/activities

Outdated 3-D technology and information content

Problematic maintenance workflows leading to frustration
by interested student community developers

In contrast, the success of Second Life, with its ever growing cyber-population and the buzz surrounding AVL, may prove that some of the assumptions upon which the 3-D MUVL of 2002 were correct.

The Second Life environment presents itself to be more suitable for social networking. The current popularity of SL might attract more library users to test an environment often seen only in the TV news, and these first-time users could perhaps become more interested in becoming active members of such an online community.

Active Worlds have not delivered technological solutions for incorporating primary web-based online library services into a 3-D interface.

Current attempts to integrate real library web service into Second Life by Alliance Library System and other providers supported by Library 2.0 technologies are very promising and worthy of further evaluation.

The 2007 edition of the New Media Consortium and EDUCAUSE's annual *The Horizon Report* included an article about the prospects for virtual worlds being adopted by the educational sector, claiming that virtual worlds might be ready for massive adoption within two to three years.[25] In this context, the 3-D Multi-user Virtual Library project for UCL must be recognised as one of the earliest experiments examining the value of 3-D social interfaces for academic libraries, although it did not attract regular attention from a large number of users.

More information and a full documentation of the project's development are available at: <http://www.virtuallibrary.de>.

## Notes

[1] P Lévy, 'Continuing Professional Development for Networked Learner Support: Progress Review of Research and Curriculum Design', in *Information Research*, Vol. 3, No. 1, 1997, p. 1.

[2] M L Maher, S Simoff, S Clark, 'Learner-Centred Open Virtual Environments as Places', in the *Proceedings of the First European CSCL Conference*, 2001.

[3] 2003-2005, more info at: <http://www.ub.uni-konstanz.de/ik/>.

[4] *Guidelines for Distance Learning Library Services*, ACRL Association of College and Research Libraries: a Division of the American Library Association, August 2005, Illinois, Chicago, 31 August 2005, available from: <http://www.acrl.org/ala/acrl/acrlstandards/guidelinesdistancelearning.htm>.

[5] Xelagot: <http://www.imatowns.com/xelagot>.

[6] More info at: <http://www.activeworlds.com/>.

[7] T Erickson, 'The Spatial Enviroment as a Medium for Interaction', in the *Proceedings of Conference on Spatial Information Theory*, 1993.

[8] K Boerner, 'Extracting and Visualizing Semantic Structures in Retrieval Results for Browsing', in *ACM Digital Libraries*, San Antonio, Texas, June 2-7, 2000.

[9] Translated from German by author, source text to be found at: <http://www.virtuallibrary.de/nutzung1.html>.

[10] More info about project to be found at 3-D MUVL project's documentary website at: <http://www.virtuallibrary.de/nutzung1.html>.

[11] More info at: <http://www.alliancelibrarysystem.com>.

[12] Machinima is a movie realised within videogame or virtual space.

[13] T Thomas, 'Cyberculture: Learning New Literacies through Machinima', in this volume, Rodopi, 2010, p. 11.

[14] B D Swanson, 'Second Life Machinima for Libraries: The Intersection of Instruction, Outreach and Marketing in a Virtual World', in the Proceedings

of the World Library and Information Congress: 73rd IFLA General Conference and Council, 19-23 August 2007, Durban, South Africa, p. 5.
[15] B D Swanson, p. 9.
[16] A Concept of the Second Life Medical Library 2.0, p. 1, viewed March 2009, <http://www.infoisland.org/drupal/node/17>.
[17] Ibid, p. 1.
[18] Linden Prize Finalist: Alliance Virtual Library <http://lindenlab.com/lindenprize /finalists/alliance>.
[19] Ibid, p. 1.
[20] ALA Island in Second Life, 2009, <http://www.ala.org/ala/mgrps/communicate/alaislandinsecondlife/index.cfm>, accessed March 2009.
[21] Europeans make up the majority of the active users in Second Life with 54 percent, just one third of active Second Life users are U.S. based, <http://secondlife.reuters.com/stories/2007/02/09/europe-takes-lead-in-secon d-life-users/>.
[22] Amsterdam Library opens Second Life Library, *Dutch Libraries*, 2007, <http://dutchlibraries.weblog.nl/dutchlibraries/2007/04/amsterdam_libra.html >, accessed 20 February 2009.
[23] R Wallis, *The Cybrary moves on: Talis supports more Library innovation in Second Life*, Talis, 2008, Available from <http://blogs.talis.com/panlibus/archives/2008/02/the_cybrary_mov.php>.
[24] J Kirriemuir, 'Digital Games in European Libraries', in Beyond 2.0: User-Focused Tools & Practices, Monterey, Canada, October 20 - 22, 2008.
[25] *The Horizon Report: 2007 Edition.* New Media Consortium and Educause Initiative, 2007, ISBN 0-9765087-4-5, available from: <http://www.nmc.org/pdf/2007_Horizon_Report.pdf>, accessed 12 September 2009.

# Bibliography

ACRL Association of College and Research Libraries: A Division of the American Library Association, *Guidelines for Distance Learning Library Services*. August 2005, Illinois, Chicago, 31 August 2005. Available from <http://www.acrl.org/ala/acrl/acrlstandards/guidelinesdistancelearning.htm>.

Amsterdam Library Association, *ALA Island in Second Life*, <http://www.ala.org/ala/mgrps/communicate/alaislandinsecondlife/index.cfm>, accessed March 2009.

Boerner, K., 'Extracting and Visualizing Semantic Structures in Retrieval Results for Browsing', in *ACM Digital Libraries*, San Antonio, Texas, June 2-7, 2000.

Dutch Libraries, 04/2007. Amsterdam Library opens Second Life Library. http://dutchlibraries.weblog.nl/dutchlibraries/2007/04/amsterdam_libra.html.

Erickson, T., 'The Spatial Enviroment as a Medium for Interaction', in the *Proceedings of Conference on Spatial Information Theory*, 1993.

InfoIsland.org, *A Concept of the Second Life Medical Library 2.0*, p. 1, viewed March 2009, <http://www.infoisland.org/drupal/node/17>.

Kirriemuir, J., 'Digital Games in European Libraries', in *Beyond 2.0: User-Focused Tools & Practices*, Monterey, Canada, October 20 - 22, 2008.

Levy, P., 'Continuing Professional Development for Networked Learner Support: Progress Review of Research and Curriculum Design', in *Proceedings of the 2nd International Symposium on Networked Learner Support*, Sheffield, England, 1997.

LindenLab.com, *Linden Prize Finalist: Alliance Virtual Library* <http://lindenlab.com/ lindenprize /finalists/alliance>.

Maher, M. L., Simoff, S., and S. Clark, 'Learner-Centred Open Virtual Environments as Places', in *Proceedings of the First European CSCL Conference*, 2001.

NewMediaConsortium.org, *The Horizon Report: 2007 Edition*. New Media Consortium and Educause Initiative, 2007, ISBN 0-9765087-4-5. Accessed 12 September 2009, Link: <http://www.nmc.org/pdf/2007_ Horizon_ Report.pdf>.

Swanson, B. D., 'Second Life Machinima for Libraries: The Intersection of Instruction, Outreach and Marketing in a Virtual World', in the Proceedings of the World Library and Information Congress: 73rd IFLA General Conference and Council, 19-23 August 2007, Durban, South Africa.

Thomas, T., 'Cyberculture: Learning New Literacies through Machinima', in *Cybercultures*, Rodopi, 2010.

Wallis, R., *The Cybrary moves on: Talis supports more Library Innovation in Second Life*. Talis, 2008. Available from: <http://blogs.talis.com/ panlibus/archives/2008/02/the_cybrary_mov.php>.

**Daniel Riha**, Ph.D., Assistant Professor at Faculty of Humanities, Charles University in Prague, Czech Republic. His research includes issues on Serious Games and Multi-user Virtual Environments Design.

# Learning New Literacies through Machinima

## Theodoros Thomas

**Abstract**
This chapter aims to describe the implementation of an introductory cyberculture course in the French language and literature faculty curriculum (University of Athens, 2008). The main objective of this course was the education of today's digital natives and future Netizens and the development of new media skills which should be seen as social skills and also include the traditional literacy. The syllabus contained an introduction to cyberspace, virtualisation and virtual communities (through MySpace), digital video and sound, digital effects, an insight into collective intelligence (through wikis), politics on the Net (by the examination of the phenomenon of hackers) and mainly the examination of digital storytelling through machinima. Machinima, a portmanteau of machine cinema or sometimes animation, is defined as 'animated filmmaking within a real-time virtual 3-D environment'. It is a new medium where filmmaking, animation, and videogames converge. Students created collaboratively characters and stories, wrote scenarios using a wiki and then produced machinima films. This chapter will present concrete course projects. Based on current research on new media literacies, we propose that the creation of machinima films by students-prosumers is a form of participatory culture and an excellent way to develop new media skills.

**Key Words:** Cyberculture, E-Learning, New Media Literacies, Wiki, Digital Storytelling, Machinima.

*****

## 1. The Case

In the last decade Cyberculture has emerged from its status of a subculture, closely related to cyberpunk and the Gibsonian cyberspace to refer to our ways of life affected by digital technology. In this chapter I talk about the implementation of an introductory cyberculture course in the French language and literature faculty curriculum (University of Athens, 2008). The course lasted for one semester, from February to June 2008, consisting of 11 sessions of 2 hours each, 22 hours of teaching and practicing in total. The audience consisted of 56 students (53 females and 3 males) aged from 19 to 23. Apart from one Socrates exchange student coming from France, the rest of the audience was Greek originated.

In the Faculty of French Language and Literature, part of the University of Athens's School of Philosophy to obtain a bachelor's degree in French language and literature a student needs to pass 33 compulsory modules and 7 out of 25 elective ones. The faculty is mainly focused on French literature courses and it aims mostly at the formation of future teachers of French language through the development of individualised skills to be used for personal expression. This curriculum can be described as very rigid and outdated.

In 2003 the faculty received funding from EPEAEK ('Operational Program Education and Primary Vocational Training'), co-funded by the European Union within a complete system of interconnecting measures and actions. The main objective of the EU program was the improvement of the educational system and its services, in order to respond more effectively to real social needs by opening up communication channels and links to the job market. Under its main priority axis of the promotion and improvement of education new educational approaches were introduced to the department.

An e-learning platform was introduced and many didactic materials were digitised. Alternative ways of learning were introduced (such as the lecture series 'The Works and the d@ys', designed on an educational, a technological and a business axis) and the curriculum was enriched by new prototype elective modules that gave priority to new media (i.e. Introduction to ICT, Usage of ICT in teaching French, Computer assisted technical translation, Cinema and literature). One of the elective courses proposed was 'cyberculture' that was introduced during the second phase of implementation of the EU EPEAEK Program (2007-2009).

## 2.        The Course Audience

The audience in current scientific literature but also in areas as varied as marketing, administration, and education is often described as 'digital generation',[1] 'cyberkids',[2] or 'digital natives'[3]. It is thought to be a generation defined in and through its experience of digital Computer Technology. According to Bourdieu, generations are socially and culturally identified and formed, and digital media help to shape the beliefs and dispositions, a different *habitus* for this generation.[4] This may be true and the current generation may be defined by digital technology but we must not fall to the trap of cyberlibertarianism, the ecstatic enthusiasm for electronically mediated forms of living combined with radical, right wing libertarian ideas about the proper definition of freedom and technological determinism. The relation of these students with technology is far more complex than it might initially appear. In their mind they are persuaded that they must use digital technologies, they interact with them on a daily basis but at the same time they often lack a deeper knowledge of how they work. They solely think about the consequence of their usage as if they fear them and they often even don't admit their technophobia. These students don't avoid the banality of digital technology use. They almost all use mobile phones and they mostly answer positively to the question whether they can use a computer but in practice their knowledge is rudimentary and they lack basic skills of literacy in the New Media Culture, the ones that we call the new media literacies: a set of cultural competencies and social skills that people need in the new media landscape.

## 3.     New Media Culture Skills

Jenkins and co-authors maintain that youth does not acquire miraculously the key skills and competencies to actively get involved to participatory culture by merely interacting with popular culture and they give three arguments to support this position. They write that this laissez faire attitude cannot solve the participation gap, 'the unequal access to the opportunities, experiences, skills, and knowledge that will prepare youth for full participation in the world of tomorrow'. Furthermore there is the transparency problem. Despite the fact that the digital natives are accustomed to using new media, their knowledge is not always active and they do not always develop critical or metacognitive skills. Finally there is the ethics challenge, the norms that rule the publication of online content without any formal guidance or supervision in a fuzzy environment where the vision of McLuhan and Nevitt[5] that with electric technology, the consumer would become a producer becomes true with the emergence of the prosumer, the consumer who is not passive but also produces.

With these three concerns in mind they propose the following competencies young people should acquire in their learning experiences:

*Play*: the capacity to experiment with one's surroundings as a form of problem-solving.

*Performance*: the ability to adopt alternative identities for the purpose of improvisation and discovery.

*Simulation*: the ability to interpret and construct dynamic models of real-world processes.

*Appropriation*: the ability to meaningfully sample and remix media content.

*Multitasking*: the ability to scan one's environment and shift focus as needed to salient details.

*Distributed Cognition*: the ability to interact meaningfully with tools that expand mental capacities.

*Collective Intelligence*: the ability to pool knowledge and compare notes with others toward a common goal.

*Judgment:* the ability to evaluate the reliability and credibility of different information sources.

*Transmedia Navigation*: the ability to follow the flow of stories and information across multiple modalities.

*Networking*: the ability to search for, synthesise, and disseminate information.

*Negotiation*: the ability to travel across communities, discerning and respecting multiple views, and grasping and following alternative norms.[6]

**4.        Course Objectives and Course Syllabus**

By taking under consideration the profile of the Department, the profile of the students and the previously mentioned new media competencies we proposed this course with the intention of creating the opportunities for students to develop the cultural competencies and social skills needed for full community involvement, participation and individual and collective expression. We departed from the traditional skills developed in a University (research skills, technical skills, and critical analysis) in order to try to cultivate skills needed for our networked society through collaborative learning. Furthermore in order to cope with the students' technophobia we decided to help them build technical computer skills that would build up their self-confidence.

We designed the course syllabus to include theories and concepts of cyberspace, knowledge in the digital era, virtual communities, and politics on the Net and we insisted on videogames and digital storytelling through Machinima.

We wanted to combine theory with practice so each session was divided in two parts of 45 minutes: a lecture (theory module) and a practical workshop (hands on software tutorials). Our aim was to show the students that the issues examined are not so virtual and elusive as they might originally think. We also adopted a blended learning strategy. The aforementioned sessions were supported by E-class, the virtual learning environment of the University of Athens.[7] E-class provides a depository for on-line learning materials (PowerPoint presentations and other notes) as well as a forum, a chat, an agenda and several other administration tools that facilitate the class management. Since we wanted to explore virtual communities, create a participatory culture and e-class cannot be easily personalised by students we encouraged them to create an account on MySpace. Furthermore we created two wikis on PBwiki in order to see in practice how a wiki space works.

Students in order to be evaluated had to accomplish three tasks (two individual and one collaborative): they had to participate in the conversations on the forum, to write an article on the wiki about cyberculture and to contribute to two other of their fellow students and finally to create a machinima film.

## 5.     Background

Wikis are websites based on the open editing concept[8], allowing common users to create and modify any of its pages. Named by Ward Cunningham in 1994 and signifying 'quick' in Hawaiian wikis have become the expression par excellence of what Pierre Lévy described as the collective intelligence.[9] The most famous, probably the most successful and surely the most controversial of these sites is Wikipedia. The collaborative nature, the simplicity and the ease of use have been remarked by numerous scholars and educators who have explored the educational potentials of the tool. [10] These characteristics go along with the constructivist pedagogy and they support learner's autonomy. Furthermore they contribute in the creation of Communities of practice.

The rise of gaming studies with the research made on the cultural and social impacts of videogames has helped mentalities to evolve and go beyond the debate of the previous decades whether videogames are just a gratuitous form of entertainment and they increase or not violence. Jef Folkerts[11] proves in his chapter that videogames are artful not only for aesthetic reasons but mainly for their ability to trigger metacognitive processes and to prompt meta-reflection. The emerging phenomenon of Machinima can be inscribed in this research.

Communities of practice on the Internet provide several definitions with the most eloquent this of the academy of machinima arts and sciences[12]. Machinima (muh-sheen-eh-mah) is filmmaking within a real-time, 3D virtual environment, often using 3D video-game technologies. In an expanded definition, it is the convergence of filmmaking, animation and game development. Machinima is real-world filmmaking techniques applied within an interactive virtual space where characters and events can be either controlled by humans, scripts or artificial intelligence. By combining the techniques of filmmaking, animation production and the technology of real-time 3D game engines, Machinima makes for a very cost- and time-efficient way to produce films, with a large amount of creative control. So more than a new medium, Machinima is rather a new technique to produce video narratives.

The term 'machinima' was coined in 1999 by two early practitioners of the technique Anthony Baily and Hugh Hanckock and it is a misspelled portmanteau of machine cinema (also implying Anima-life).[13] Back in the early 1990's players of video games *Quake* and *Doom* used to record their game exploits and to create movies. Gamers were gradually transformed into actors and 'the viewpoint of the player became the viewpoint of the director'.[14] Series like the *Halo* based *Red vs. Blue* made the genre quite popular and films like *The French Democracy* about the 2005 riots in the suburbs of Paris gave an alternative touch.

## 6.     Procedure

Since this was a course addressed to inexperienced students, in parallel to the lectures we launched initiation activities. Students were asked to create online profiles on MySpace and to get registered to class groups. In an attempt to break the ice and help students get to know the other members of their group we used E-class forum. We tried to ignite conversations by posing questions such as: 'how digital technology affects your life?' or 'Do you think that videogames are a waste of time?'. This activity lasted the first two weeks of the semester and gave them the opportunity to get adapted to the online environment. Most of the students responded quite well, although some were still hesitant to participate.

Then we addressed the issues of knowledge in the digital era and we studied the case of Wikipedia. Given that E-class did not offer at that time the functionality of a wiki we chose Pbwiki because it is web-based, it is easy and simple and does not require any knowledge of HTML but it allows at the same time to upload any kind of documents, and multimedia content, access can be forbidden to non members and lastly it has no ads. We invited students to the wiki and we proposed them a list of topics about cyberculture from the definition of cyberpunk to the biography and work of Foucault.[15] We asked them to choose one to develop it and two from the ones that their colleagues developed to comment them and correct them. The deadline was three weeks later, after spring holidays. Then they had to present their work and their experience to the rest of the group orally. Most of the students accomplished this assignment but they were reluctant to post any negative comment for their fellow student work even if it was obvious that sometimes they did not agree. This can be attributed to the mental model Greek students have for corrections in academia. Usually there are no iterations and corrections are translated to loss of marks.

When we explored digital narratives, we had tutorials on Audacity, an open source audio editing software and Windows Moviemaker, video editing software in order to introduce students to digital storytelling. Storytelling and learning are inseparably interconnected since the process of making up a story is at the same time a process of making sense. Especially for language students the ability to make coherent stories is related with the pragmatic competences (discourse and functional competence) of the Common European Framework for language learning.

We delved deeper into digital narratives through Machinima. Our intention was to initiate students to the procedure of a creation of a film (preproduction, filming and postproduction) by enabling them to create their own film. Our ambition was not to create new directors or producers but to teach cineliteracy. To quote again Jef Folkerts the artistic 'is situated in the perception and comprehension of it'.[16] We chose for that the Lionhead's studio game *The Movies*. *The Movies* is a business simulation where the aim is to create the most successful studio in the world. The player must recruit and nurture the best stars and keep them happy, build the most impressive studio lot, create movies, win awards and make as much money as he can. Probably the most interesting feature of the game is the advanced creation of a movie where you can write a script based on the Hollywood scriptwriting templates (horror, action, romance, sci-fi, comedy movies), choose the settings, the actors, direct and postproduce a film. I found *The Movies* game engine perfect for an introduction to Machinima because it provides lots of capabilities and requires little or no technical or modding skills to create interesting movies. Additionally it isn't demanding in computer technical requirements and its price is not prohibitive.

The students were asked to form groups of 2-4 and to work collaboratively in order to create and to develop a short film based on their ideas. They were invited to a wiki[17] where they could describe the characters of their story, write their story, and develop a script. Finally they could optionally post their film on these pages. The ideas and stories were critiqued during team meetings with the instructor. One of the main concerns was to establish the notion of narrative action and conflict and resolution. These critiques occurred informally as the instructor observed student progress but it was still very difficult for the students to apply successfully these principles. Finally, on the last course session students had to present orally their work, speak about the challenges and the problems they faced while producing the film and project it. Their fellow students were invited to peer-review these final products. We noticed that students were much more motivated to finish this assignment than the first wiki assignment, even though they lacked time. What's more, they were more eager to criticise their fellow students work and to point out negative and positive aspects. We judge that is due to the oral nature of the commentaries as opposed to the written commentaries on the wikis.

The best way to illustrate the concepts that student learned is to look at the films they created. 11 films were produced ranging from horror movies to romance, crime stories, sitcoms and dramas. For instance one group created *Nightmare* a fusion of horror/love story that demonstrates perfect time economy and in three minutes it delivers a complete film from the visual and narrative point of view. In addition students showed extreme ingenuity and capacity to overcome problems. The group was of feminine composition and one character in their story was male. They could not find a male actor, so they recorded themselves the voice over of this actor and then they turned into a male voice by applying to it sound filters. Many students applied successfully techniques of remix culture by incorporating elements of famous popular films into their movie (e.g. scenes and music from Quentin Tarantino's *Pulp Fiction* or Alfred Hitchcock's *Psycho*).

## 7.     Results

With these assignments we applied an underlying principle of constructivism which supports that for learning to happen, learners themselves must be actively engaged in the process of learning and we gained a better understanding on the procedure of creating a machinima as a tool to promote learning. We think that these activities develop new media skills including the following:

> *Play* - despite the time pressure students were motivated to bring to a termination their film, not so much out of desire for a higher mark but for the sake of the project.

> *Performance* - they adopted different roles in order to carry off their project (i.e. director, video editor, audio editor, script editor). They also had the chance to participate and to perform identity tourism.

> *Multitasking* - they took turns to adopt those roles.

> *Simulation* - out of the video game they realised how a thriving cultural industry works.

> *Appropriation* - Students incorporated in their films experiences from other media and they remixed them in their own products.

> *Distributed Cognition*, *Collective Intelligence* and *Networking* - they used the digital tools offered by a wiki in

order to collaborate, communicate and break the constrictions imposed by distance and time. This interaction thanks to the wiki was not only among members of their team but of all their class.

*Judgment* - they had to make decisions of which tools to choose and which sources were better to support their choices. Additionally they built critiques and reflections on other's work.

*Transmedia Navigation* - they weaved a story that they expressed using different modalities (text, video, music, photos).

*Negotiation* - finally, students learned teamwork, scheduling project management, iterations and refinement skills that depend heavily on negotiation.

## 8.      Assessment

Work produced by students surprised us positively. They learned how to use the game in order to create a movie fairly easy. They produced original, completed short movies and they were often very creative. On the other hand it must be noticed here that the greatest drawback of many films was the narrative, a domain that requires constant refinement so as to achieve high quality results. As far as the use of wikis is concerned, I must state that there was a problem with the evaluation of sources for the cyberculture wiki. The problem of source evaluation by the net generation has been also brought out by other scholars. Generally speaking I realised that students encountered greater difficulties with the use of French language than the use of digital tools. One last remark is that the use of several virtual spaces (Eclass, wikis, MySpace) is not recommended since it triggered a feeling of *virtual disorientation* to the more technologically inexperienced students. Linked to this is the *identity disorientation*. Many students turned out unable to understand that cyberspace also has its own registers and conventions as every human interaction does and so they have to adopt the proper code.

Students assessed their experience of this course very positively. Most of them were happy to have chosen it (4.33/5, N=32) and they thought that its contents were very interesting (4.42/5), with clear objectives (4/5) and well structured (3.7/5) (chart 1). They thought that it requires a lot of effort to follow it (3.33/5) (chart 2), but that it is almost as difficult as other courses are (3.2/5) and it develops their critical thinking (3.9/5) (chart 1). At the same time they thought that more time was required to cover its contents (3.45/5) (chart 2).

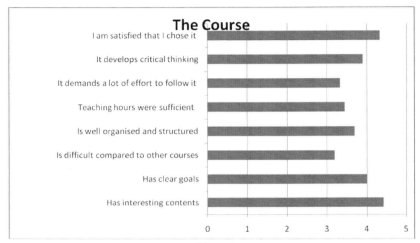

*Chart 1*

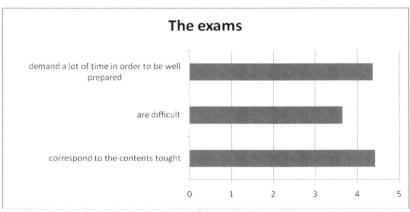

*Chart 2*

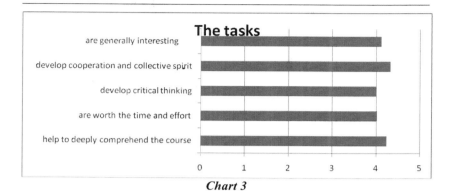

***Chart 3***

As far as the assignments are concerned students thought that they foster collaboration and team spirit (4.33/5), that they are indispensable for the deeper understanding of the course (4.24/5) and they are worth the time spent (4.03/5) because they are generally interesting (4.12/5) and they develop critical thinking (4/5) (chart 3).

## 9.    Conclusion

In conclusion, in this chapter I have suggested that the process of Machinima making proves to be an excellent tool to teach cyberculture. The initial evaluation of this idea was built on student performance and our observation and interaction with them through the preparation of their assignments and conversations in the lab. Machinima films are produced quickly, cheaply, effectively and combined with the usage of a wiki they can initiate students to digital storytelling and help them develop cultural competencies and social skills for the digital arena. I believe that Machinima film production motivated students to learn and allowed them to apply the concepts learned.

## Notes

[1] K C Montgomery, *Generation Digital Politics, Commerce, and Childhood in the Age of the Internet*. MIT press, Cambridge, MA, 2007.

[2] S Holloway & G Valentine, *Cyberkids: Youth Identities and Communities in an On-line World*. Routledge Falmer, London, 2002.

[3] M Prensky, Digital Natives, Digital Immigrants, *On the Horizon, 9(5):* Oct. 2001.

[4] P Bourdieu, *Questions de sociologie*. Éditions de Minuit, Paris, 1984.

[5] M McLuhan & B Nevitt, Take Today: The Executive as Dropout. Longman Canada, Ontario, 1972.

[6] H Jenkins, R Puroshotma, K Clinton, M Weigel, & A J Robison, *Confronting the Challenges of Participatory Culture: Media Education for the 21st Century*. The John D. and Catherine T. MacArthur Foundation, 2005, retrieved on 15 March 2009. Available at <http://www.new medialiteracies.org/files/working/NMLWhitePaper.pdf>.

[7] E-class: <http://eclass.uoa.gr/>, retrieved on 15 March 2009.

[8] B Leuf & W Cunningham, *The Wiki Way: Quick Collaboration on the Web*. Addison Wesley, Upper Saddle River, NJ, 2001.

[9] P Levy *L'intelligence collective. Pour une anthropologie du cyberspace*. La Découverte, Paris, 1995.

[10] E.g. N Augar, R Raitman & W Zhou, 'Teaching and Learning Online with Wikis', in *Beyond the Comfort Zone: The Proceedings of the 21st ASCILITE Conference*, R Atkinson, C McBeath, D Jonas-Dwyer & Rob Phillips, ASCILITE, Perth, 2004.

[11] Jef Folkerts, paper C03 in this volume.

[12] <http://machinima.org/>, retrieved on 15 March 2009

[13] H Hancock & J Ingram, *Machinima For Dummies*. Wiley Publishing, Indianapolis, 2007.

H Lowood, 'High-Performance Play: The Making of Machinima', in *Videogames and Art: Intersections and Interactions*. A Clarke & G Mitchell (eds), Intellect Books, UK, 2007.

[14] P Marino, *3D game-based filmmaking: The Art of Machinima*. Paraglyph, Arizona, 2004.

[15] <http://cyberculture.pbwiki.com/>, retrieved on 15 March 2009.

[16] Folkerts, loc. cit.

[17] <http://machinimafilms.pbwiki.com/>, retrieved on 15 March 2009.

## Bibliography

Augar, N., Raitman, R., & Zhou, W., 'Teaching and Learning Online with Wikis', in *Beyond the Comfort Zone: The Proceedings of the 21st ASCILITE Conference*. R Atkinson, C McBeath, D Jonas-Dwyer & Rob Phillips, ASCILITE, Perth, 2004.

Bourdieu, P., *Questions de sociologie*. Éditions de Minuit, Paris, 1984.

Hancock, H., & J. Ingram, *Machinima for Dummies*. Wiley Publishing, Indianapolis, 2007.

Holloway, S. & G. Valentine, *Cyberkids: Youth Identities and Communities in an On-line World*. Routledge Falmer, London, 2002.

Jenkins, H., Puroshotma, R., Clinton, K., Weigel, M., & A. J. Robison, *Confronting the Challenges of Participatory Culture: Media Education for the 21st Century*. 2005.

Leuf, B., & W. Cunningham, *The Wiki Way: Quick Collaboration on the Web*. Addison Wesley, Upper Saddle River, NJ, 2001.

Levy, P., *L'intelligence collective : Pour une anthropologie du cyberspace*. La Découverte, Paris, 1995.

Lowood, H., 'High-Performance Play: The Making of Machinima', in *Videogames and Art: Intersections and Interactions*. A Clarke & G Mitchell (eds), Intellect Books, UK, 2007.

Marino, P., *3D Game-based Filmmaking: The Art of Machinima*. Paraglyph, Arizona, 2004.

McLuhan, M., & B. Nevitt, *Take Today: The Executive as Dropout*. Longman Canada, Ontario, 1972.

Montgomery, K. C., *Generation Digital Politics, Commerce, and Childhood in the Age of the Internet*. MIT press, Cambridge, MA, 2007.

Prensky, M., Digital Natives, Digital Immigrants. *On the Horizon, 9(5):* Oct. 2001.

Walraven, A., Brand-Gruwel, S., and H. P. A. Boshuizen, *How Students evaluate Information and Sources when searching the World Wide Web for Information*. Computers & Education, 52 (1), Jan. 2009.

**Theodoros Thomas** is a PhD student at the French Department of the University of Athens. He is interested in digital culture and how it affects learning.

# PART IV

# Web 2.0 and Social Networking

# Youth Connecting Online: From Chat Rooms to Social Networking Sites

*Natalia Waechter, Kaveri Subrahmanyam,*
*Stephanie M. Reich and Guadalupe Espinoza*

## Abstract

As media is rapidly changing and different technologies are gaining and losing favour, youth are adapting to these changes in ways that support their developmental needs. This chapter will present research, which demonstrates that as online contexts have changed and evolved, so have young people's behaviours within them; yet at its core, these behaviours remain connected to important offline developmental concerns. We do this by presenting results from our own research on chat rooms and social networking sites as well as drawing from other recent research on young people's online lives. We begin by describing an Austrian-American study on chat rooms, which was first published in 2005 in German. Using participant observation and analysis of chat room conversations between teenage boys and girls, the study concentrated on adolescents' gender and ethnic identity negotiations in the public space. The second study was conducted at the Children's Digital Media Centre (CDMC@LA) and examined young people's use of social networking sites; it was presented at the 'Cybercultures' conference (4th Global Conference: Cybercultures - Exploring Critical Issues, Salzburg, Austria, March 13-15, 2009) and was recently published in the *Journal of Applied Developmental Psychology.*[1] The study investigated emerging adults' online activities, their use of social networking sites for communication, and the overlap between their online and offline social networks. After describing both studies, we will relate them to other relevant literature on chat rooms and social networking sites and compare the different ways that young people use the currently popular social networking sites compared to chat rooms, which have been around longer. We will show how - regardless of the seeming differences in online activities - both forms of online communication are important playgrounds for young people's development of identity and intimacy.

**Key Words:** Emerging Adults, Identity Development, Intimacy, Online Communication, SNS, Web 2.0, Chat Rooms, MySpace, Facebook.

*****

## 1.      Introduction

A growing number of young people worldwide spend their leisure time on the Internet communicating with others online. The most commonly used online communication tools are email, social networking sites, blogs, instant messaging, and chat rooms. In this chapter, we will focus on our research on chat rooms and social networking sites as well as relate this work to other relevant research that has examined teenagers' communication through these online contexts. Whereas chat rooms have been used for more than a decade, social networking sites are a relatively recent tool for online communication. However, both offer similar and unique ways for users to connect with others. In this chapter, we will highlight two aspects of these tools: First, we show that the technical and communication characteristics of chat rooms and social network sites lead young people to use each of them very differently and for different reasons. Second, as different as these applications and the behaviours within them are, we argue that young people use them, nonetheless, to ultimately connect to others and support their own individual development.

Since the introduction of the Web 2.0, social networking sites (SNSs) such as MySpace and Facebook have become especially popular among adolescents and emerging adults. The numbers of new members are still increasing: For example, in 2008, 68% of German online youth, age 14-19 years, reported having used social networking sites (for private reasons), whereas in 2007 it was just 40%.[2] In addition to online social networking platforms, young people in some countries are still using chat rooms as a tool for online interactions. In 2008, almost half of the young German population aged 12 to 19 reported chatting at least sometimes, and 29% reported chatting several times a week.[3]

Capitalising upon quantitative and qualitative research, this chapter will focus on two of our studies, one on chat rooms and the other one on social network sites to demonstrate how youth use these platforms for addressing developmental needs such as identity formation and social connect. The Austrian-American study on chat rooms, which was first published in 2005 in German[4], investigated adolescents' use of chat rooms (chapter two) in two countries, Austria and the U.S.A. Using participant observation and analysis of chat room conversations between teenage boys and girls, the study explored adolescents' gender and ethnic identity negotiations in both contexts. The second, study carried out at the Children's Digital Media Centre (CDMC@LA), examined young people's use of social networking sites, and was presented at the 'Cybercultures' conference (4th Global Conference: Cybercultures - Exploring Critical Issues, Salzburg, Austria, March 13-15, 2009); it was originally published in the Journal of Applied Developmental Psychology[5], and investigated emerging adults' online activities, their use of social networking sites for communication, and the overlap between their online and offline social networks (chapter three). College students in Los Angeles, CA, USA, participated in a two-step design, in which they were first asked to complete an in-person survey and then an online survey later that day. A variety of questions about online activities and with who people interacted with the most face-to-face, via instant messaging, and on social networking sites were included in the surveys. While not a central focus of this chapter, we will also refer to two more chapters, which describe research conducted at the Children's Digital Media Centre @ LA.[6] These chapters consider young people's use of chat rooms and focused on how adolescents use chat rooms in the service of adolescent developmental issues such as identity exploration and interconnection. Another qualitative study, which will also be described, was conducted at the Children's Digital Media Centre[7] and focused on how social networking sites are used to address core developmental issues, especially gender identity.

We will discuss our studies and the related research using a two-pronged approach (chapter four): On the one hand, we will show that the characteristics of Web 2.0, which are represented in social networking sites (such as more visualisation instead of mostly text-based communication or providing a broader semi-public audience), lead to a differentiated use of chat rooms compared to social networking sites. On the other hand, we argue that young people use both online communication tools, chat rooms as well as social networking sites, for primary developmental concerns such as identity and intimacy development.

## 2.        Identity in Teenage Chat Rooms

Adolescence as well as emerging adulthood has been described as a central period for identity development.[8] Particularly in western worlds, emerging adults are believed to be still working on their identity achievement.[9]

Many authors have commented on the diverse uses being made of the term 'identity'.[10] Two opposed positions can be identified: The 'strong' concept of identity implies a fundamental and durable sense of selfhood[11], whereas the more recent 'weak' concept stresses the fluidity, impermanence, complexity, and context sensitivity of identities, often focusing on the construction of identity in social interactions as well as on certain aspects of identity.[12] For analyses of the social construction of 'the self' it is useful to acknowledge a combination of diversity and fluidity on the one hand and of core and continuity on the other.[13] The concept of the self-stresses that people have only one self, but many aspects of self-identity, some of which may be more primary.[14] Identity formation happens through questioning and restructuring of the self, which is a process of experimentation, trial and error, searching, and testing.[15]

Chat rooms are public online spaces, where participants can participate in multiple simultaneous conversations with other users. Chat providers usually offer not only one, but many different rooms, and the participants can choose which room they want to chat in.[16] The separate rooms tend to target certain groups, (e.g. a certain age group coming from a particular city or region) and can deal with a range of topics, although general chat rooms also exist. Most chat rooms that teenagers use tend to be 'flirt chats': the young chatters want to get to know new people for romantic interest and communicate with them.

Early authors like Turkle, who wrote about the information and communication technologies, speculated that virtual communication provides the opportunity for young people to try and live new identities, such as 'gender swapping' in which teens can identify themselves as a different gender.[17] In contrast, more recent studies have found that young people do not often change their identities when they communicate online, but rather, display their offline gender and ethnic identity.[18] The study described below also shows empirically that adolescents do not use chat rooms for gender swapping, but instead seem more focused on the development of their own offline gender and ethnic identity.

A. Research Design

Qualitative data collection took place 2002-2003 in two geographic areas and with different ethnic groups: in Vienna, Austria, with migrant youth from Turkey and former Yugoslavia, and in Los Angeles, USA, with young Mexican-Americans.[19] Data collection, in Vienna and in Los Angeles, took place in youth centres, where teenagers came regularly in the afternoons with the intention to chat. Most of the 80 young people in the study at the time were between 14 and 16 years old, with a mean age of 15. Whereas the small group of Mexican-Americans was quite homogeneous - they were all girls and first generation immigrants from Mexico - the much bigger group of young people in Vienna was very heterogeneous. Turkey was the country of origin for most of the boys, for the girls it was the former Yugoslavia.[20] Some of them were first generation immigrants and some were second (or third) ones. The gender distribution was equal.

Based on the participant observation method[21] for data collection, the true identity of the participants was confirmed. In conducting research about online communication this is quite the exception because when one collects online-data (e.g. online-conversations), one often does not know who stands behinds the online personas. Sometimes online profiles do not represent the owner's offline identity in all aspects, e.g. the adolescents in the study often did not provide their real age when chatting but adapted their age to their chat partners' age which, of course, may be 'fake' as well.

Throughout the participant observation, the main focus was on collecting and analysing chat room conversations. For data collection, Waechter sat down next to the teenagers, followed their online conversations, and then asked them to copy and save the conversations. Additionally, she interviewed the girls and boys about their online-conversations and took detailed field notes. For data analysis, Waechter used the method of conversation analysis, and, more precisely, the 'Santa Barbara School.' Whereas classic conversation analysis as it was grounded by Sacks[22] is not led by theory but only by data, the 'Santa Barbara School'[23] also takes into account the institutional context and provided theoretical assumptions into the analysis. This approach is also referred to as studies of 'institutional talk' and studies of 'talk and social structure'.[24]

## B. Chat Rooms as Experimental Rooms

The analysis showed that for teenagers, chat rooms were opportunities for experimenting. New and otherwise forbidden behaviours could be tried with few repercussions. For instance, adolescents with migration backgrounds were free to try out conversations that their more traditional value system would not approve of. Typically, the teenage chatters reported that they did not know their chat partner in real life, but may have met before in an online chat room or were 'buddies' on instant messenger. For boys, the objective of chat communication appeared to be finding a girl who was willing to chat with them, and then, throughout the chat conversation trying to get a date with the girl (which, as they reported, never happened). As analysis of the interviews and the chat conversations showed, the girls' focus seemed to be more on the conversation itself, without having the goal of a date. They reported that they did not use chat rooms to meet a chat partner in real life, but to have exciting and entertaining conversations.[25]

## C. Gender in Teenage Flirt Chats

In both samples (Los Angeles & Vienna) researchers found that the use of teenage chat rooms provided a chance for loosening traditional values that determine gender-specific behaviour of migrant youth. The results indicate that girls were taking the opportunities that the online context provided them, and they were clearly experimenting. Their behaviour in chat rooms differed from how they were expected to behave in offline contexts (and as observed in the youth centres). This was especially true for the Mexican-American girls, but also for the Yugoslavian-Austrian girls, who used the conditions of chat rooms for their benefit. Unlike typical teenage cross-gender interactions offline, in chat rooms they cannot be judged by their physical appearance. This may have allowed girls to focus on the content of their conversations in a more self-confident way and to bring in their own desires and needs. Some boys appeared to be surprised by the strong and demanding behaviour of the girls, as illustrated by the following interview excerpt:

> *[...]*
> *mickeygirl90921: i asked you a question*
> *[...]*
> *mickeygirl90921: you didn't answer my question*
> *[...]*
> *mickeygirl90921: are you busy*
> *sophmoor16: not really*
> *mickeygirl90921: answer my question*
> *sophmoor16: wut question??????*
> *mickeygirl90921: scroll up ur screen*
> *sophmoor16: o 1987*
> *mickeygirl90921: so your going to be 15*
> *sophmoor16: no im gonna b 16*
> *mickeygirl90921: when next year*
> *sophmoor16: no in a couple of months my birthday is in january*
> *mickeygirl90921: ok*
> *[...]*
> *sophmoor16: u dont really like me 2 much do ya?*
> *mickeygirl90921: why*
> *sophmoor16: I dunno*
> *mickeygirl90921: you seem a nice guy*
> *sophmoor16: o*
> *[...]*

'Sophmoor16' seemed to misinterpret his chat partner's behaviour. She insisted upon receiving an answer which he thinks is a bit rude and made him believe that she was not interested in him. An alternative interpretation of her behaviour also seems appropriate; because she was interested in him, she really wanted to know his age. This observation demonstrates how the girls were more active in their conversations compared to face-to-face cross-gender conversations.[26]

Nevertheless, in such teenage flirt chats, the display of gender is as important online as offline. For example, the observed boys and girls as well as their chat partners used their first chance to display their offline gender identity in presenting themselves with nicknames that enabled the chat partners to attribute gender membership. Analysis shows that girls have to make their gender membership explicit in order to be recognised as girls, which means they have to use girls' first names or add 'girl' to the name. The results also show that boys do not need to do that, if a nickname is gender neutral everyone regards the person as male. There were no cases of 'gender swapping' or gender bending. Rather, the observed young people usually assumed their offline gender in the online chat space.

The girls used the nicknames to present themselves as sexually attractive; in the Austrian sample typical names were 'Sexygirl' or 'Sarisinbomba' ('Blond Bomb'). The nicknames the boys chose referred to their life style, interests and activities. Typical names were 'SubCuLtuRe' or 'Snoop016' where the part with numbers in it (which is called a 'flag') provides information about the age of the boy. With that stereotypical use of nicknames - the girls presented themselves as sexually attractive, the boys as active in public life - the young people displayed their gender membership. In the sample of the Mexican-American girls, they used the first question to confirm the partner's gender membership: using the code *asl* they asked for the partner's age, sex and location.[27] These are just some of the ways that the youth participants attempted to overcome the limitations of the disembodied environment.

D. Negotiations of Ethnicity

In this section we will show that ethnicity is also constructed in adolescents' chat room conversations. The Turkish teenagers from Austria displayed their ethnic identity already by choosing a particular chat room that was mostly used by Turkish migrant kids, but also by using a Turkish nickname, and by chatting only in Turkish. They and their chat partners used their nicknames not only to communicate their gender and their Turkish origin but also to show which town in Turkey their family originally came from by attaching Turkish license plate numbers to their nicknames (e.g. 'Sevda66' or Betül68'), or by using other references to their specific origin (e.g. 'Trabongüzeli' = 'Beauty from Trabon' or 'Daglarkizi' = 'Girl from the Mountain'). Interestingly, in the sample of Mexican-American girls, it was observed that the longer they had lived in the USA, the more likely they were to chat only in English and not use Spanish or a mix of English and Spanish anymore. However, even for those more acculturated to the host country and using the host's language, 'racialised' problems may occur as illustrated in the following conversation thread:

> *[...]*
> *anastasia15> how do you look like*
> *SubCuLtuRe> black spiky hair with blue ends, 1,75 tall*
> *brown eyes, skater*
> *SubCuLtuRe> you??*
> *anastasia15> what*
> *SubCuLtuRe> how do you look like*

---

*anastasia15> brown hair, green-brown eyes, white in the*
*face*
*SubCuLtuRe> white in the face?*
*anastasia15> yes why*
*SubCuLtuRe> what does that mean?*
*anastasia15> how do you look like?*
*[...]*

The boy 'SubCuLtuRe' does not know how to interpret the information that his partner is 'white in the face'. Whereas for her, it is normal to present her complexion her description was not conventional or easily interpreted by her chat partner, this does not seem to make any sense to him. As a supposedly native Austrian, so far he has had no reason to assume that his chat partner has a migrant background. Also, he is not familiar with complexion being part of a person's description. In this case, the conversation ended very quickly, quite possibly because of the misunderstanding. However, there were also examples of conversations where the sudden appearance of different ethic memberships did not disturb the flow of the chat.

E. Gender and Ethnic Identity in Chat Rooms
        Comparing the relevance of gender and ethnicity in chat room conversations, it seems that gender is even more important for a successful teenage flirt chat conversation. For instance, the analysis found that someone's perception of ethnic membership may switch without causing too much problems for the continuation of the conversation. That would not be possible if someone becomes suddenly aware regarding their conversation partner's gender. In contrast, because of adolescents' goal to chat with a potential romantic partner and their overall heterosexual orientation, we have to assume that a young person's 'gender bending' would disturb and probably end the conversation. The observed girls and boys try hard to not chat with a user who displays the same gender. If they cannot tell for sure by the nickname, they ask immediately for the chat partner's gender before continuing with the conversation. In the context of teenage flirt chats, girls have to chat with boys and boys with girls. In the whole period of participant observation only once was it observed that a girl pretended to be her offline best friends' male chat partner - for fun and with the knowledge of her best friend.[28]

F. Other Research on Chat Rooms and the Development of Identities
        Along these lines, in their chat rooms study, Subrahmanyam, Smahel, and Greenfield added a developmental perspective and found that identity information was provided more often by participants who described themselves as younger.[29] They noted that many chat nicknames seem to

utilise strong gender stereotypes and are used to attract potential partners. It appeared that nicknames may help to compensate for the absence of the body and the face. Chat rooms help adolescents address important developmental issues such as romantic partner selection or the development of gender identities.

A quantitative analysis of recorded chat conversations has found that gender was the most popular category of the adolescents' identity declarations.[30] These researchers also found that nicknames were used to express gender identities. For example, for participants who stated that they were male, 32% used male connoted nicknames, whereas for the participants who stated that they were female, 49% used female connoted nicknames.[31] Since it was typical for those participants to first ask their chat partners for age, gender, and location, it may not be as important to have a gendered nickname (although the nickname may matter as they serve to attract potential chat partners). The finding that girls are more likely to use their nickname to display their gender identity than the boys, provides support for the conclusion that gender-neutral nicknames are interpreted as male ones. Girls have to make their gender explicit because female identities are not perceived as the norm.

Regarding ethnic identities, Greenfield et al.[32] also report Tynes, et. al.'s[33] finding that teenage chatters identified themselves on the basis of race using racialised discourse. The researchers distinguish between implicit forms such as the use of Spanish or African American English and explicit forms such as self-identification, identifying in-groups, partner selection or expressing racial attitudes. They point out that unlike in conventional face-to-face settings, race is no longer taboo. The authors conclude that 'all teens and not just teens of colour [...] appear to be exploring ethnic and racial identities'[34] and that the use of chat rooms seems to encourage inter-ethnic interaction, which may otherwise be limited in face-to-face contexts.[35]

The research presented so far has shown that the process of achievement of identity, which is a primary adolescent concern, is continued in the online context of chat rooms. Adolescents use these flirt chats to interconnect with potential romantic partners and to experiment and practice such interactions. Those chat conversations may contribute not only to the development of their gender identity but also to their ethnic identity.

## 3.      Relation between Young People's Online and Offline Networks: Social Networking Sites

In the period of adolescence and emerging adulthood there are two basic developmental challenges: identity achievement and the development of intimacy. Friends are especially important for young people but also through interconnections with romantic partners, relatives and family youth seek to establish intimacy. There is evidence that adolescents and emerging adults also use online communication and online interconnections for offline concerns such as the need to interconnect with others.[36]

One central new communication tool of the Web 2.0 is social networking sites, which are especially popular among adolescents and emerging adults. What differences do we find in young people's use of chat rooms versus social networking sites? There are several specific features that may also influence how these communications tools are being used: Whereas the use of chat rooms is mainly text based, social networking sites allow and support visualisation, for example, users can upload pictures and videos to their social networking site. Another difference is that a profile on a social networking site typically has a larger audience than a chat conversation. Also, we have shown that in teenage chat rooms, users typically have not met their chat partners offline before. For the study presented next, we investigated whether young people using social networking sites use them for communicating with people whom they also know offline. Because research of social networking sites has just been emerging in the Anglo-American as well as in the German-speaking area, questions still remain as to what exactly young people do on these sites and with whom they interact.[37] The question that often has been raised but not sufficiently answered yet is about the 'online-offline-connection', especially the influence that online activities through social networking sites has on offline lives. Also at the 'Cybercultures' conference one topic of discussion was whether online interactions have to be regarded as 'real' experiences with a significant impact on one's offline live.

These concerns prompted the survey study of emerging adults, carried out at the Children's Digital Media Centre (UCLA). Some of the questions examined were:

> The prevalence and frequency of college students' use of social networking sites.

> Their reasons for using these sites.

> Whether they present their 'offline self'.

> Who they interact with online and whether these are offline friends as well.

> Whether they feel their online activities have any affect on their offline relationships.[38]

At the 'Cyberculture' conference, the results of two questionnaires were presented: The first was a paper-and-pencil survey given to students in the

Department of Psychology at California State University, Los Angeles. The second questionnaire was administered online later that day. It specifically asked about online and offline activities and the use of the Internet on that particular day.

The sample consisted of 110 college students; equally divided by gender. They ranged in age from 18 to 29 years with a mean age of 21,5. The majority (78%) were between 18 and 23 years old and the sample was ethnically diverse. The majority of participants were Latino (51%) and Asian (20%). Other ethnicities in the sample were (in order of their frequency): White/Caucasian, Mixed, African American, Native Hawaiian/Pacific Islander, and Middle Eastern (all between 10% and 2%). With regard to religious affiliation, 66% identified themselves as Christian, and almost a quarter reported no religious affiliation.

A. Usage of Social Networking Sites

Of our sample of 110 college students, 86 (78%) reported having a profile on a social networking site. Although more young men (82%) reported having such a profile than young women (75%), this was not a significant difference. Having a profile page on a social networking site was not related to the students' ethnic group membership or religious affiliation.

Of those students who had a profile, 61% reported having only one and 34% reported having two or three profiles. A few (5%) had four, five, or six accounts on social networking sites. The majority of participants used MySpace (88%). This was similar to the findings of Lenhart and Madden (2007), who found that 85% of teenagers using social networking sites have a MySpace profile. In our sample, only 8% had a profile on Facebook, and even less had one on Xanga, Bebo, or other sites. Although more recently, trends indicate that Facebook is becoming increasingly popular among adolescents and young adults.

The majority of participants in our sample could be characterised as frequent users: 57% reported checking their account or other people's profile at least once a day (half of those had their profile open all day or checked it several times a day). Another 23% reported visiting social networking sites every two to three days, and only 20% said that they go to such sites once a week or less.[39]

B. Reasons for Using Social Networking Sites

In order to assess why emerging adults had an account and their reasons for using it, participants with SNS profiles (n=86) were asked to indicate all of the statements that applied to them from a list provided with 12 items. The results suggested that the most common use of these sites was to interact with offline friends with 81% listing 'to stay in touch with friends I don't see often'. Other social reasons were also common, such as 'because all of my [offline] friends have accounts' (61%), 'to stay in touch with relatives and family' (48%), and 'to make plans with friends who they see often (35%). 'To fill up free time/not be bored' was also another frequent reason with 52% reporting this purpose. These data suggest that college students used their account to maintain and enforce their existing 'offline' social network. MySpace and other social networking sites are not only used to connect with friends and relatives who they do not have the chance to see very often but also to connect with their day-to-day friends with whom they frequently spend time with.

Interestingly, meeting new people was not a common reason for having a social networking site profile. Only 29% of students reported that they had a profile 'to meet new people' and 'make new friends', and 21% admitted that they use the profile 'to flirt'. It appears that the use of MySpace and similar sites is strongly related to participants' offline worlds, whereas research on Internet chat rooms has shown that adolescents and emerging adults use it to a larger extent to meet new people and to flirt.[40]

One key feature of social networking sites such as MySpace is the ability to create a presentation of oneself through a profile. The profile gives basic information about a person such as their name, age, school/job affiliation, interests such as music and sports, etc. Interestingly, the college students in our sample reported presenting their 'real self'. The majority (70%) reported never having made anything up about themselves or others on their profile and only 2% admitted to having frequently made something up. Of those who had ever made something up, they did so as a joke, 'to make myself look better', or 'to see if people notice'.[41]

C. The Friends' List

Another important feature of social networking sites is the friends' list. We were interested in how many 'friends' participants had on their friends' lists, how they decided who to add to their list, and if those offline friends were also online friends.

On average, participants with SNS profiles (n=86) reported having 137 friends with a range from 0 to 642 friends. However, two thirds of the participants had less than 100 friends. Forty percent had up to 50 friends on their friends' list and 26% had between 50 - 100 friends on their list. When asked how many of the people in their list they have met face-to-face, 27% reported having met everyone of their friends' list. On average, they reported having met 78% of the people in their friends' list face-to-face.

When asked why emerging adults add friends to their profile, more than two thirds (73%) answered that they 'will only add a person who they have met in person.' About half of them even reported to 'only add a person if they are a face-to-face friend.' Eleven percent of the SNS users said that they will add anyone who sends a friends request, and if the person who sends a request 'looks cool' only a few more said that they are willing to add him or her (17%). So looking cool helps a little but knowing the person offline, or at least having a friend who knows that person makes it a lot more likely that they will put them on their friends list (33% reported they 'will add a person who is a friend of a friend'). Regarding our research question about the link between online and offline social networks, these results provide further evidence that young people's online and offline social networks are interrelated as the participants' reasons for adding a person to their profile friend list are based on their offline connections.

The social networking sites that college students in our study used not only feature a friends' list but also a 'top friends list'. The results regarding the 'top' friends show that the best friends offline are the most likely ones to make it into the top friends' list; 68% of the students in the sample reported that they chose their best friends offline for their top list. Another, less frequent way of choosing their top friends was to reciprocate a friend who listed them on their top list (15%). Only 7% of respondents said they add people who ask for it or who put pressure to be in the top list. Quite a few did not use the top friends feature at all (15%) or had other criteria of selection (some participants mentioned family and relatives).[42]

## D. Reported Impact of Social Networking Sites on Offline Relationships

When asked whether experience on social networking sites had influenced their relationships, the majority of the SNS using college students in the sample (n=86) reported that it had not affected the relationship they have with friends (73%). Twenty percent reported that it has made them closer and only 25% reported that SNS had created problems with their friends.

We also asked if anything in their profile had caused trouble between them and their friends or family, and if anything in their profile had fixed a problem or cleared a misunderstanding. Twenty-one percent reported troubles, especially problems with their romantic partners. When asked to describe the nature of the problems experienced on social networking sites, quite a few young women reported romantic trouble in which their boyfriend was jealous of male online friends ('I had an ex-boyfriend as a friend, my current one got mad'; 'Guys would leave me compliments and my boyfriend would ask about them. It seemed to annoy him.'). Young men also experienced romantic difficulties ('My girlfriend is possessive and jealous'; 'Ex-girlfriend thought I was cheating on her'). Difficulties were not constrained to romantic relationships. Troubles with parents also resulted from online use. Specifically when family members viewed the college student's profile and discovered things the young adult did not wish them to see ('My sisters would look through and see that I had a boyfriend, I was not allowed to have one before, and they told my Dad').

A few respondents reported that having and using a profile affected their offline relationships in a positive way. Specifically, 11% of students reported that something on their profile page had fixed a problem or misunderstanding. All problems that the college students in the sample mentioned had to do either with their friends ('make sure my friend wasn't mad at me, where it would be harder to ask in person or by phone') and/or with their boyfriend/girlfriend ('A partner/friend at the time had feelings of betrayal, but once they saw my page they found out that they were wrong'). However, there were also incidents in which the problem that could be fixed by the profile page had been caused through the use of the profile in the first place ('My boyfriend could read my comments that I've left for the guys and see that I've done nothing to provoke obnoxious comments they've left me').[43]

E. Overlap between Online and Offline Social Networks

In order to further understand the levels of overlap between young people's online and offline social networks, students were asked to list the names of up to 10 people whom they interact with the most offline, on social networking sites, and through instant messaging. Based on these data, 2 x 2 x 2 contingency matrices were created that assessed the amount of overlap between these three settings for each person. If participants named 10 people in each area and there was no overlap, they could name up to 30 people. For this chapter, only the overlap between face-to-face and social networking site friends will be discussed.

Of the total sample, 73 students provided the names of their online and offline friends. Of these, eight (11%) had no overlap between their face-to-face friends and the friends with whom they interacted with on social networking sites. Sixteen people (22%) reported 100% overlap between those online friends and face-to-face friends. On average, we found half (49%) of their listed social networking site friends also among their top offline friends.

These results suggest that there is a connection between college students' online and offline social networks. In fact, a key characteristic of social networking sites is that they consist largely of people with whom the emerging adult is friends with or related to offline. Even some college students, who do not own a social networking site profile, reported that they visit MySpace or similar social networking sites.[44]

F. Further Research on the Connection between Online and Offline Networks

The results of the CDMC's study on social networking sites are corroborated by a recent study conducted in Austria questioning online users aged 14 to 39 years. In the press preview, the authors of the study report that the users of social networking sites know the majority of their contacts in person. They estimate that only a quarter of the contacts are just used online.

Furthermore, respondents' main reason for using social networking sites was to stay in contact/communicate with friends.[45] Similarly, in a recent qualitative study in Germany of how 13-16 year old girls and boys' participation in local online social networks ('www.localisten.de') related to local offline integration into peer networks, found that in the virtual day-to-day communication with friends continues.[46] As such, the teenagers' activities in such local online communities document and stabilise existing relationships with friends.

Other results from US populations support our findings. For instance, Ellison et al.'s study that examined whether offline social capital could be generated online with the use of the social networking site, Facebook, found that college students, particularly girls, reported using Facebook mostly to connect with people from their offline world, above all to keep in touch with old friends rather than to meet new people.[47] Similarly, Lenhart and Madden found that adolescents, particularly girls use social networking sites to keep in contact with peers from their offline life, either to make plans with friends that they see often or to keep in touch with friends they rarely see.[48]

G. Social Networking Sites and Identity

Recent research indicates that social networking sites should be seen as a cultural context in which young people engage in processes of identity development.[49] Manago et al. regard MySpace as a rich cultural context in which norms of social interaction and opportunities for self-presentation create new possibilities for experimentation and reflection about possible selves.[50] Each participant in a social networking site presents himself/herself through a profile, which can be modified every time the owner of the profile visits the site. In their qualitative study of MySpace using focus groups with college students, Manago and colleagues detected several aspects of self-presentation and identity formation.[51] Above all, the students used MySpace for presenting themselves in interactions with friends. Through the public performance they reify their selves, i.e. through the self-presentations intended for a more or less public audience they make themselves real. The use of social networking sites also creates opportunities for identity exploration. However, because of the online-offline connection, obvious contradictions between the profile and the offline characteristics would be realised by viewers. Some other aspects of social networking sites are that they are used for social comparison, to display social relationships through communication on the public comment wall or the friends' list, and to display membership in exclusive groups.

Regarding gender identity, Manago et al. conclude that gender role constructions on MySpace seem to correspond to gender role constructions in mainstream US culture: 'females as affiliative and attractive, males as strong and powerful'.[52] However, they also detected increasing pressure for young men to display their physical attractiveness.

Because young people's online world seems to represent an extension and elaboration of offline interaction, Manago et al. further conclude that social realities and roles translate into the online context.[53] Even though in our research on social networking sites, only a few students reported that the use of such sites has directly affected their face-to-face relationship, we suggest that it nonetheless has implications for young people's offline development.[54] First, emerging adults use such sites to interconnect with their peers, which is a core developmental issue during this life phase. Second, on social networking sites youth can present themselves in an experimental way, which contributes to the development of their sense of self. In both respects, social networking sites seem to provide a new developmental playground for adolescents and emerging adults.

## 4.    Comparing Chat Rooms and Social Networking Sites: Conclusions and Outlook

The studies on chat rooms and social networking sites that have been presented in this chapter did not only have different detailed research questions but also concerned different age groups. Whereas the chat room sample for the participatory observation consisted of adolescents, the study of social networking site was with emerging adults. Nevertheless, examining the findings from research on both contexts enabled us to develop assumptions about changes in young people's online behaviour and its implications from a developmental perspective.

First of all, we want to outline important differences between chat rooms and social networking sites. Whereas research on social networking sites has come to the conclusion that the people with whom the users of such sites connect are partly friends from offline life, previous research on teenage chat rooms has shown that young chat room users, above all, interact with strangers. Chat rooms have been used especially for meeting potential romantic partners (or at least for pretending that the chat partners may become potential romantic partners). They have provided a perfect space for experimental behaviour of how to be attractive to the opposite sex and how to flirt successfully. Social networking sites on the other hand are used more to keep in touch and for exchanging (textual and visual) information with offline friends. Whereas the interaction in chat rooms was focused on textual communication, social networking sites have made it easy to interact using text, pictures, and videos.

The differences lead to the conclusion that (online) self-presentation has become more important in newer online contexts. The study on chat rooms has shown that even though in some chat rooms it was possible to set up a profile, it was very common for adolescents to present themselves in the text-based conversations by giving a description of their physical appearance. In contrast, on social networking sites used by young people, the visualised self-presentation is one of the most important aspects. Comparing chat rooms with social networking sites, we therefore have to rethink some of our considerations about the implications of chat rooms. Our own as well as other research on chat rooms has stressed that the physical disembodiment of chat room participants might have implications for their behaviour. Furthermore, it has been posited that the physical disembodiment may even support the decline of gender hierarchies.[55] Whereas one may be tempted to think that online communication implies physical disembodiment, we now know that almost the opposite has happened. The rise of social networking sites suggests that adolescents' self-presentation of their bodies and faces becomes increasingly more important. On social networking sites much is communicated about the self through photos.[56] Of course, while in many chat rooms, it was common for users to have a profile with a picture of themselves; adolescents would have intense conversations about primary teenage concerns without the intervening influences of physical presence and physical embodiment. This argument seems harder to maintain now because adolescents use physical self-presentation for expressing and negotiating their identity when interacting online. If there is no possibility for a physical presentation, pictures will be presented as well descriptions of the missing physical appearance. This suggests that as online contexts have changed, so have youth behaviour - chat rooms and social networking sites have entirely different affordances, and youth have adapted to these affordances accordingly.

The development from chat rooms to social networking sites has another implication. Chat rooms usually have public rooms where several people can chat at the same time yet, they also offer separate rooms where private, one-on-one conversations may take place. Our research has shown that youth preferred private rooms for flirting and practicing romantic relationships. Social networking sites also provide the possibility for private communication, through sending messages to others but this is not solely the reason why they have become popular. The rise of social networking sites seems to be encouraging the semi-public playing out of identity negotiations and peer interactions. As Manago et al. have shown, the self-presentations of young users are intended for an audience of peers.[57] Many users keep their profile private which enables only their profile-friends to access all information. However, as the average number of friends that a teenager may have listed on their profile page can reach the hundreds or even thousands, even a private profile may be considered semi-public.

It is also interesting to compare social networking sites and chat rooms regarding gender identity. The research on both forms of online interaction confirms each other to a large part. Gendered expectations and behaviour are transferred from the offline to the online world. In chat rooms[58] as well as on social networking sites, young people seem to present themselves to a large part according to stereotypical gender norms.[59] It appears that on social networking sites, because of the limited forms of expression often concentrated on the profile picture, the stereotypical gendered display is more relevant than in offline contexts. However, on social networking sites young men seem to be experiencing an increasing pressure to display physical attractiveness.[60] Research on chat rooms has also found certain contexts with potential for a decline of stereotypical gender roles, e.g. girls cannot be interrupted by their male chat partners, as it is typical in face-to-face conversations.[61]

From a developmental perspective it may be more important to point out the similarities in young people's online behaviour in these two contexts rather than the differences. Young people use both chat rooms and social networking sites for essential developmental issues. Chat rooms are used for having first experiences with romantic partner selection, while the users of social networking sites have a stronger focus on visualised self-presentation. Whereas in chat rooms only the chat partner reacts to the text-based self-presentations, on social networking sites there is a quite a large audience (at least all contacts of one's friends' list) that may provide feedback - praise or criticise - to one's presentation through the profile. However, both forms of young people's actions, partner selection as well as the negotiation of the self through peer interaction, are primary developmental concerns and we see how young people are playing out different concerns based on the particular characteristics of the online context.

One chapter in this volume also investigates social aspects of the Web 2.0 and online social networking. Regarding online-offline-connections, the text by Somaiah is interesting. Her research interest was a subcultural group of young people, eating disorder survivors, who are usually extremely isolated because of their illness. However, using the Web 2.0 they form online communities and tell their life stories and stories of illness, which is assumed to contribute to the healing process. This research implicitly supports our assumption of the connectedness of young people's online and offline worlds. Developmental research on online communication and behavior of young people also assumes that users of interactive online forums such as social networking sites are co-constructing their online environments, which implies that their online and offline worlds are psychologically connected.[62]

Regarding future research, there is still a lack of studies combining different age groups into one research design. This is currently being done by the CDMC research team in Los Angeles. The same research design as used in the study on social networking sites has been extended to high school students (13-19 years of age) within the Los Angeles area. While data are still being analysed, our hope is to compare uses of social networking sites across these age groups (adolescents and emerging adults) using a developmental approach. Along these lines, results from an additional project by Waechter, Jäger, & Triebswetter on the use of the Web 2.0 and social networking is underway which focuses on socio-economically disadvantaged young people aged 12 to 19 years. Initial quantitative as well as qualitative results have been summarised in a research report[63] and further publications are currently being prepared.

# Notes

[1] K Subrahmanyam, S M Reich, N Waechter, & G Espinoza, 'Online and Offline Social Networks: Use of Social Networking Sites by Emerging Adults', in *Journal of Applied Developmental Psychology,* Social Networking on the Internet - Developmental Implications, K. Subrahmanyam, P. M. Greenfield, (eds), 29(6), 2008, pp. 420-433.

[2] M Fisch, & C Gscheidle, 'Mitmachnetz 2.0: Rege Beteiligung nur in Communitys. Ergebnisse der ARD/ZDF Online-Studie 2008', in *Media Perspektiven 7,* 2008, pp. 356-364.

[3] JIM 2008, *JIM-Studie 2008. Jugend, Information, (Multi-)Media. Basisuntersuchung zum Medienumgang 12- bis 19-Jähriger.* Herausgegeben vom Medienpädagogischen Forschungsverbund Südwest (LFK, LMK), Stuttgart, 2008.

[4] N Waechter, 'Doing Gender & Doing Ethnicity bei Jugendlichen in Chatrooms. Kann das neue Medium zur Verringerung von sozialer Ungleichheit beitragen?', in *Zeitschrift für Frauenforschung und Geschlechterstudien, 23* (3), 2005, pp.157-172.

[5] Subrahmanyam et al., 2008, op. cit.

[6] P M Greenfield, E F Gross, K Subrahmanyam, L K Suzuki, & B Tynes, 'Teens on the Internet. Interpersonal Connection, Identity, and Information', in *Computers, Phones, and the Internet. Domesticating Information Technology,* R. Kraut, M. Brynin & S. Kiesler (eds.), Oxford University Press, 2006, pp.185-200.

[7] A M Manago, M B Graham, P M Greenfield, & G Salimkhan, 'Self-Presentation and Gender on MySpace', in *Journal of Applied Development Psychology,* Social Networking on the Internet - Developmental Implications, K. Subrahmanyam, P. M. Greenfield, (eds), *29*(6), 2008, pp. 446-458.

[8] E H Erickson, *Identity, Youth and Crisis.* Norton, New York, 1968.
J J Arnett, 'Emerging Adulthood: A Theory of Development from the late Teens through the Twenties', *American Psychologist, 55,* 2000, pp. 469-480.

[9] Subrahmanyam, et al., 2008, op. cit.

[10] R Brubaker, F Cooper, 'Beyond Identity', in *Theory and Society* Vol. 29/1, February 2000. S Hall, 'Introduction: Who Needs 'Identity'?', in *Questions of Cultural Identity*, Hall, S., Du Gay, P. (Ed), Sage Publications, London, 1996. R Jenkins, *Social Identity*, Routledge, London, 1996.

[11] eEg. J E Marcia, 'Development and Validation of Ego Identity Status', in *Journal of Personality and Social Psychology*, 3 1966, pp. 551-558.

[12] for ethnic identity see e.g. Hall, 1996, op. cit.

for gender identity see e.g. C West, D H Zimmerman, 'Doing Gender', in *The Social Construction of Gender*. J. Lorber, S. A. Farell, Sage Publications, Newbury Park, 1991.

[13] L Jamieson, *Orientations of Young Men and Women to Citizenship and European Identity*. State of the Art Report of EC-project SERD-2000-00260, 2003.

[14] Jenkins, 1996, op. cit.

P Berger, & T Luckmann, *Die gesellschaftliche Konstruktion der Wirklichkeit*, Fischer, Frankfurt/Main, 1969.

[15] J P Jordan, 'Exploratory Behavior: The Formation of Self and Occupational Concepts', in *Career Development: Self-Concept Theory*, De E Super, R Starishevsky, N Matlin, & J P Jordan, (eds), Princeton: College Entrance Examination Board, 1963, pp. 42-78.

[16] For literature about how chat rooms function see e.g. M Beißwenger, (ed), *Chat-Kommunikation. Sprache, Interaktion, Sozialität & Identität in synchroner computervermittelter Kommunikation. Perspektiven auf ein neues Forschungsfeld*, ibidem-Verlag, Stuttgart, 2001.

I Willand, *Chatroom statt Marktplatz. Identität und Kommunikation zwischen Öffentlichkeit und Privatheit*, KoPäd Verlag, München, 2002.

[17] S Turkle, Life on the Screen: Identity in the age of the Internet, Simon & Schuster, New York, 1995.

[18] Greenfield, et al., 2006, op. cit.

Fix, T., Generation @ im Chat. Hintergrund und explorative Motivstudie zur jugendlichen Netzkommunikation, KoPäd Verlag, München 2001.

C L Halbert, *The Presentation of Self in Computer-Mediated Communication: Managing and Challenging Gender Identity*, Dissertation, University of Kentucky, 2000.

[19] In labeling their immigrant populations, Austria and USA have different traditions. In contrast to 'Mexican-Americans' in the USA, Turkish immigrants in Austria are not labeled Turkish-Austrians. One may conclude that Austria is less open towards immigrants or that the United States seeks to assimilate their immigrants. However, the different terms reflect a different perception of the immigrants.

[20] Of course, there must be reasons for this relation: It is easy to explain why no Turkish girls show up: Their parents simply do not allow them to visit institutions with opportunities to meet with young men. Even though the Austrian youth center has established a day when the Internet café opens for girls only, they may not come. Most of the Turkish immigrants in Austria have emigrated from rural areas and are a lot more traditional than the young Istanbul generation of today. As for the lack of former Yugoslavian boys the youth workers assume that they do not mix up with their Turkish peers and the youth center has become - to a certain extent - the Turkish guys' territory.

[21] N K Denzin, *Interpretive Interactionism*. Sage, Newbury Park, CA., 1989.

[22] H Sacks, 'Sociological Description', in *Berkeley Journal of Sociology,* 8, 1963, pp. 1-16.

[23] C West, and D H Zimmerman, 'Small Insults: A Study of Interruptions in Cross-Sex Conversations between Unacquainted Persons', in Language, Gender and Society. B. Thorne, C. Kramarae, N. Henley, (eds), Newbury House Publishers, Rowley/London/Tokio, 1983.

[24] G Psathas, *Conversation Analysis: The Study of Talk-in-Interaction*. Sage, Thousand Oaks, 1995.

[25] Waechter, 2005, op. cit.

[26] see e.g. C Thimm, Alter - Sprache - Geschlecht. Sprach- und kommunikationswissenschaftliche Perspektiven auf das höhere Lebensalter, Campus, Frankfurt/Main, 2000.

[27] Waechter, 2005, op. cit.

[28] Waechter, 2005, op. cit.

[29] Translated from German into English

[30] K Subrahmanyam, D Smahel, & P M Greenfield, 'Connection Developmental Constructions to the Internet: Identity Presentation and Sexual Exploration in Online Teen Chat Rooms' in *Developmental Psychology,* 42, 2006, pp. 1-12.

[31] ibid.

[32] Greenfield, et al., 2006, op. cit.

[33] B Tynes, *'What's Everyone's Race': Racialized Discourse and Self-Representation in Teen Chat Rooms*. Unpublished Master's Thesis. 2003.

[34] Greenfield, et al., 2006, op. cit., p. 19

[35] ibid.

[36] Subrahmanyam, et al., 2008, op. cit.

[37] Eg. Manago, et al., 2008, op. cit.

D Hoffman, 'Kult und Kultur, Spaß oder auch Ernst? Inszenierung und Kommunikation in sozialen Online-Netzwerken', in *Merz. Zeitschrift für Medienpädagogik, 52(*3), 2008, pp. 16-23.

A Tillmann, *Identitätsspielraum Internet: Lernprozesse und Selbstbildungspraktiken von Mädchen und jungen Frauen in der virtuellen Welt.* Juventa, Weinheim & München, 2008.

D M Boyd, 'Why Youth (Heart) Social Network Sites: The Role of Networked Publics in Teenage Social Life', *MacArthur Foundation Series on Digital Learning - Youth, Identity, and Digital Media Volume* (ed. D. Buckingham). MIT Press, Cambridge, MA, 2007.

N B Ellision, C Steinfield, C Lampe, 'The Benefits of Facebook 'Friends': Social Capital and College Students' Use of Online Social Network Sites', *Journal of Computer-Mediated Communication, 12*, 2007, pp. 1143-1168.

[38] Subrahmanyam, et al., 2008, op. cit.

[39] Subrahmanyam, et al., 2008, op. cit.

[40] Greenfield, et al., 2006, op. cit.

N Waechter, 'Chat Rooms and Girls' Empowerment', in *Youth Activism: An International Encyclopedia* (Vol. 1) L. R. Sherrod, C. A. Flanagan, & R. Kassimir, (eds), Greenwood Press, 2006, Westport, CT/ London, pp. 109-113.

Waechter, 2005, op. cit.

[41] Subrahmanyam, et al., 2008, op. cit.

[42] Subrahmanyam, et al., 2008, op. cit.

[43] Subrahmanyam, et al., 2008, op. cit.

[44] Subrahmanyam, et al., 2008, op. cit.

[45] D Karobath, *Social Media Studie: Nutzung von Web 2.0 Plattformen.* Presseaussendung von marketagent.com vom Juli 2009, 2009.

[46] E Sander, & A Lange, ''Die Jungs habe ich über die Lokalisten kennen gelernt'. Virtuelle Freundschaften oder Intensivierung der örtlichen Vernetzung unter Gleichaltrigen? ', in *merz, zeitschrift für medienpädagogik, 52*(3), 2008, pp. 24-31.

[47] Ellison et al., 2007, op. cit.

[48] A Lenhart, & M Madden, *Social Networking Websites and Teens: An Overview,* Pew Internet & American Life Project, Washington, DC, viewed on 6 November 2008, <http://www.pewinternet.org/pdfs/PIP_SNS_Data_Memo_Jan_2007.pdf>.

[49] Manago, et al., 2008, op cit.

Tillmann, 2008, op. cit.

A Thomas, *Youth Online: Identity and Literacy in the Digital Age.* Peter Lang, New York, 2007.

[50] Manago, et al., 2008, op. cit.

[51] Manago, et al., 2008, op. cit.

[52] Manago, et al., 2008, op. cit., p.455.

[53] Manago, et al., 2008, op. cit.

[54] Subrahmanyam, et al., 2008, op. cit.
[55] Waechter, 2005, op. cit.
[56] See Manago, et al., 2008, op. cit.
[57] Manago, et al., 2008, op. cit.
[58] Waechter, 2005, op. cit.
[59] Manago, et al., 2008, op. cit.
[60] Manago, et al., 2008, op. cit.
[61] Waechter, 2005, op. cit.
[62] K Subrahmanyam, & P M Greenfield, 'Communicating Online: Adolescent Relationships and the Media', in *The Future of Children; Children and Media Technology*, 18, 2008, pp. 119-146.
Subrahmanyam, Smahel, Greenfield, 2006, op. cit.
[63] N Waechter, B Jäger, & K Triebswetter, 'Internetnutzung und Web 2.0 Nutzung von Jugendlichen in Wien. Final report of the Austrian Institute for Youth Research, funded by the City of Vienna, MA 13 (Fachbereich Jugend/Pädagogik), Vienna, <http://vipja.files.word press.com/2009/12/internetnutzung_web-2_0_waechter.pdf>.

# Bibliography

Arnett, J.J., 'Emerging Adulthood: A Theory of Development from the Late Teens through the Twenties'. *American Psychologist, 55*, 2000, pp. 469-480.

Beißwenger, M. (ed.), *Chat-Kommunikation. Sprache, Interaktion, Sozialität & Identität in synchroner computervermittelter Kommunikation: Perspektiven auf ein neues Forschungsfeld.* ibidem-Verlag, Stuttgart, 2001.

Berger, P. & T. Luckmann, *Die gesellschaftliche Konstruktion der Wirklichkeit.* Fischer, Frankfurt/Main, 1969.

Boyd, D. M., 'Why Youth (Heart) Social Network Sites: The Role of Networked Publics in Teenage Social Life' in *MacArthur Foundation Series on Digital Learning - Youth, Identity, and Digital Media Volume.* D. Buckingham (ed), MIT Press, Cambridge, MA, 2007.

Brubaker, R. and F. Cooper, 'Beyond Identity', in *Theory and Society* Vol. 29/1, February 2000.

Denzin, N. K., *Interpretive Interactionism.* Sage. Newbury Park, CA., 1989.

Ellision, N. B., Steinfield, C. and C. Lampe, 'The Benefits of Facebook 'Friends': Social Capital and College Students' Use of Online Social Network sites'. *Journal of Computer-Mediated Communication, 12*, 2007, pp. 1143-1168.

Erickson, E. H., *Identity, Youth and Crisis.* Norton, New York, 1968.

Fisch, M. & C. Gscheidle, 'Mitmachnetz 2.0: Rege Beteiligung nur in Communitys. Ergebnisse der ARD/ZDF Online-Studie 2008', in *Media Perspektiven 7*, 2008, pp. 356-364.

Fix, T., *Generation @ im Chat: Hintergrund und explorative Motivstudie zur jugendlichen Netzkommunikation.* KoPäd Verlag, München 2001.

Greenfield, P. M., Gross, E. F., Subrahmanyam, K., Suzuki, L.K., & B. Tynes, 'Teens on the Internet: Interpersonal Connection, Identity, and Information', in *Computers, Phones, and the Internet. Domesticating Information Technology.* R. Kraut, M. Brynin & S. Kiesler (eds.), Oxford University Press, 2006, pp.185-200.

Gscheidle, C. & M. Fisch, 'Online 2007: Das 'Mitmach-Netz' im Breitbandzeitalter: PC-Ausstattung und Formen aktiver Internetnutzung: Ergebnisse der ARD/ZDF Online-Sudie 2007'. *Media Perspektiven, 8*, 2007, pp. 393-405.

Hall, S., 'Introduction - Who Needs 'Identity'?', in *Questions of Cultural Identity.* S. Hall and P. Du Gay, (eds), Sage Publications, London, 1996.

Jamieson, L., *Orientations of Young Men and Women to Citizenship and European Identity.* State of the Art Report of EC-project SERD-2000-00260, 2003.

Jenkins, R., *Social Identity.* Routledge, London, 1996.

JIM 2008, *JIM-Studie 2008: Jugend, Information, (Multi-)Media. Basisuntersuchung zum Medienumgang 12- bis 19-Jähriger.* Herausgegeben vom Medienpädagogischen Forschungsverbund Südwest (LFK, LMK), Stuttgart, 2008.

Jordan, J. P., 'Exploratory Behavior: The Formation of Self and Occupational Concepts', in *Career Development: Self-Concept Theory.* D. E. Super, R. Starishevsky, N. Matlin, & J. P. Jordan, (eds.), College Entrance Examination Board, Princeton, 1963, pp. 42-78.

Halbert, C. L., *The Presentation of Self in Computer-Mediated Communication: Managing and Challenging Gender Identity.* Dissertation, University of Kentucky, 2000.

Hall, S. and P. Du Gay, *Questions of Cultural Identity.* Sage Publications, London, 1996.

Hoffman, D., 'Kult und Kultur, Spaß oder auch Ernst?: Inszenierung und Kommunikation in sozialen Online-Netzwerken'. *Merz: Zeitschrift für Medienpädagogik*, 52(3), 2008, pp.16-23.

Karobath, D., *Social Media Studie: Nutzung von Web 2.0 Plattformen.* Presseaussendung von marketagent.com vom Juli 2009, 2009

Lenhart, A., *Adults and Social Network Websites:* Report 'Social Networking, Communities, Web 2.0' of the Pew Internet and American Life Project. viewed on 7 April 2009, <http://www.pewinternet.org/Reports/2009/Adults-and-Social-Network-Websites.aspx>.

Lenhart, A. & Madden, M., *Social Networking Websites and Teens: An Overview.* Pew Internet & American Life Project, Washington, DC, viewed on 6 November 2008, <http://www.pewinternet.org/pdfs/PIP_SNS_ Data_ Memo _Jan_2007.pdf>.

Manago, A. M., Graham, M. B., Greenfield, P. M. & G. Salimkhan, 'Self-Presentation and Gender on MySpace'. *Journal of Applied Development Psychology,* Social Networking on the Internet - Developmental Implications, K. Subrahmanyam and P. M. Greenfield, (eds), 29(6), 2008, pp. 446-458.

Marcia, J. E., 'Development and Validation of Ego Identity Status'. *Journal of Personality and Social Psychology*, no. 3, 1966, pp. 551-558.

Psathas, G., *Conversation Analysis: The Study of Talk-in-Interaction.* Sage, Thousand Oaks, 1995.

Sacks, H., 'Sociological Description'. *Berkeley Journal of Sociology*, no. 8, 1963, pp.1-16.

Sander, E. & A. Lange, "Die Jungs habe ich über die Lokalisten kennen gelernt'. Virtuelle Freundschaften oder Intensivierung der örtlichen Vernetzung unter Gleichaltrigen?' *Merz: Zeitschrift für Medienpädagogik*, 52(3), 2008, pp. 24-31.

Subrahmanyam, K., Reich, S. M., Waechter, N. & G. Espinoza, 'Online and Offline Social Networks: Use of Social Networking Sites by Emerging Adults'. *Journal of Applied Developmental Psychology*, Social Networking on the Internet - Developmental Implications, K. Subrahmanyam and P. M. Greenfield, (eds), 29(6), 2008, pp. 420-433.

Subrahmanyam, K. & P. M. Greenfield, 'Communicating Online: Adolescent Relationships and the Media'. *The Future of Children; Children and Media Technology*, 18, 2008, pp. 119-146.

Subrahmanyam, K., Smahel, D., & P. M. Greenfield, 'Connection Developmental Constructions to the Internet: Identity Presentation and Sexual Exploration in Online Teen Chat Rooms'. *Developmental Psychology*, 42, 2006, pp. 1-12.

Thimm, C., *Alter - Sprache – Geschlecht: Sprach- und kommunikationswissenschaftliche Perspektiven auf das höhere Lebensalter.* Campus, Frankfurt/Main, 2000.

Thomas, A., *Youth Online: Identity and Literacy in the Digital Age.* Peter Lang, New York, 2007.

Tillmann, A., *Identitätsspielraum Internet: Lernprozesse und Selbstbildungspraktiken von Mädchen und jungen Frauen in der virtuellen Welt.* Juventa, Weinheim & München, 2008.

Turkle, S., *Life on the Screen. Identity in the Age of the Internet.* Simon & Schuster, New York, 1995.

Tynes, B., *'What's Everyone's Race': Racialized Discourse and Self-Representation in Teen Chat Rooms.* Unpublished Master's Thesis. 2003.

Waechter, N., 'Chat Rooms and Girls' Empowerment', in *Youth Activism: An International Encyclopedia* (Vol. 1). L. R. Sherrod, C. A. Flanagan, & R. Kassimir, (eds), Greenwood Press, 2006, Westport, CT/ London, pp.109-113.

——, 'Doing Gender & Doing Ethnicity bei Jugendlichen in Chatrooms. Kann das neue Medium zur Verringerung von sozialer Ungleichheit beitragen?'. *Zeitschrift für Frauenforschung und Geschlechterstudien*, 23 (3), 2005, pp.157-172.

Waechter, N., Jäger, B., & K. Triebswetter, K. *Internetnutzung und Web 2.0 Nutzung von Jugendlichen in Wien.*Final report of the Austrian Institute for Youth Research, funded by the City of Vienna, MA 13 (Fachbereich Jugend/Pädagogik), Vienna, <http://vipja.files.wordpress.com/2009/12/internetnutzung_web-2_0_waechter.pdf>.

West, C. and D. H. Zimmerman, 'Doing Gender', in *The Social Construction of Gender*. J. Lorber and S. A. Farell, Sage Publications, Newbury Park, 1991.

——, 'Small Insults: A Study of Interruptions in Cross-Sex Conversations between Unacquainted Persons', in Language, Gender and Society. B. Thorne, C. Kramarae, and N. Henley (eds), Newbury House Publishers, Rowley/London/Tokio, 1983.

Willand, I., *Chatroom statt Marktplatz. Identität und Kommunikation zwischen Öffentlichkeit und Privatheit*. KoPäd Verlag, München, 2002.

**Natalia Waechter**, sociologist, is a Senior Researcher at the Institute for Advanced Studies, Vienna, and she is Lecturer at the Department for Educational Science, University of Vienna, Austria. As a Post-doc Researcher at the UCLA she has collaborated with the Children's Digital Media Center. Her research interests are youth research, gender studies, sociology of migration, and research on online communication.

**Kaveri Subrahmanyam** is a Professor in the Department of Psychology, California State University, Los Angeles, United States, and Associate Director of the Children's Digital Media Center, Los Angeles, United States. Her research interests are children's and adolescents' interactions with digital media; games and their impact on children's cognition; as well as dual language learning.

**Stephanie M. Reich** is an Assistant Professor in the Department of Education, University of California, Irvine, United States. Her research interests focus on child development with the explicit goals of understanding children's social lives and how to promote healthy developmental trajectories.

**Guadalupe Espinoza** is a doctoral student in the Department of Psychology, University of California, Los Angeles, United States, specialising in Developmental Psychology. Her main research interest is adolescent development, specifically, the dynamics of peer relationships in the school and online context.

# Cybergrace among Eating Disorder Survivors in Singapore

## Chand Somaiah

**Abstract**
This chapter, in a spirit similar to Arthur Frank in *The Wounded Storyteller*[1], shows how the injuries of the eating disordered can become seeds of their self-stories. Through everyday life stories and reflections on their personal blogs, recovering eating disordered individuals forge bonds of empathy between themselves and their readers. Growing pains and telling pains in defining despair and disorder, in expressing trials while journeying through individualised and therefore unchartered paths for recovery make for painful and active typing and reading. Illness experiences in post-modern cyberspaces can serve as cultural (re)sources of healing and can aid in empirical studies of the socio-cultural roots and routes of illness and recovery. Illness, Frank asserts, is about learning to cope with lost control. Cyberspace then offers a medium to reclaim some semblance of lost control, a space where potential narrative wreckage can be rescued. The chapter conceptualises such online confessionals as proof of embodied community, sites where medically treated monadic bodies re-connect. Jennifer Cobb's concept of 'cybergrace'[2] allows for a tuning in to what can be observed as spiritually charged curative networks of support towards full recovery.

**Key Words:** Eating Disorders, Illness Narratives, Cyberspace, Cybergrace, Networks of Support, Recovery.

*****

**1.    I was chanting the mantra in my head [...] I need to finish all now to gain weight to get well to let go to set myself free - Helen**
This chapter is a modest attempt to illustrate a fiercely embodied and youthful hungering for connection and community in a technological age of supposed ever increasing (dis)connect. It aims to show how socially defined vulnerable groups such as those bearing the label of mentally disordered, specifically the eating disordered (ED) in the Republic of Singapore - a city-state in Southeast Asia whose Tourism Promotion Board has actively promoted as a 'foodie's paradise'- make use of cyberspace to assert and express themselves as creative, proactive, often spiritually-charged individuals who form bonds of cyber-commensality via social networking tools and interconnected blogospheres.

Ethical acts of storytelling are explored through the textual analysis of virtual modes of expression. These outlets of localised vocalisation include thirteen personal blogs of recovering and recovered ED individuals aged between late teens to mid-twenties, various online community forums and social networking groups based on common interest or self-help which serve to actualise a community of not only pain, but of promise - of full recovery. I therefore did not restrict my research in cyberspace to blogs but to any kinds of online communication. This included e-mail interaction and support found in online-forums and sometimes perhaps maintained via instant messaging tools such as Microsoft Messenger (MSN). My research was therefore multi-locale. Focusing on ED recovery as a topic rather than on a specific site or two enabled me therefore, using discourse analysis, to recognise how the presentation of self, discussions on the trials of treatment, complaints about the lack of understanding from a largely uninformed, insensitive general public and declarations of religious faith were arranged to enable an embracing of a genuine pledge to getting better.

The findings are constantly triangulated with data from my ongoing fieldwork in the form of in-depth biographical face-to-face interviews with eleven identified recovered and recovering ED youth and my participant observation during monthly support group sessions held at the only specialised ED medical centre on the island where I informally interact with inpatients, outpatients, medical professionals, parents, friends. 'Survivors' is the term used during support group sessions to identify those who are suffering from or who have suffered from an ED of any kind. I adopt and employ the term here because I feel it truly encompasses with dignity and honour, the emotional, moral, physical and spiritual bravery demanded during recovery. The term is positive and empowering, and a move away from feminising, infantilising and victimising stances associated with the word 'patient' in the arguably patriarchal and sometimes patronising world of biomedicine. The potential impact of online eating disorder communities for shaping individual and collective identities, for cyber-activism among youth, for professional-patient interactions, and for the ongoing debate of what constitutes ethical web-based research with vulnerable groups is also explored.

This chapter while desisting being a utopian rave about the power and potential of online support circles among ED survivors in Singapore, critically celebrates it. It affirms and acknowledges the largely pro-recovery stance in the blogosphere as being positively life-affirming and enriching. The spiritual content so prevalent on some of the blogs will be analysed with the help of Jennifer Cobb's 'Cybergrace' to better appreciate what I found to be curative cybernautic networks of support among certain circles charmed by a highly personal yet very public commitment to actively choose paths towards recovery.

**2.      (B)Logging On - Researching Recovery in Cyberspace**
      While the World Wide Web (WWW) can be regarded as a supplementary resource for social research, for this chapter, the Internet was prime fieldwork site for data. The discovery of a blog (sub)culture was a surprise to me. I found out about it through someone at my first support group session. None of the blogs or online group URLs, names of bloggers or dates of blog posts are mentioned here to guard the privacy of these individuals some of whom are below 21 years old. In instances where I have quoted at length it is with permission by the adult author. Since 2007, as part of my 'internetography'[3] or 'virtual enthnography'[4], I actively visited the blogs of those who spoke of their eating disorder and recovery journeys. To place their blog posts in context, some of the internet usage occurred away from personal laptops at home or in the hospital but at university or at the gym using personal phones. The geographic spread of the bloggers was limited, and deliberately so, to Singapore. Blogs often were updated late into the night and response time from other bloggers varied.
      In some blogs the ED featured as a strong presence, in others less so. It has been highlighted that personal blogs provide a potential area of research that moves beyond using community as a conceptual frame but instead utilises narrative analysis to understand (inter)relationships and the nature of community.[5] I thus embarked on this call and was able to examine the gamut of individual tactics to make sense of an ED and recovery. Some blogs had a blog roll that linked me to other blogs by other recovering or recovered ED individuals. The bloggers whose blogs I visited often interacted on each others' sites through comments of encouragement, empathy and sympathetic humour in response to sometimes considerably lengthy narratives of trauma. I was thus able to not only observe their relationships to their blogs and each other but topical trends, the local lingo of ED, compare my data and marvel at the sense of community support here.

**3.      We have God with us, not alone, never alone - Dawn**
      Jennifer Cobb's 'cybergrace'[6] speaks of the divine and divinities that are manifested in computer mediated communication. She embraces a holistic view of embodiment, spirituality and godly love that is transmitted and touches users of the Web. I employ the word because it was what I intuitively felt was occurring in the blogospheres of the ED community in Singapore. One blogger quotes a missionary she meets in a foreign land who advises against becoming a 'spiritual anorexic' or 'spiritual bulimic' and she discusses how this term resonates within her deeply, after her dark experiences in anorexia. Her posts uplift and inspire not only me (a non-ED individual), - she has a large following of readers in Singapore and abroad who comment, praise and leave comments of thanks on her posts. She ponders upon a 'god-shaped hunger' within everybody and makes interesting

links with her experience with anorexia and her spiritual quest. Her quotes from the Bible relate to nourishment, fasting, feasting but above all a commensality and endless love. Such quotes from the Bible were found on a number of the sites from ex or recovering ED girls.

The ED was also referred to as the 'devil,' as 'stupid satan'. Dawn, a twenty-three year old community outreach executive who used to suffer from anorexia and depression, summons the name of Jesus to 'curcumsise'(sic) her ED thoughts. She tells herself, 'Jesus doesn't want Dawn to starve,' decides 'God needs to be put again as priority', and promises, 'I WILL FIGHT WITH THE UNFAILING STRENGTH OF THE LORD TO EAT LIKE A NORMAL HUMAN BEING'. In a (dis)similar vein, Gayle, a twenty year old university student, Gayle sometimes juxtaposes prayers seeking mercy with profanities against herself, the medium of the Internet or against people who do not understand. She sometimes makes direct (rhetorical) pleas to her readers - a common motif in the inner sanctums of these online confessionals where Judgment Day is spoken about and where gluttony, sin, guilt, grace, hell/heaven is contemplated.

**4.     Off/Online Marginality & Writ Bodies**

Cyber-communicating and blogging can help overcome barriers resulting from stigmatised physical human bodies.[7] Bodily sensorial was projected in the blogs I encountered to a large extent. The body in these blogs becomes the point of reference for the shedding of problems with food and the invention of new imaginings of the self, post-recovery.

Some blogs such as those of Stan, Gayle, Dawn and Helen have food diaries with caloric content charted out to pain-staking detail to the point of counting croutons. These food journals are self-assessed harshly. Insomnia, obsessive exercise, baking adventures, experiences of being at the ward and meals there, and reactions to various medications are shared.

In some blogs, clothing and identities feature more prominently than in others. In Chloe's blog, she often posts what she wears to work daily from the 'bowels of (her) wardrobe', sometimes generating comments about what clothes can make her look less 'fat'. Roberta Seid in her book *Never Too Thin* does not underestimate clothing as merely an exercise of compliance to social norms but asserts that it influences our sense of identity profoundly, 'Dressing is also a virtual process of self-creation, of self-portraiture'.[8] To the lay observer EDs can be both visibly or invisibly writ on the body and the tensions that both possibilities bring out continues to be a source of concern for survivors.

**5.      Come to the Table of Feasting - Tessa**

Those who are recovering from or who have recovered from an ED, both diagnosed and undiagnosed, often reveal on their blogs and during support group sessions how alone they felt in the depths of their problems around food and eating. It has been offered that ED individuals tend to feel they are facing an ED alone because they are subject to other's biomedical and/or folk constructions of it.[9] In a conversational-style interview Isabel revealed something that others have confided to me as well, 'You're so isolated when you have the ED.' The Internet can then be attractive to those who yearn for safe social contact but are in the clutch of the disorder's self-imposed retreat from society.[10] Through everyday life stories and reflections on their personal blogs, recovering ED individuals form bonds of empathy between themselves and their readers. From the rich corpus of online material that came my way from hyperlink to hyperlink, it is evident that the articulation of the self after the trauma of the ED finds community in cyberspace.

**6.      Seeds of Self-Stories Midst Pathographies of Pain - Re-enchanting Narratives on the Net**

In a spirit similar to Arthur Frank in *The Wounded Storyteller*[11], there are many illustrations of how injuries of the ED can become the seeds of their self-stories. Frank asserts that the medical narrative becomes 'The story of illness that trumps all others in the modern period'.[12] Complying with narrative moulds of medical authorities in most respects, the online narratives I studied revealed effervescent spiritual dimensions that are provocatively and positively re-enchanting. Illness experiences in post-modern cyberspaces can serve as cultural (re)sources of healing which can aid in empirical studies of the socio-cultural roots and routes of illness and recovery.

While cyberspace offers a medium to reclaim some semblance of control lost during illness, a space where potential narrative wreckage can be rescued, online membership to eating disorder causes can serve to turn illness into meta-control. An example includes membership to Facebook causes to raise awareness about eating disorders. Blogging can be a means through which the 'dyadic body'[13] proffers its own body and obtains the comfort that others recognise what torments it. These online confessionals can be conceptualised as proof of embodied community, sites where medically treated monadic bodies re-connect.

**7.      Damage (Meta)Control, 'Spoiled Identity', Self-Censorship & the Sacred**

Recovering eating disordered individuals give voice to experiences that Prozac prescriptions cannot communicate. While voices of recovering eating disordered individuals are embodied in particular persons, in the democratic space of the Internet, they are simultaneously social. Examining explicit sculpting of the body-self online through illness narratives can serve to shed new light on Erving Goffman's ideas of management of stigma, presentation of the self and 'spoiled identity'.[14]

The identity positions of the bloggers were that they had or were suffering from an ED. Gayle is self-reflexive and is extremely particular not to be perceived as 'promoting ED'. Self-censorship is sometimes a moral issue dealt with at a personal level by the bloggers who keep open blogs. Her reflections on readership of the blogs of other ED survivors however shows how cyberspace has allowed her to plug into a community of other wounded storytellers who struggle to tell their recovery journeys while providing hope for others that they are not alone in their trials.

The blogs sometimes challenge the bloggers into new spaces of interiority where their inner demons are confronted in front of an audience of other recovering ED bloggers and strangers. Gayle speaks of her 'amazing' 'ed fighter friends' and sometimes speaks directly to them in her posts. Sometimes when feeling at a loss, or weak in the battle, the positive, life-affirming friendships she's made on and offline with other ED survivors proves, along with her blogging, to provide a sense of accountability to herself with relation to others. Soft social pressure in the form of Durkheimean mechanical solidarity seems to be a tremendous aid in recovery journeys. A consultant psychiatrist whom I conducted face-to-face interviews with links recovery models using support groups to the kinds of support received from Alcoholics Anonymous where peer pressure to recover produces positive outcomes.

Gayle writes about her damaged teeth as a result of her excessive purging. She regrets how hard recovery is, because even if the ED is kept at bay, 'the aftermath' left in the body takes time to settle. From her consumption of other blogs she realises she is not alone in being 'denied' a clean release from 'the chains'. Her metaphoric language of the prison is reflective of how many others I've come across refer to their condition. Cyberspace allows for empathy to be felt between two kindred spirits negotiating spoiled identities, to connect. Gayle feels like she can relate to others like her. She understands completely the steep peaks and low valleys of other recovering bulimics and wishes release for a particular ex-ED girl from the long-term biological consequences of her previous condition. Cobb credits cyberspace in birthing new 'faith communities' that exist on a geographically unbounded platform and yet are founded upon intensely personal interactions.

There have been discussions that alliance to an ED identity is an obstacle to recovery.[15] The bloggers whose blogs I studied however self-identified as recovering or having recovered from an ED. Their identity therefore weighed in favour of recovery and post-recovery midst other multi-hyphenated identities. I read these blogs as a taste of what it feels like journeying towards recovery, to get a glimpse in understanding the many diverse problems on their plate that need addressing. Out of all the blogs I read, only one seemed to identify as fully recovered and was able articulate eloquently her past ED experiences with the benefit of complete hindsight.

## 8.        Recovery is a journey not a destination - Isabel

Susan Sontag's ideas about metaphors of illness can be useful when conceptualising recovery as a non-linear narrative journey. She speaks in her *Illness as Metaphor* of the ill as possessing 'a more onerous citizenship', being obliged to use the un-preferred passport to journey from the 'kingdom or the well' to the 'kingdom of the sick.'[16] She verbalises that she is interested in what it is truly like to emigrate to that second-class kingdom and discusses the often-oppressive uses of illness as a metaphor. Illnesses - and eating disorders are no exception - are often subjected to macabre metaphoric thinking. While Sontag warns against dishonest understandings of illness via the prejudiced figures that dot the backdrop of our social imagination, I posit that from the strong lyrical language and magical realism on curative cyber-spaces I visited, metaphor could indeed be a rich weapon ED individuals arm themselves with as they resist the assorted biases they encounter on a daily basis and which they fight against internalising. While Sontag seeks to dedicate her inquiry towards a liberation of illness from metaphor using the case of tuberculosis and cancer, that is not my aim here. Here I seek to move inside and beyond metaphor to perhaps elucidate why certain images among the ED community here keep cropping up. I was interested in how the individual bloggers seek new visual, religious, emotive imaginings to make sense of their clinical diagnosis.

Friends talk Gayle out of succumbing to her ED, personifying the ED as an abusive lover, 'ed is such an asshole, why do you keep listening to him?!' Helen, a twenty-five year old recovering anorexic with binge-purge subtype, speaks sarcastically of a harrowing weekend 'rendezvous with (her) lover, Mr ED' when left home alone. Stan, a recovering ED individual who is undergoing mandatory military national service, leaves a comment on particularly trying day at the hospital for her where tensions run high between patient and psychologist:

> I guess she doesn't want to let ED have a foot in the door
> this time. No chances, whatever. Show it to her that you're
> fucking doing it, stiff upper lip and stilettos on ED's ass,
> and she'd be proud of you! =p and all of us too!

She makes the brave decision to 'seek divorce from ed'. This quintessential image of the femme defeating an eating disorder is remarkable. The metaphorising of the ED in terms of a romantic relationship gone sour where one needs out was a recurrent theme that emerged from my study of the blogs. Lea, a twenty year old university student and an ex-gymnast, address 'Mr. Ed' directly, telling him to 'please go play with someone else, I'm quite done playing with you.' The metaphors employed thus serve to provide emotional and spiritual ammunition against the enemy, the eating disorder.

With respect to cyberspace, Cobb argues that metaphors are the 'primary currency' we employ to 'access' the digital world and therefore the moral content of the metaphors used in this medium 'carry additional weight'.[17] I posit that metaphors associated with EDs are the fundamental means by which survivors and those who support them map escape routes from illness towards recovery.

## 8.1     Baldev

One of my informants, Baldev, a recovered male anorexic who is in his late twenties and who is working, spoke of befriending an American woman, who had documented her recovery process on her blog. He used to email her a lot to seek assurance for the changes he was himself going through during his personal recovery journey. He remembers asking her, 'What am I feeling, is it correct?', 'I think I'm putting on weight too fast, is it alright?,' 'Will it ever go away?' She used to respond to his queries with encouragement. My informant even added her on MSN so as to be able to continue discussions with her.

He tells me that someway halfway during his recovery, he went to an online forum and came across a 'kinda distressing' entry from a girl who was 'like crying out for help'. He emailed her telling her, 'I'm in the same situation as you.' He seemed to have been able to pay-it-forward with cyber-friendship and support, helping a perfect stranger in Australia the best way he could. He could even place his recovery journey in perspective, understanding that she was at that stage, in a far worse condition than he was. He tells me how she used to come online frequently and how he used to 'share with her my stuff.' He explained to me how at an early stage of his recovery, when others were pressuring him to eat right, he got so terrified of eating that he 'would just chew and not swallow the food.' He learnt after his confession to her, that she did the same thing as well. After a period of non-communication when she moved away to live with her boyfriend, Baldev met her online again and asked her in general, how she was. He was cautious not to ask too bluntly, admitting, 'I know how difficult it is to approach. So I thought I'd ask about everything around but not that topic.' After some sensitive side-stepping he gathered that she had gotten a lot better from the previous time. She was doing drugs on the side though. Baldev's interaction with her apart from allowing him to comprehend his own recovery introspectively from another angle where he was providing support by being a wounded storyteller to someone else, allowed him to come to the conclusion that 'people overseas have it a lot worse'. He said this with respect to a supposed more liberal lifestyle that involved drugs, 'clubbing and drinks.' He remains my only face-to-face interviewee who believes that recovery in Singapore is easier than recovery abroad. He says this not with a respect to a comparative institutional help for ED survivors but with regard to a broader, social environment where addictive behaviours during the difficult phase of recovery such as substance abuse might be more easily facilitated due to access, availability and different social mores.

Facebook facilitates occasions for re-connecting with friends pre- and post-recovery. Baldev speaks of going to the temple and seeing someone whom he had not seen for about seven years. He describes how he was 'just talking to her normally, like how (he) would now.' The next day she messaged him on Facebook saying that she's really happy that he had opened up. He asked her what did she mean to which she responded, 'The person I knew back then was like this: very conserved, a shy person. And now I see this confident Baldev, a total surprise!' He used this example to illustrate to me the obvious changes in him in terms of his personality and public persona. The Facebook message from a person from his past confirmed to him that presently, socially he is fine, 'I'm kinda enjoying myself.' Baldev also spoke of coming across 'a support site where they teach you to love yourself and to love' and which he describes as 'spiritual'. To this day he receives emails from 'this particular lady, some sweet lady' because '(he) didn't unsubscribe' despite having fully recovered some five years ago.

## 8.2    Isabel

The only local person Baldev interacted with online was Isabel, a recovering bulimic, who has been described in a local women's magazine as being a 'cyber-guardian angel' and 'an online Big Sister' to youth struggling with ED. Isabel started seeking treatment in 2002 and became actively involved at Support Group sessions a year later. She set up the email address for the support group and has been helping to monitor ever since. Some weeks she receives no emails yet sometimes receives up to six a week. She explained that 'many use the email as a way to 'let off steam' but now with blogs being the rage, emails are not as popular.' The emails increase in frequency during local festive occasions, school holidays and exam times, 'Many people will send emails in with some fears that they have.' While admitting her fears and reservations about insensitive comments posted on blogs by non-ED individuals she believes cyberspace and email interaction can help those on their recovery journey 'because people with ED like to express ourselves and many that I know, like myself like to WRITE!!' She continues, 'I know many of the survivors also like the secrecy and anonymous aspect of this medium.'

### 8.3     Dawn
where's the surrendered love?
have you tanned in the grace of submission?
rested knowing below are nets of salvation?
drank a cup of tea on the cushioned chair of trust?

During our first interview, Dawn invited me to her closed blog that she updated regularly during her days with anorexia. When seeking permission to quote her from her blog, she said 'Use it, use it. If it's helpful to you or somebody else, just use.' On her blog, she writes with sensitivity about her journey into the depths of anorexia and depression often posting songs, original poetry and thoughtful, self-critical entries. She displays a great degree of social consciousness in questioning what normality is, in questioning morality and medical help. Her blog also contained lots of references to God. One can find quotes about beauty from the Bible that have strengthened and sustained her and her commitment to 'tell all (her) girlfriends how just how beautiful they are.'

In a post titled 'screw normality' she types in bold 'just because we are different, that don't mean we are crazy.' She goes on, 'God accepts us. He made us as we are. Then we accept and love ourselves. We will get by.' Sometimes her offline support experiences are articulated on her blog. She narrates, in good humour, how a friend of hers who is a lower primary school teacher lectured her on how food gives the body energy to function. Dawn concludes this story with a laugh and an 'amen to that.' She had been in 'a FAT daze,' feeling faint and low because she had been 'depriving' her 'precious' body of 'the essentials.' Dawn realises that not having felt full for so long makes her feel 'queasy' when she is. She writes a curt cyber-manifesto when while fighting her anorexia she realises she is fighting 'da GUILT of normal eating':

> What the hell we are doing to our warped bodies. It's just an indirect way of stabbing ourselves. And the best part is that we perpetuate it oh so willingly. To fit into an ideal that doesn't even exist. What the [...] screw the dieting or the slimming industries which FEED of humanoids' insecurities. Screw magazines and air brushes and stick thin anorexic models who become girls' role models. Screw them. Screw the media and the businesses that make them do that. Screw society. Screw us all who act as SOCIAL

POLICE, scanning the crowds, picking out those who do
not fit into the thin ideal and condemning them.

Dawn has become a cyber activist of sorts forming a Facebook Group that is
critical of the mental health industry.

## 8.4    Joan

Another informant of mine, Joan, came out first on a Facebook post
where she revealed her life-changing experience of surviving an ED. She
publicised a blog she set up where those suffering in silence can seek help,
advice, support and ask questions. She has received immensely positive
responses and feedback in her food-related non-governmental organisation
which among other things has launched an on-going successful ED
awareness campaign in the form of public talks and so on:

> Choosing prayer and sweets instead of cigarettes. Choosing
> prayer and fruits over drinks. Choosing to eat without guilt
> instead of starving. Choosing to accept myself instead of
> hating myself - Dawn.

For many of the bloggers whose blog contents I studied, their blogs seemed
to be one of the spaces where they felt they could be at their most honest.
EDs are often misunderstood in popular culture and in general Singapore
society where food and eating is considered a national pastime, where body-
work and social policing of the body (politic) is part of the everyday fabric of
social life on the island.

Disenchanted patients of biomedical psychiatry can learn to turn
inwards, to use their pathographies of pain for better rather than for worse, by
becoming wounded storytellers. By typing her thoughts through highly self-
conscious writing, where she often ponders upon the purpose of blogging and
her own self-reflexivity, Lea self-medicates through storytelling and through
her active listening of others' who have gone through similar experiences like
herself.

Gayle sometimes refers to other blogs. She finds inspiration in the
blog of a girl who had binge-eating disorder for eight years but recovered.
She speaks of how that blog made her 'more determined to change (her)
ways'. Likewise her blog inspires others like Eva, a university student and
ex-anorexic, who has commented, 'u put the things i feel into words, & i can
totally relate to you!' Eva and Gayle have spoken about their faith and
admiration for each other, wishing Godspeed. Eva and Lea have also
committed that they are 'to strive for godliness, not perfection'.

## 9.     Dialectics of Flesh and Silicon - From Dystopia to Etopias

Nakamura[18] and Collins-Jarvis[19] proffer that cybercultures best be understood as a chain of negotiations which take place both off and online. Many of the bloggers have a shared history and knowledge of the other bloggers on their blog roll as they have met and continue to meet in person in a hospital setting - as in/outpatients or at support group sessions - or other institutional settings like schools, tertiary or university settings. It has been argued that flesh-and-blood communities are nourished on the principal of reciprocity, just as virtual ones are. Cyberspace then gifts upon the users an extension of everyday living, and so the safety nets of society penetrate into the digital realm where introspection can reach richer planes without the encumbrance of a clinical setting, or a public unsafe space or a visibly abused body-mind. Although the possibility of diminishing into the cyburbia of one's personal blog exists, it is quite improbable given the amount of peer policing and concerned surveillance that goes on among the survivors.

Gayle has directly thanked her visible readers, speaking of her gratitude for 'companionship'. She says 'thanks for being there, sometimes all that matters is just to have someone there'. Support comes streaming in from a friend who encourages her to battle on, promising to see her 'on the other end someday really freaking soon'. Gayle has asked Eva in an online thread if they had met before in support group. Eva has encouraged Gayle to come. Eva has also asked Gayle to be study buddies offline thus displaying a wish to extend the online support into offline support as well. There is clearly more than surface-level cheerleading going on in cyberspace. Practical and pragmatic concerns such as desires to do well in school and save money inform and shape their social interactions with each other.

A Facebook search revealed a couple of related online local groups. One describes itself as existing 'for those who feel they need a sense of support.' It professes not to discriminate what ED one might be suffering from, listing a few. It is a closed group meaning members have to be invited or approved by the administrator. It appeals to a sense of in-group solidarity to battle the disorder in a secure and confidential mode, acknowledging that 'Professionals can't be there for us 24hrs,' thus promising the benefit of availability.[20] The other group is an open one with 25 members.

The professionals at the ED unit I e-mail interviewed had mixed feelings about the idea of recovery in cyberspace. One senior principal psychologist spoke of accepting invitations from her patients to view their blogs. She keeps herself updated by frequent visits and sometimes leaves comments of encouragement there, not advice or recommendations which she might give via email or during therapy sessions. She felt, 'It is the way the current generation communicate. And the 'anonymity' helps them to be more open.' She appreciates the 'insight' to be gained on blogs, especially by her patients who are less vocal. She does not however interact with her patients past or present on social networking sites, as that would be 'violating boundaries', even blocking them so that they will be unable to find her. Cyberspace for her can play a role in support and recovery in the form of 'professional moderated forums, peer support groups and psychoeducation.' A family therapist did not, as a personal policy, view the blogs of her patients even though she knows some of them keep them. With regards to social networking sites she is uncomfortable accepting friend requests from patients citing, her preference 'to retain my private life apart from my professional work.' She does worry if online interaction which can be done at any time of the day might cause burn out among professionals. Also her concern is whether the ED professional present themselves as expert or friend. The consultant psychiatrist felt online communication had boiled down to a 'generational cultural thing' - 'sometimes they are able to communicate with us that way between our sessions and the younger generations of patients, we do notice, tend to express themselves much better on the Internet rather than face-to-face.' Homework given as part of therapy sessions are sometimes uploaded on blogs which are accessed via a hospital computer during the sessions themselves. The accessing of blogs during face to face therapy sessions just shows how much weight they carry for so many survivors and for the people who are supporting them through recovery.

## 10. In Lieu of a Conclusion

Cyberspaces can serve an important role as compass towards connection amidst arguably increasing modern society's disconnectedness to each other. Just as EDs are bound up with dualisms such as mind/body, culture/nature, agency/structure spilts and require a new 'somaesthetic'[21] and bodily wisdom to recuperate, cyberspace can be its complementary tool, a guide 'toward a reconciliation of the major schisms of our time, those between science and spirit'.[22] The cyberculture in the blogs I came across seemed to inspire feelings of empowerment among the users. To me it seems a healthy reclaiming of cyberspace from high profile pro-Ana, pro-Mia sites which have recreated many a moral panic which have led to debates on web communication among ED individuals as being 'sanctuary or snare?'.[23]

Gayle sometimes quotes inspiring nuggets of wisdom from what she terms 'a fellow survivor's blog' - quotes that 'whac(k) (her) hard.' There is definitely camaraderie across these blogs however sharp-eyed, cautious and silent or luminously articulate, it is strong and it remains there. Also present in the writing is the 'rapport' that people with ED feel to have with one another. This sentiment was constantly articulated at support group sessions and its important thematic occurrence cannot be understated.

The duet of recovery and renewed spirituality finds meaning in the wounded storyteller concept. Gayle speaks of the double-edged sword of opening up to those around her, such as her work colleagues. There is so much fear about even talking about this illness. That in the talking, those who are on the verge might somehow slip into this disorder. I do believe however the blogs, while often scathing to read, and I imagine to type, do provide hope and help to those who are willing to go through the zeniths and nadirs of these cyber-confessionals which sometimes cross-currents, which sometimes connect dots, which sometimes curse but which in all cases in the course of my data do not wrongly promote EDs as a life-style choice, rather they advocate recovery and provide safe support networks by those who are wounded storytellers themselves. Hope, help, honesty and the arduous return from hell characterise the content of these writings from recovered/recovering youth. It must be noted however that while online social support might provide a counter-effect to harsh diagnostic psychiatric labels, sometimes blog posts go uncommented and this might aggravate feelings of alienation especially among those who might be psychologically fragile.[24] Cobb would argue that despite cyberspace being a 'technology of connection' that simultaneously can 'breed separation and isolation,' in the broader schema of 'spiritual evolution, the dark and the light coexist in a constant dialectical tension that serves to move the entire process forward'.[25]

It has been suggested that the 'stigma and shame that come with both diagnostic labelling and society's misunderstanding of eating 'disorders' contribute to women's need to find creative ways to connect'.[26] I hope that I have shown in this chapter that the apparent atomised story-telling on the net by ED survivors in Singapore, through hyperlinks, and on and offline friendships creates a constellation of faith sometimes detached and ethereal, sometimes embodied and incensed but always towards full recovery. Just as the creatively expressed meditations painted on the blogs in the form of stream of consciousness style narratives, poetry or a pastiche bricolage of Bible verses bridges outsiders into a glimpse of their lived experiences[27], through my sustained observation of online voices which was continuously cross-checked with my primary fieldwork data, I hope I have managed to 'reduce the puzzlement'[28] and distance that separates ED and ex-ED individuals from their friends, family and perfect strangers by bringing their voices to light. Online activity by recovering ED individuals are an exercise in self-management and bonding to reclaim a sense of self apart from the ED identity that is addressed in a clinical setting. By cybergrace, new non-ED identities are being bolstered by the open dialogue and accountability of blogging to a place where an appetite for living is slowly but surely rehabilitated.

# Notes

[1] A Frank, *The Wounded Storyteller: Body, Illness, and Ethics*. University of Chicago Press, Chicago, London, 1995.

[2] J Cobb, *Cybergrace: The Search for God in the Digital World*. 1998.

[3] R Tapper, 'Anthropology and (The) Crisis: Responding to Crisis in Afghanistan' in *Royal Anthropological Institute*, 2001, viewed on 21st November 2008, <http://www.therai.org.uk/pubs/at/editorial/tapper.html>

[4] C Hine, *Virtual Ethnography*. Sage, 2000.

[5] A C Davies, *Reflexive Ethnography. A Guide to researching Selves and Others*, 2nd Ed. London, Routeledge, 1998, p. 163.

[6] Cobb, op. cit.

[7] V Bolhuis, E Herman and V Colom, *Cyberspace Reflections*. VUB University Press, Brussels, Belgium, 1995, p.115.

[8] R P Seid, *Never Too Thin: Why Women are at War with their Bodies*, 1989, p.44.

[9] E Rich, 'Anorexic Dis(connection): Managing Anorexia as an Illness and an Identity' in the *Sociology of Health and Illness*, vol. 28, 2006, pp. 284-305.

[10] L Clarke, 'Creating Communities in Cyberspace: Pro-Anorexia Web Sites and Social Capital' in the *Journal of Psychiatric and Mental Health Nursing*, vol. 15, 2008, pp. 340-343.

[11] Frank, op. cit.

[12] Frank, op. cit. p. 5.

[13] Frank, op. cit. p. 35.

[14] E Goffman, *The Presentation of Self in Everyday Life*. Harmondsworth: Penguin, 1969.

[15] A Keski-Rahkonen & F Tozzi, 'The Process of Recovery in Eating Disorder Sufferers' Own Words: An Internet-based Study' in *International Journal of Eating Disorders*, vol, 37, 2005, S80-S86.

[16] S Sontag, *Illness as Metaphor*. Farrar, Straus and Giroux, 1978, p.3.

[17] J Cobb, *Cybergrace: The Search for God in the Digital World*, 1998, p.231.

[18] L Nakamura, 'Race in/for Cyberspace: Identity Tourism and Racial Passing on the Internet' in *CyberReader*, Vitanza, V. J. (ed), Allyn and Bacon, Boston, MA, 1999, pp. 442-453.

[19] L A Collins-Jarvis, 'Gender Representation in an Electronic City Hall: Female adoption of Santa Monica's PEN system' in the *Journal of Broadcasting & Electronic Media,* vol 37:1, 1993, pp. 49-66.

[20] S R Cotten, 'Implications of Internet Technology for Medical Sociology in the New Millennium' in *Sociological Spectrum*, vol. 21, 2001, pp. 319-340.

[21] R Shusterman, *Body Consciousness: A Philosophy of Mindfulness and Somaesthetics*. Cambridge University Press, 2008.

[22] Cobb, op. cit. p.1.

[23] S Tierney, 'The Dangers and Draw of Online Communication: Pro-Anorexia Websites and their Implications for Users, Practitioners, and Researchers' in *Eating Disorders. The Journal of Treatment and Prevention*, vol. 14:3, 2006, pp. 181-190.

[24] L Clarke, 'Creating Communities in Cyberspace: Pro-Anorexia Web Sites and Social Capital' in the *Journal of Psychiatric and Mental Health Nursing*, vol. 15, 2008, pp. 340-343.

[25] Cobb, op. cit, p. 92.

[26] K Dias, 'The Ana Sanctuary: Women's Pro-Anorexia Narratives in Cyberspace' in the *Journal of International Women's Studies*, vol. 4(2), 2003, p. 32.

[27] E R Uca, *Ana's Girls: The Essential Guide to the Underground Eating Disorder Community Online*. Authorhouse, Bloomington, IN, 2004.

[28] C Geertz, *The Interpretation of Cultures*, Fontana, 1993, p. 14.

## Bibliography

Clarke, L., 'Creating Communities in Cyberspace: Pro-Anorexia Web Sites and Social Capital'. *Journal of Psychiatric and Mental Health Nursing*, 15, pp. 340-343, 2008.

Cobb, J., *Cybergrace: The Search for God in the Digital World*. Crown Publishers, New York, 1998.

Collins-Jarvis, L. A., 'Gender Representation in an Electronic City Hall: Female Adoption of Santa Monica's PEN System'. *Journal of Broadcasting & Electronic Media* 1993, 37:1, 49-66.

Davies, A. Ch., *Reflexive Ethnography: A Guide to Researching Selves and Others*. 2nd Ed, Routledge, London, 1998.

Dias, K., 'The Ana Sanctuary: Women's Pro-anorexia Narratives in Cyberspace'. *Journal of International Women's Studies*, 2003, 4(2), pp. 31-45.

Frank, A., *The Wounded Storyteller: Body, Illness, and Ethics*. University of Chicago Press, Chicago, London, 1995.

Geertz, C., *The Interpretation of Cultures*. Fontana, 1993.

Goffman, E., *Stigma*, Prentice-Hall, 1963.

Hine, Ch., *Virtual Ethnography*. Sage, 2000.

Keski-Rahkonen A. & F. Tozzi, 'The Process of Recovery in Eating Disorder Sufferers' Own Words: An Internet-based Study'. *International Journal of Eating Disorders*, 37, 2005, pp. S80-S86.

Nakamura, Lisa., 'Race in/for Cyberspace: Identity Tourism and Racial Passing on the Internet' in *CyberReader*. V. J. Vitanza (ed), Allyn and Bacon, Boston, MA, 1999, pp. 442-453.

Rich, E., 'Anorexic Dis(connection): Managing Anorexia as an Illness and an Identity' in the *Sociology of Health and Illness*, 2006, 28, pp. 284-305.

Sontag, S., *Illness as Metaphor*. Farrar, Straus and Giroux, 1978.

Tapper, R., 'Anthropology and (The) Crisis: Responding to Crisis in Afghanistan'. *Royal Anthropological Institute*. 2001.
Available from: <http://www.therai.org.uk/pubs/at/editorial/tapper.html>.

Tierney, S., 'The Dangers and Draw of Online Communication: Pro-Anorexia Websites and their Implications for Users, Practitioners, and Researchers.' *Eating Disorders. The Journal of Treatment and Prevention*, 14:3, 181-190. 2006.

Uca E. R., *Ana's Girls: The Essential Guide to the Underground Eating Disorder Community Online*. Authorhouse, Bloomington, IN, 2004.

Van Bolhuis, H. E. and V. Colom, *Cyberspace Reflections*. VUB University Press, Brussels, Belgium, 1995.

**Chand Somaiah**, M.A., Post-Graduate Research Scholar, Department of Sociology, Faculty of Arts and Social Sciences, National University of Singapore.